BUYING REALITY

Donald McGannon Communication Research Center's
Everett C. Parker Book Series

Buying Reality

POLITICAL ADS, MONEY,
AND LOCAL TELEVISION NEWS

Danilo Yanich

FORDHAM UNIVERSITY PRESS   NEW YORK 2020

Fordham University Press has no responsibility for the persistence or
accuracy of URLs for external or third-party Internet websites referred to
in this publication and does not guarantee that any content on such websites
is, or will remain, accurate or appropriate.

Fordham University Press also publishes its books in a variety of electronic
formats. Some content that appears in print may not be available in
electronic books.

Visit us online at www.fordhampress.com.

Library of Congress Cataloging-in-Publication Data available online
at https://catalog.loc.gov.

Printed in the United States of America
22 21 20   5 4 3 2 1
First edition

To our Mom, Mary Yanich—
the purest soul of us all.

Većnaja Pamjat

Contents

The most corrupting lie is the truth poorly told.

I have a motto: My job is not to make up anybody's mind but to make the agony of decision making so intense that you can escape only by thinking.

Introduction

Speaking at the Morgan Stanley Technology, Media, and Telecom Conference at the Park Hotel in San Francisco in February 2016, Les Moonves, the then-president of CBS, described the 2016 presidential election campaign as a "circus" that "may not be good for America, but it's damn good for CBS." He could have stopped there, but he just *had* to continue: "Sorry. It's a terrible thing to say. But, bring it on, Donald. Keep going" (Bond 2016, 2). Moonves spoke like the businessman that he is: We're in it for the money.

In the presidential race in 2016, the losing candidate and her supporters bought 75 percent of the political ads, while Donald Trump was the beneficiary of an estimated $5 billion of media coverage for which he did not have to pay (Stewart 2016). Trump's tweets were irresistible to the broadcast and cable networks as he made one over-the-top statement after another. Even he was surprised by it.

However, if we look at the down-ballot races—the races for the US House of Representatives and Senate—the 2016 election looked very much like previous elections. Political ads, not tweets, carried the messages of candidates because the vast majority of candidates did not enjoy the name recognition and celebrity of the presidential contenders. Local candidates depended upon campaign ads to convey their messages. As a result, local television stations inundated citizens with political ads that often proclaimed mutually exclusive visions of reality.

Specifically, of the 4.29 million ads that aired on broadcast television (not cable) in the 2015–2016 election cycle, only about 1 million targeted the presidential campaign. The remaining ads targeted down-ballot races, including 926,426 ads for Senate races (at a cost of $655 million), 621,556 for House

1

candidates (at a cost of $335 million), 463,683 for governor races, and about 1.25 million ads for state attorney general, state representative, and mayoral races (Fowler, Ridout, and Franz 2016). In other words, more than three-fourths of the political ads that we saw during a white-hot presidential campaign were directed at races that were *not* for the presidency. More importantly, we did not even recognize that imbalance. To be sure, the presidential race had enough media coverage—broadcast television, cable news, social media, and talk radio—to make it seem that there were no other races being contested. It literally consumed all of the air in the room—precisely as Moonves had anticipated. But that is the point. For the down-ballot races, political ads became critically important in a media environment in which they were the principal means for candidates to advance their messages. And the significant majority of those ads were aired on local television newscasts.

Of course, political advertising is only possible with money. And the money has increased significantly over time. In 2006 political advertising on local television amounted to $2.6 billion. In 2012 it was just over $3 billion (Matsa 2014). In 2014 it increased dramatically to $3.8 billion. There was an expectation that 2016 would see $6 billion in political advertising on local television. Because of the immense amount of free coverage that Donald Trump received from the broadcast networks, he did not spend as much money on political ads as was anticipated. As a result, political ad spending remained around the level of the 2012 campaign, but the amount was significant—$9.8 billion in total political ad spending with $4.4 billion going to broadcast television stations (Cassino 2017). The spending increase continued for the 2018 midterm election to over $3 billion, a record (Miller 2018a). That is a lot of money.

Why Study Political Ads?

What is so compelling about political ads? Why should we look at them at all? First, they are ubiquitous—even in this age of social media, they remain the primary mechanism through which candidates communicate their message (Fowler, Ridout, and Franz 2016). Second, political ads are the largest expense in a typical campaign for a major office (Cassino 2017). Third, they can persuade voters and affect voter turnout (Dunaway et al. 2019; Valentino, Hutchings, and Williams 2004; Huber and Arceneaux 2007). Fourth, they can drive media coverage of the campaigns (Fowler and Ridout 2009; Ridout and Fowler 2012). Fifth, they can serve as signals for what elected officials will do once elected (Ridout, Franz, and Fowler 2014). In short, political ads matter, especially in down-ballot races for the House of Representatives where candidates who "flood and frankly overwhelm ad space" will increase their vote share and their chances of winning (Jones and Jorgensen 2012, 182). That is why candidates, action committees, and consultants spend billions of dollars to produce and to disseminate them in every election campaign.

My concern in this book is, what did we, as citizens, get for the money? I know what the political advertisers got for their money—an audience that they can persuade. I know what the broadcasters got—an economic windfall. All of this is perfectly legal in the system that we have set up for elections in the United States. However, given the sheer volume of millions of political ads that citizens see, what political information did broadcast stations provide for their viewers beyond the political ads that they aired? And, given the imbalance of presidential campaign versus down-ballot election ads, how did that play out in those races?

The 2016 Campaign

Hillary Clinton and Donald Trump both survived brutal primary campaigns to secure their party's presidential nomination.

Hillary Clinton and the Democrats

Hillary Clinton announced her candidacy for president in a YouTube video on April 12, 2015. It was her second bid for the presidency, having lost the Democratic nomination to Barack Obama in 2008. Her resumé included her public service as secretary of state, senator from New York, and former First Lady when her husband Bill Clinton occupied the Oval Office from 1993 to 2001. She was considered the front-runner from the beginning of her campaign.

Her main campaign themes reflected a populist tone and included raising the incomes of the middle class, expanding women's rights, instituting campaign finance reform, and expanding and improving the Affordable Care Act.

She ran against five other candidates in the Democratic Party's primary races: Maryland Governor Martin O'Malley, former Rhode Island Governor Lincoln Chaffee, former Virginia Senator Jim Webb, Harvard Law Professor Lawrence Lessig, and Vermont Senator Bernie Sanders. All, except Sanders, dropped out early in the campaign. Through the primary contests, which took place in all fifty states, the District of Columbia and five US territories, Clinton won 55 percent of the delegates. She was officially nominated as the party's presidential candidate at the Democratic National Convention in Philadelphia on July 26, 2016. Her running mate for vice-president was Senator Tim Kaine of Virginia.

Clinton had only one chief competitor, Vermont Senator Bernie Sanders, who articulated a progressive agenda that focused on income and wealth inequality. He was particularly popular with voters under forty and drew large crowds who chanted "Feel the Bern." But Sanders could not overcome Clinton's presumptive status as the nominee. After the final primary election in June that gave her the required number of delegates for the nomination, that presumptive status was ensured. However, many of Sanders's supporters were not willing to throw their support to Clinton. That was exacerbated when WikiLeaks published leaked emails of the Democratic National Committee (DNC) in July 2016. The bias against Sanders that the leaked emails revealed prompted the resignation of the DNC chair, Debbie Wasserman Schultz, and an apology to Sanders and his supporters. Sanders's supporters were extremely upset at the revelations that the emails revealed, but Sanders endorsed Clinton, put her name in nomination at the Democratic National Convention and actively campaigned for her during the general election.

There are divergent findings regarding the proportion of Sanders supporters who voted for Trump. The Rand 2016 Presidential Election Panel Survey put the figure at 6 percent. Other research concluded that the proportion was 12 percent (Ansolabehere and Schaffner 2017). That said, there is some evidence that a large proportion of the Sanders-Trump voters did not self-identify as Democrats. They were still registered as Democrats even as their politics in their states turned from blue to red because changing registration took time and effort. And less engaged voters did not take the time to do it. So, in closed primary states, they could not vote in the Republican primary. When they voted in the Democratic primary, they supported Sanders, as was the case in Oklahoma and West Virginia. In Kentucky, Clinton won by only 1 percent. They were not going to vote for Clinton. Therefore, it was no surprise that they moved to Trump in the general election (Wheel 2017).

Donald Trump and the Republicans

Donald Trump had no experience in government. He was a real estate developer from New York and a reality TV star of *The Apprentice* fame. He was also a household name because of a decades-long public relations strategy that kept his name prominent in every endeavor he pursued, from the Trump casino in Atlantic City to Trump University.

The primary race that he navigated was very different from Clinton's. While she had just one other serious contender, he had sixteen Republican opponents. The "circus" began on June 16, 2015, when Trump announced his candidacy at Trump Tower in New York City.

His campaign slogan was "Make America Great Again." That slogan contained his characterization of the United States as victim of unfair trade practices, Islamic terrorism, and loss of American jobs to other countries and illegal immigration. During his announcement, his assessment of illegal immigration was direct, and it told us all that we needed to know about the tenor of the forthcoming campaign. Talking about Mexican immigrants he said: "When Mexico sends its people, they're not sending their best. . . . They're bringing drugs. They're bringing crime. They're rapists. And some, I assume are good people" (Newsday Staff 2016).

Through the following fourteen months of the Republican primary process, Trump would engage in combat with his Republican opponents by making outlandish statements and then doubling down on the point. On May 3, 2016, on Fox News, citing unsubstantiated claims in a *National Enquirer* story, he said that Texas Senator Ted Cruz's father was with Lee Harvey Oswald before Oswald assassinated President John F. Kennedy. At a Family Leadership Summit in Ames, Iowa, on July 18, 2015, he denigrated John McCain's imprisonment and torture during the Vietnam War saying that he was not a war hero because he had been captured. In Birmingham, Alabama, on November 21, 2015, he said that he watched in Jersey City, New Jersey, when thousands of people cheered as the World Trade Center towers came down on September 11, 2001. That claim has been debunked. On October 19, 2016, during the last debate with Hillary Clinton, moderator Chris Wallace asked if he would honor the tradition of the election loser, whoever that is, to concede to the winner. Trump dodged the question by saying that he would keep us in suspense. On the following day, at a campaign rally in Delaware, Ohio, he said he would accept the results of the election, adding the ominous caveat, "if I win" (Newsday Staff 2016).

Think about that—a candidate for the presidency of the United States said he would accept the election results *only* if he won. A fundamental hallmark of stable democracies is the smooth transfer of power—a feature of the American system that we hold up to the world as a symbol of our greatness. That aspect of our greatness was lost on the very person who espoused it.

The Republican primaries were held in all fifty states, the District of Columbia, and five US territories from February 1 to June 7, 2016. By mid-March, only three candidates remained in the race: Texas Senator Ted Cruz, Ohio Governor John Kasich, and Trump. By the time they were over, Trump had won 1,441 delegates, 204 more than the 1,237 needed to win the nomination. He was formally nominated on July 21, 2016, at the Republican National Convention in Cleveland.

The convention, like the primaries, was contentious and notable for who *did not* attend. Former Presidents George W. Bush and George H. W. Bush sat it out. The 2012 presidential nominee, Mitt Romney, also skipped the event along with more than twenty Republican senators, including the 2008 presidential nominee, John McCain. Six Republican governors were no-shows, including John Kasich, the sitting Republican governor of Ohio, the state where the convention was held. It was a stunning display of their displeasure with Trump.

There was a floor fight over the rules as a group of delegates pushed to have a roll-call vote on the convention rules package that had been adopted previously by the Rules Committee. In an effort to stymie the Trump nomination, they wanted to "unbind" delegates from voting for Trump on the first ballot and "vote their conscience." That effort failed.

The admonition to "vote your conscience" was made crystal clear in a remarkable speech at the convention by former candidate Ted Cruz. Normally convention speaking slots are given to people who support the nominee and the expectation was that Cruz would announce his endorsement. That did not happen. Remember, Cruz was the person whose wife and father Trump had ruthlessly denigrated. Instead, Cruz urged the delegates to "vote your conscience, vote for candidates up and down the ticket whom you trust to defend our freedom and be faithful to the Constitution" (Healy and Martin 2016). Cruz was booed off the stage. Two months later, he endorsed Trump, even though Trump said that he did not want his endorsement. So much for conscience.

The worm had turned drastically. Trump went to Texas in October 2018 to campaign for Cruz in his close battle against Democratic challenger Beto O'Rourke. He went from characterizing Cruz as "Lyin' Ted" to "Beautiful Ted." Cruz won—by a smaller margin than expected—but he won.

The Senate and House Elections

All of the 435 seats in the House of Representatives and 34 seats (24 held by Republicans and 10 held by Democrats) in the Senate were contested in 2016. In the Senate, prior to the 2016 election, the Republicans held 54 seats, the Democrats held 44, and there were two Independents, although they caucused with the Democrats. The Democrats needed to pick up 6 seats to gain control of the Senate. They fell short; they gained only 2, in the battleground states of Illinois, where military veteran Tammy Duckworth defeated incumbent Mark Kirk by 15 percent of the votes, and New Hampshire, where former governor Maggie Hassan defeated incumbent Kelly Ayotte by a razor-thin margin of 0.1 percent (Ballotpedia 2016). As a result, the Senate remained in the hands of the Republicans with a 52 to 48 majority (placing the two Independent senators in the Democratic column as they caucus with that party).

In the House of Representatives, the Republicans held a majority of 246 seats to the Democrats' 186 heading into the election. There were three vacant seats pending special elections. After the election, the Republicans held a majority of 291 seats to the Democrats' 194—a 45-seat gain for the Republicans.

The Senate races were thought to be much more volatile than they turned out, especially with the Republicans having to defend 24 incumbent seats. However, the Republican majority was up to the task. That may be explained, in part, by the interplay between presidential and down-ballot races which has undergone a remarkable change between 1980 and 2016. In 1980, during the presidential contest between Jimmy Carter and Ronald Reagan, almost six out of ten Senate races went for the same party's candidate as their state's most recent presidential choice. That is, there was a consistency between the party of the president and the senator who was elected. In the 1982, 1984, and 1986 elections, the results were the opposite—most races saw the Senate votes that were not the same party as the most recent presidential choice. In 1988 it was about even. But that is where things changed. Between then and 2016, the proportion of senators elected whose party was the same as the party's most recent presidential choice was always above 60 percent and it steadily increased. In fact, it reached its absolute zenith in 2016 when all of the Senate races were won by candidates of the same party as their state's most recent presidential vote (Desilver 2018). Such was the appeal of Donald Trump. That was important in battleground states such as Pennsylvania where incumbent Republican senator Pat Toomey was trailing his Democratic challenger by 4 percent in a poll taken just days before the election. Trump unexpectedly won the state by less than 1 percent; Toomey won by 1.5 percent. Even though Toomey kept some distance from Trump during the campaign, he benefitted from the Trump turnout. That voting block did not split their ticket when voting in the Senate race.

This phenomenon may be explained as "negative partisanship" (Abramowitz and Webster 2016, 14). The feelings of Americans about their *own* party have changed little over time. However, they have changed drastically regarding the *other* party, and that has taken a much more negative turn. Negative partisanship has significant potential to strongly influence voting behavior and not in a way that we might expect. In its most basic form, partisans vote *against* the other party rather than *for* their own. In that way, the issues in the local elections become almost irrelevant as those races become nationalized. That is precisely what happened in the 2018 mid-term elections. Trump said it was all about him and the Democrats gained 40 seats in the House of Representatives.

This nationalization of politics also reduces the power of incumbency as voters increasingly are reluctant to cross party lines. Straight-ticket voting and president-centered electoral nationalization occur as our politics become more divided and vehemently partisan (Jacobson 2015). But beyond the partisan divide, incumbents are also threatened by the unleashing of historic amounts of money that can be dedicated to any campaign against them. The change has been exponential, "total independent spending from all sources in House races grew from $37.9 million in 2004 to $260.6 million in 2012" (870)—an increase of 680 percent in eight years.

Political Stories in the 2016 Election

This nationalization of politics has important implications for the down-ballot races that I considered in my research. As mentioned earlier, the overwhelming majority of the political ads and money were directed to the down-ballot races rather than the presidential campaign. The ad sponsors placed great importance on those races—particularly those for the House and Senate. You might expect that the stations that aired the ads might also direct their attention to these races, as measured by the political stories that they produced about the campaign, but you would be wrong. In covering the campaign, the stations only devoted 13 percent of their political stories to the down-ballot races; 87 percent went to cover Clinton and Trump. In effect, the stations nationalized their reporting at the expense of covering local races. For them, the campaign was only about Clinton and Trump and it is not that far of a leap to conclude that the national coverage affected voters' preferences for down-ballot races. If you supported Trump, then you also supported the Republican House or Senate candidate. If you supported Clinton, you did the same for Democratic candidates. There were almost no political stories directed at the down-ballot races from which you could learn something about the candidates that was separate from the presidential contest.

Political Ads in the 2016 Presidential Race

Several aspects of the political ads made this election different from previous campaigns. At the presidential level, there was a striking imbalance between the number of ads that were aired for the Democratic and Republican nominees. In prior campaigns that proportion was relatively even. During the 2016 campaign, however, over three-quarters of the political ads supported Hillary Clinton. Further, while Clinton was ahead in the polls, she never experienced the bump that such an imbalance would suggest (Fowler, Ridout, and Franz

2016). That said, Fowler and her colleagues offer two notes of caution: "(1) Clinton's unexpected losses came in states in which she failed to air ads until the last week, and (2) Clinton's message was devoid of discussions of policy in a way not seen in the previous four presidential elections" (445). Clinton's ads hammered at the theme that Trump was unfit to be president. For example, over 90 percent of Clinton's negative ads focused on Trump's personal characteristics, not his policies. Even in the ads in which she contrasted Trump and herself, most of the comparisons were personal rather than their differences in policy. On the other hand, over 95 percent of Trump's contrast ads focused on policy differences (Fowler, Ridout, and Franz 2016). In the closing week of the campaign, Clinton released an ad that contained clips of Trump's comments about women, from the Access Hollywood tape to his statement that "putting a wife to work is a dangerous thing." The ad closes with the tag line, "Anyone who believes/does/says what he does is unfit to be president" (Berenson 2016).

Clinton may have made a strategic error in the personal attacks in her ads. As long as she focused on Trump's fitness for office, there was no discussion—either by her or the media—of her policy knowledge.

Trump essentially did not match Clinton's political ad strategy, both the volume of ads and the money spent on them were below levels in 2012. There were about 900,000 presidential ads in the top seventy-five television markets in 2012; that number was about 600,000 in 2016—a significant decrease, but about on par with levels in 2008 and 2004 (Fowler, Ridout, and Franz 2016). Broadcast television political ad revenue fell 19 percent from the 2012 level to just over $1 billion (Cassino 2017).

The imbalance in political ads in the presidential race becomes even clearer when we consider that political advertisers had increased their use of local cable considerably since 2012. For example, Clinton purchased fewer ads than Obama on local broadcast but almost 150,000 more ads on local cable. On the Republican side, Trump bought fewer ads than Romney on local broadcast and only a very small number on local cable. That made the political ad imbalance between Clinton and Trump even more historic. However, it should be noted that, while Clinton enjoyed an overall ad advantage, Trump aired more ads in pivotal states such as Michigan and Wisconsin up until the last week of the campaign (Fowler, Ridout, and Franz 2016).

The imbalance of the political ads at the presidential and down-ballot levels reflected the unusual nature of the presidential race: a former First Lady, Secretary of State, and senator versus a celebrity and reality television star who had been on television for decades. That made the advertising effects, which historically are relatively small at the presidential level, even smaller in 2016

(Ridout and Mellen 2007). Both Clinton and Trump had been in the public eye for decades, and they entered the race with large disapproval ratings from groups of voters. Hardened and predetermined views of each may have made it difficult for political ads to influence a voter's view (Fowler, Ridout, and Franz 2016). And Donald Trump had Twitter as well as the compliance of a media system that used Moonves's model of campaign coverage. It was a reality show and Trump knew it. He didn't need the ads as long as the media system covered him extensively for free.

Political Ads in the 2016 Down-Ballot Races

The political ad contour of the presidential race was different from previous cycles. However, the down-ballot campaign followed a very familiar script. Political ads on television were the dominant method that candidates used to convey their messages, for both the Senate and the House races. The political ad television strategies and methods in 2016 were much like those in 2008, 2010, 2012, and 2014 (Fowler, Ridout, and Franz 2016). No major candidate drastically disengaged from using them. And the pattern of sponsorship and tone was similar to previous races. In effect, it was business as usual.

Political Ads on Local Television News

About half of all political ads for the presidential and down-ballot races were aired on local newscasts—that was about twice as many as all other news programs on networks combined (network news and morning news programs such as the *Today Show* and *Good Morning America*) and twice as many as all entertainment and sports programs combined. That is higher than previous campaigns but consistent with the dominance of local television news for the placement of ads over time. For example, the program with the most presidential advertising during the campaigns of 2000, 2004, 2008, and 2012 was local television news at 43.5 percent, 37.9 percent, 35.1 percent, and 36.1 percent, respectively. In 2000 local television news' nearest competitor was the *Today Show* at 4.7 percent. In 2012 *Good Morning America* came in second at 2.1 percent (Ridout, Franz, and Fowler 2014).

That said, the significant use of local newscasts for the airing of political ads that I encountered in this research most probably reflects the fact that nine out the ten markets I studied were in battleground states. That makes intuitive sense—the stakes are high, races are competitive, voters need to be persuaded, and political ads are the prime mechanism for that task (Dunaway et al. 2019).

In the 2016 election cycle, broadcast television captured almost 45 percent of the $9.8 billion that was spent on political advertising—a decrease from almost 58 percent of $9.4 billion in 2012. Both cable and digital advertising increased in that period, but they still only accounted for about 14 percent each of the share (Cassino 2017). That was different than the political spending patterns over the past six decades and the question is whether that signaled a blip in the pattern or a sea change in how political advertising will unfold in future campaigns. I think it is a bit of both (see the conclusion). In the 2018 midterm election, local television political ads reached an all-time high for a midterm cycle of over $3 billion (Miller 2018a).

The point for the 2016 campaign is that, even in the face of increases in other media, broadcast television still had a three-to-one advantage in political advertising dollars because of its distinct advantages over cable as a prime vehicle for political ads: (1) smaller competitive markets are an advantage for local broadcast TV, because ads are more affordable to candidates and PACs and many congressional districts fall across multiple television markets, further benefitting the local TV option; (2) local broadcast news is key, because its audience still comprises the highest density of voters; (3) local television stations can target audiences by program, time of day, and genre, while local cable targets by network, but the average cable interconnect reaches only about 44 percent of the television market. Local television reaches *all* of the market—that is, all of the voters (Poor 2014).

One reason that local television news is prominent is because there is a lot of it during a station's broadcast day. However, there are other reasons—most importantly, the audience. David Plouffe (2009, 315), President Obama's campaign manager in 2008 and 2012, said that local television news was where the undecideds were, those voters who could still be persuaded: "What really mattered—and our research was clear as a bell on this—was the local news. True swing voters watched their local TV station and read their regional paper." Further, "local television is the only source that draws a majority of both self-identified Republican and Democrats and a near-majority of independents" (Ridout, Franz, and Fowler 2014, 187).

The Media in a Democratic Society

This book is about the relationship between one aspect of the media, television news, and one aspect of the political environment, political ads, within the larger media and social context in which that relationship plays out. Do the media help bring about or hinder democracy? The short answer: the media can be absolutely necessary to the democracy that it informs, but it may do so poorly.

Prominent media scholar Robert McChesney (2008, 34) maintains that "journalism in any meaningful sense cannot survive without a viable democracy." That is, a democratic society not only provides a forum in which journalists can act, but it also delivers an audience that listens. However, the corollary is also true. Democracy cannot survive without viable journalism. At the core of a democratic society is a self-governing public, and it cannot govern properly without an entity to provide insight into the actions of the officials whom it has elected.

To expand on this framework, the political scientist Shanto Iyengar (2011, 20) enumerates how journalism serves the needs of the people in a democratic society: (1) It provides a forum, before a national audience, where candidates and political parties can debate their qualifications for office; (2) it educates citizens by providing a variety of perspectives on the important issues of the day; and (3) it serves as a watchdog that scrutinizes the actions of government officials on behalf of citizens, most of whom do not have the opportunity to closely follow the actions of politicians and the government. The watchdog role of the press is particularly important as Graber (2010, 17) points out: "If media surveillance causes governments to fall and public officials to be ousted, democracy is well served."

In addition to the watchdog function of the media, Pippa Norris (2010, 18) adds agenda setters and gatekeepers. The agenda-setting function raises awareness of critical issues that the public and politicians should address. As gatekeeper, or "gate openers," as she calls it, "the news media can serve as the classical agora where journalists and broadcasters bring together a plurality of diverse interests, political parties, viewpoints and social sectors to debate issues of public concern." Indeed, Norris (2000, 318) argues that as the public encounters these functions of the news media, a "virtuous circle" forms in which "prior positive attitudes stimulate attention to the news and campaign messages, and that attention reinforces positive engagement."

The watchdog role places the media, to an extent, outside of the formal political system that it is supposed to observe. According to Cook (2006, 160), the view that the media are a political institution suggests, at first blush, that the "news media are sufficiently independent of other political actors that we should think of them as distinct." However, that view may emphasize the image of walls between the media and political system that "downplays the interpenetrating journalistic and governmental realms too much" (160). Indeed, Cook concludes that governmental actors are central to the news-making process.

The idealized view of the role of the media in society is tempered. There are much more pointed critiques of the media system in the United States. Edward Herman and Noam Chomsky (1988) famously characterized the media system as a propaganda machine whose main function is to manufacture the consent of the public. McChesney (2012) pointedly calls out the "problem of the media." He goes beyond whatever content the media produces and focuses on its very structure. How a democratic society decides to create and organize its media system is crucial to its survival. He writes: "The measure of a media system in political terms is not whether it creates a viable democratic society—that would be too much of a burden to place upon it. Instead, the measure is whether the media system, on balance, in the context of the broader social and economic situation, challenges and undermines antidemocratic pressures and tendencies, or whether it reinforces them. Is the media system a democratic force?" (1–2).

Lance Bennett (2016) argues that the assumption that a free press results in quality information is false, and he portrays America's media system as a carefully crafted construction. He characterizes the US media system as a balance among three distinct groups—politicians, journalists and the public. Although there is a balance, by no means are the actors equal in their influence. The pecking order is clear—first, politicians; second, journalists; and then, the public. There is a symbiotic relationship between politicians and journalists— politicians cannot survive without journalists and journalists cannot survive without politicians. Without the attention of the press, politicians cannot communicate their messages to the public. Alternatively, journalists need politicians as their fundamental source of political news.

The relationships between the public and politicians and the public and journalists do not rest on any such symbiosis. Politicians *need* the public to obtain their official roles. But neither they nor journalists *need* the public to *carry out* their roles. They *need* the public as the *object* of their work—the audience that registers its preferences as voters or as consumers with ratings, circulation, and clicks. In this depiction of America's media system, the power lies not with the people but rather with the interests of the government elite and the news media (Bennett 2016).

Given that the public is the least powerful entity in this arrangement, the question emerges if the public is receiving the information that best serves its needs or those of the press and politicians. Many media experts contend that the answer is the latter. Robert Entman (1996, 222) contended that the "media cannot live up to the demands that modern American democracy imposes on them." In that process, as McManus (2017) argues, news has shifted from an information resource to one of "infotainment," where entertainment is camouflaged as news and, alternatively, news reports are presented in a sensationalized, dramatic manner.

The sensationalism of news and its drive to maintain ratings prompted Neil Postman (1986) to conclude that we are "amusing ourselves to death" as media firms must make accommodations to the show business nature of the market. The result is that television altered the meaning of what it is to be informed by creating a type of information that is misplaced, irrelevant, fragmented, and superficial.

Seeing the United States in 1999, Michael Janeway (2001, 171) posited that the press must function in a condition in which "the real problem, the very devil, is the fragmentation of society and the disintegration of political culture." He echoes Robert Putnam's (2000) notion that we are "bowling alone." But Janeway issued a warning that the corporate profit imperative in the news business will demand that the press, "instead of not considering an argument for combating social fragmentation . . . figure out how to profit from it . . . the press will continue to lose ground as long as its core product—news— fails to engage people beyond the sensational, the frivolous and the merely selfish" (171).

Thomas Patterson (1993) argues that the press' adversarial stance toward candidates, particularly in presidential elections, undermines its usefulness to citizens. He concludes that "the United States cannot have a sensible campaign as long as it is built around the news media" (25).

James Fallows (1996) characterizes the news as broken and undermining American democracy. He argues that the press presents "public life as a depressing spectacle, rather than a vital activity in which citizens can and should be engaged" (8). He goes on to say that the press functions that way because it believes that the people will pay attention to public affairs only if they are presented in an entertaining way. But when competing "head-to-head with pure entertainment programs, the serious press locks itself into a competition it cannot win" (8).

The critique of television is long-lived. In 1976 political scientist Michael Robinson (1976, 425) coined the term "videomalaise" to capture the concept of the "frustration, cynicism, self-doubt and malaise" that television journalism created. Some of that critique is based on Dennis Lowry's (1971) conclusion that television reports are *interpretive* in order to give meaning to the story that matches the needs of the organization. Robinson (1976, 428) refers to Paul Weaver as he explained the interpretive inclination in structural terms: "There is, writes Weaver, the television news form . . . a television news story cannot assume . . . discursive structure. Its principal need is for a clear, continuous narrative line sustained throughout the story—something with a beginning, a middle, and an end that will create, maintain, and if possible, increase the viewer's interest . . . it needs a *theme* which can be sustained throughout the story." However, its reporting was characterized, interpretive or thematic, Robinson considered whether television would be "potent enough to define, as a matter of course, the political environment—to make the issues of our times the issues which best accommodate the medium. Television may, however unintentionally, come to define our politics as a byproduct of its own organizational and idiosyncratic need" (431). Flash forward to the second decade of the twenty-first century and we see that his rather mild warning has come to pass—in spades.

Television's idiosyncrasies may also be a critical advantage in conveying information. Doris Graber (2001) argues persuasively that television's fundamental attribute—its audiovisuals—makes it a powerful conveyor of information because audiovisual message transmission facilitates learning, including political learning. Specifically, "audiovisuals ease two major information-processing problems: failure to embed information in long-term memory and inability to retrieve it" (33). That is, presenting the essential information of the story with "visuals rich in relevant information" enhances memory and recall (33).

Roderick Hart (1999, 3) took the point further—"television has changed politics itself." It is an emotional medium that creates an intimacy between its viewers and the objects of its attention. And that intimacy seduces us into thinking that we know more than we do. He states: "Many Americans, far too many Americans, feel eminently knowledgeable about politics, and that is a danger of some consequence. A democracy, I shall argue here, becomes imperiled (a) when its people do not know what they think they know, and (b) when they do not care about what they do not know" (8–9). He comes to a devastating conclusion, "Television miseducates the citizenry, but, worse, it makes that miseducation functionally attractive" (9).

Having delivered his assessment, Hart makes a critical point. Changing television will be hard, whatever the number of its critiques, because "its phenomenology is too seductive and its technologies too entrenched" (171). Instead, he says that change must come from the commonwealth—from us—from the quiet conversations "in the home, in the classroom, in the church, in the wardroom, in the union hall" (171).

Given the polarized political landscape of the United States in 2020, when everyone knows everything about politics and opposing views are characterized as treason, those quiet conversations may be difficult to muster.

About the Book

Political advertising and local television newscasts are intertwined. There are many reasons for that which I address in the following chapters. Some have to do with the nature of television news, the audience it commands, and its effect on voting and citizen engagement. Some have to do with the nature of political ads, the campaigns and the money required to run them, and their tone and their capacity to persuade and inform voters, among other things.

The 2016 campaign was characterized by three imbalances. Two were the result of decisions by the political candidates and the PACs that supported them. The third was the result of decisions made by local television stations about how they would cover the campaign:

(1) The volume of ads: Hillary Clinton sponsored three times more ads than Donald Trump and lost. Trump did not need the ads because he recognized the circus and got more free media coverage than any other candidate in history and won.
(2) The target of ads: About two-thirds of the money and the political ads were directed at the down-ballot level. This was the "business as usual" aspect of the campaign. Political ads were the primary mechanism that candidates and PACs used to persuade voters for local races.
(3) The coverage of the campaigns: Although the overwhelming majority of ads were directed at the down-ballot races, local television newscasts almost ignored them in their political coverage—only 13 percent of political stories addressed the local races.

Certainly, there are many ways that citizens acquire political information. Local television news, as I will show, plays a prominent if not dominant role in that calculus, especially for local politics. So, the interaction of imbalances 2 and 3 causes some concern. What is the nature of that distance between the reality that is bought by the political ads and the journalism that local television news brought to the table?

Chapter 1 addresses the question of why we should look at local television news. I look at its audience, how much local news is broadcast, the importance of local information, the trust we place in it, its relationship with civic and political engagement, what the news audience wants, what happens when there is loss of local news, its coverage of local politics and the public interest obligation of media producers.

Chapter 2 examines political advertising in the United States. It includes a short history of the medium and a discussion of the campaign finance rules that apply to its use. I address the overall impact of the *Citizens United* US Supreme Court decision of 2010 and its effect on political advertising at the down-ballot level. I also examine the rules for airing political ads on television and the effects of political ads, the campaign context, and the tone of political ads.

Chapter 3 explains my research methods. I lay out the research questions that guided the study followed by a discussion of the relevant factors that are essential for any rigorous social science research: the time period of the study (the last sixty-four days of the campaign between September 5 and November 7, 2016); the television markets, the stations and the broadcasts that comprised the sample; the units of observation (the elements of the broadcast and political stories). I also explain the structure and attributes of the data on political ads that I designed and purchased from Kantar Media as they constructed the database to meet my specifications. The chapter also contains a detailed profile of each of the ten television markets that comprise the sample.

Chapter 4 reports the findings of the examination of the political ad data based on a comparison of the presidential and down-ballot races—the number of races, the money spent to air them, the programs on which they were aired, when they were aired during the broadcast day, their sponsors, their tone, and how they were distributed across the markets. I also look at the social and policy issues that were the subjects of the ads.

Chapter 5 presents an analysis of the stories that appeared on the newscasts across the stations in the ten markets over the course of the last two months of the campaign period. I address the relationship between political ads and the news content of the broadcasts and focus on the nature and distribution of the political stories that appeared on the more than fifteen hundred broadcasts that comprised the sample. I compare those stories with the political ads that also appeared on those broadcasts—also across each of the markets.

Chapter 6 is organized around the television markets and the political races in each, in addition to the presidential contest. What was the outcome of the races? Who won? Who Lost? By how much? How much money was spent—in the markets and on the stations? I compare the stories and political ads that were directed at the presidential and down-ballot races and develop ratios to indicate the relationship between them.

Chapter 7 places my findings regarding the political ads and political stories in the context of the business of local television news. I discuss the business model that produces the news that we see as citizens—the system that produced what we found in the ten markets during the campaign. The chapter includes an examination of the increasing consolidation that characterizes the local news space and what that might mean for the future of political communication in local places.

In the conclusion I place my research in the context of what I call a "perfect storm" of three factors: (1) our politics is based on what Francis Lee (2016) describes as "insecure majorities"; (2) we have a political campaign finance system that almost guarantees that version of politics; (3) we have a media system that benefits greatly from the first two features. I examine the relationship among those elements and provide a look into the future of local television news and the media ecosystem that proposes to offer citizens information about the body politic.

Even in the age of the Internet and social media, political ads on local television are the most important way candidates convey their messages. That has been true for almost a half of a century. We are already seeing their importance in the 2020 campaign. The 2016 campaign revealed imbalances in the political ads, the money, and the political stories between the presidential and down-ballot campaigns. In this book I look at how that played out and what it means for how we understand political reality, particularly in local places.

1

Why Local Television News Matters

Tip O'Neill, former Speaker of the House of Representatives, once famously said, "All politics is local." What he meant was that the political decisions that have the most impact on our lives are local. Policy preferences about crime and justice, housing, taxes, education, health, and employment, among many others, are implemented at the local level. Even in this age of instant communications and globalization, we often lose sight of the fact that we live our lives in local places.

Sizable Audience

Even though the overall audience has decreased over time, as it has for all broadcast television, television news still has a sizable audience—especially in comparison with cable news. Between 2007 and 2016, the audience for the late-night newscasts on the four network affiliate stations (ABC, CBS, Fox, and NBC) decreased, on average, from about 30 million to about 20 million viewers. The early evening newscast audience decreased from about 27 million to about 20 million viewers in that same time period, while the morning newscasts maintained an audience of about 10 million viewers during that time span (Matsa 2018).

In contrast, in 2016 the average number of televisions that were tuned to the evening news programs on cable for CNN, Fox, and MSNBC was 1.3 million. For their daytime news programs, the audience dropped to about 800,000 television households. Further, when it comes to local issues, local television consistently has a larger share of the audience than their cable counterparts.

The size of the television audience is expressed in ratings and shares. A rating is the percentage of households watching a program based on all of the television households in the market. A share, however, is the percentage of households who have their television on and who are watching a specific program. For example, KUTV in Salt Lake City had an audience share of eight whereas the audience share in that market for the typical cable news varies between one (for Anderson Cooper) and three (for O'Reilly and Hannity) (Glassman 2017).

Looking at the raw numbers for the nation, local news has an average daily audience of 18.1 million viewers (Matsa and Fedeli 2018). The top three cable networks—CNN, Fox News, and MSNBC—have a combined daily average of 1.9 million viewers (Grieco 2018).

Still, the local news television audience is slowly declining, albeit not consistently across all television markets (Wenger and Papper 2018). Even as online news consumption increases, television remains the dominant news source for Americans—half of US adults get their news from television, compared to online (43 percent), radio (25 percent), and newspapers (18 percent) (Gottfried and Shearer 2017). Local news reaches almost half of adults over 18 (46 percent), significantly more than national broadcast news (39 percent) and more than twice as much as cable news (22 percent) (Nielsen 2017). It also skews younger than national broadcast news or cable news; albeit the proportion of viewers who are 18 to 34 years of age is only 8 percent compared to 19 percent for viewers aged 35 to 49, they are higher than either of its broadcast competitors. A substantial majority of the audiences for all three sources is over fifty. However, among the three, local news has the lowest proportion of an audience that is 50 or older (73 percent) compared to national broadcast news (76 percent) and cable news (81 percent) (Nielsen 2017).

As we move up the age ladder from the 18 to 29 age group to 65 or older, the proportion of the cohort that gets most of its local news from television rises from 22 to 67 percent (Mitchell et al. 2016). That pattern also holds for citizens who follow local news "very closely"—15 percent for the 18 to 29 age group and up to 42 percent for those 65 and older (Barthel, Grieco, and Shearer 2019). On the other hand, the local news audience in some markets is increasing as the baby boomer population ages, and they continue to retain their news viewing habits (Wenger and Papper 2018).

The attention that older Americans direct to local news has implications for local politics and elections. Consistently, these viewers vote more than any other age cohort in the nation. In 2018, for example, the voting turnout rate for citizens 60 and older was 66 percent, the highest for any age group. And, it was double the proportion of the 18- to 29-year-olds (United States Election Project 2019).

The local news audience tends to be female (57 percent) rather than male (43 percent), and it tends to be lower on the income scale than either national broadcast or cable news—almost one-fifth have yearly incomes below $25,000 compared to just 11 percent in that category for cable viewers. Furthermore, local news audiences have the smallest proportion of viewers earning more than $75,000 per year (34 percent), compared to cable (47 percent) and national broadcast news (37 percent) (Nielsen 2017).

Average Viewing Time

There is a lot of local news. In fact, as of 2017, there are 1,072 local television stations in the United States that air local newscasts for an average of almost 6 hours per day on weekdays, an all-time high. On weekends, that number drops to an average of about 2 hours (Papper 2018). Put differently, on any weekday in the United States, the public has access to over 6,400 hours of local news broadcasts. That is an immense amount of content.

The audience spends significant time watching television news. Nielsen reports that, in its local people meter markets, adults watch, on average, almost 6 hours of news per week (Nielsen 2017). The average time spent per week on each type of television news source (local, national broadcast, cable) only differs by two minutes for local and cable news, 2:21 and 2:23, respectively (Nielsen 2017). However, local news viewers are diverse, and there is a substantial difference in the amount of time that racial and ethnic groups devote to viewing. African Americans comprise about one-fifth of the audience of local television news, but they spend the most time per week watching, on average, just over 7 hours (7:17). White viewers make up 71 percent of the local news audience, and they watch for just over 6 hours per week (6:12). Hispanic and Asian viewers, who account for 13 and 4 percent of the audience, watch about 3 hours (2:57) and 2.5 hours (2:25), respectively (Nielsen 2017).

In six of the ten markets, viewers spent more time watching local TV news than either cable or national news (fig. 1.1). In Cleveland, the average per week was almost 3.5 hours (3:27). The weekly average in San Francisco for watching local TV news was just over 2 hours (2:05). In Phoenix, Las Vegas, and Tampa, the audience watched more cable news (Nielsen 2017).

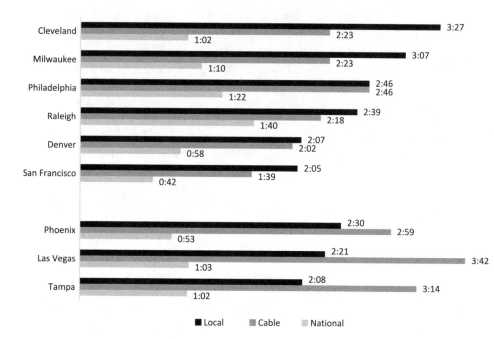

Figure 1.1. Average time per week devoted to news types (h:mm). Source: Nielsen Local Watch Report, Q1 2017: Television Trends in Our Cities.

Primary Source for Local Information

In 2011 a comprehensive report by the Federal Communications Commission (FCC) catalogued the shortcomings of local television news (Waldman 2011). The report also found that many stations genuinely strive to serve their communities with information that is important to citizens in the face of the reportorial gaps that have been left by the decline of newspapers. The report states that they are not where they need to be to fill that role but, given their local focus, "in many ways, local TV news is more important than ever" (13).

Local television news far outpaces other media as the primary source of local and regional news. Forty-four percent of the public got their news from local television; 12 percent turned to its closest competitor, newspapers; and 5 percent said they get their news from social media (TVB and Keller Fay Group 2015).

The FCC found that "there is an identifiable set of basic information needs that individuals need met to navigate everyday life, and that communities need to have met in order to thrive" (Friedland et al. 2012, v). They identified eight categories: emergencies and risks, health and welfare, education, transportation, economic opportunities, the environment, civic information and political life (Friedland et al. 2012). Moreover, based on the FCC's regulatory principle of localism, local television is the perfect vehicle to meet these informational needs (Sohn and Schwartzman 1994).

In considering the needs of communities in a democracy, the Knight Commission (2009) stated that community functions depend on information and exchange and that they need to accomplish four things that depend on information. Communities need to coordinate elections activities; they must solve problems that face them; they must establish systems of public accountability; and they must develop a sense of connectedness.

In each of the characterizations of critical information needs, both the FCC and the Knight Commission recognize that journalism is the critical intermediating practice that makes the overwhelming exchange of information possible for communities.

Most-Trusted News Source

A key factor in the relevance of any institution is whether the public trusts its work. For the media, in general, trust has taken a real hit. According to the Knight Foundation (2018), almost seven out of ten US adults say that they have lost trust in the media over the last ten years, and there is a significant divide between conservatives (95 percent) and liberals (46 percent). The overwhelming reasons that are given for the decline revolve around inaccuracy (seen as inaccurate/misleading reporting, alternative facts, fake news) and bias. However, 69 percent of the public also believe that trust can be restored.

There is some nuance to the findings. Rather than not trusting *any* media, two-thirds of the public indicates that it trusts only *some* media and not others. That includes 64 percent of Democrats and 75 percent of Republicans (Knight Foundation 2018). This may help explain the trust levels that are reported for local TV news. Most of the public (79 percent) trusts the news it gets from their local television stations and the significant majority (67 percent) say that they reference or repeat those news reports; that level of trust is consistent across Democrats (82 percent) and Republicans (80 percent) (TVB and Keller Fay Group 2015).

According to the Video Advertising Bureau (2018), television is identified as the most trusted source of accurate *political* information for adults in the United States—at 61 percent it outperforms newspapers (47 percent) and social media (31 percent). The difference is even more striking when it comes to forming an opinion about key issues—at 68 percent television news consumers are more opinionated than newspaper readers (18 percent) and social media followers (21 percent).

An increasing number of Americans get their news from social media sites. Elisa Shearer and Elizabeth Grieco (2019) found that Facebook is the most popular site with 52 percent of Americans using it, followed by YouTube which is used by 28 percent of Americans. However, Americans' evaluation of the news they get from these sites is tempered. Six out of ten say that social media companies have too much control over the news that people see and over half of them say that the control results in a worse mix of news for users.

In general, local television news is viewed as the least likely source of fake news. In a list of twenty-five news sources ranked in terms of likelihood to deliver fake news, only 8 percent of those surveyed viewed local television as a likely source of fake news. By contrast, Facebook was at the top of the list (58 percent), followed closely by Internet news sites (51 percent) and Twitter (45 percent). Fox News, CNN, and MSNBC were tied at 24 percent. The *New York Times* was at 17 percent. Local newspapers, CBS's *60 Minutes* and *Face the Nation*, and NPR were tied at 11 percent, and the *PBS News Hour* was at 9 percent (Statista 2019a).

The trust of television news extends across countries even as the use of social media and online sources has increased. Nic Newman, David Levy, and Rasmus Nielsen (2015) in their study of the news habits across twelve developed countries, including the United States, found that social media users value television news for accuracy and reliability (37 percent) over social media (12 percent). Further, "social media are not seen as a destination for accurate and reliable journalism but more as a way of getting access to it" (11).

There is a startling disconnect between the overall trust in news in the United States and the public's interest in it. Out of the twelve countries in Newman, Levy, and Nielsen's study, the United States came in last in overall trust in news—only 32 percent said that they trusted the news they get. Yet 67 percent stated that they were *interested* in local television news. Compared to fifteen other television, radio, and print sources, local television news scored the highest proportion of weekly usage (39 percent), followed by Fox News (32 percent). Even when compared to online sources, local television news sites were used weekly by 16 percent of the public, the fourth highest among the sources with the highest being Yahoo at 23 percent.

Ironically, the Russian disinformation effort during the 2016 campaign sought to capitalize on Americans' trust in local news. The Internet Research Agency (IRA) is a Kremlin-linked Russian troll farm and 30 percent of the URLs that it posted linked to local media outlets (Yin et al. 2018). Operatives who worked in the IRA in St. Petersburg created a number of Twitter accounts that posed as sources for Americans' hometown headlines. They had names such as @ElPasoTopNews, @MilwaukeeVoice, @CamdenCityNews, and @Seattle_Post (Mak and Berry 2018).

Civic and Political Engagement

The relationship between citizenship and democracy is fraught with challenges. James Madison put the point starkly: "A popular Government, without popular information, or the means of acquiring it, is but a Prologue to a Farce or a Tragedy; or, perhaps both. Knowledge will forever govern ignorance: and a people who mean to be their own Governors, must arm themselves with the power that knowledge gives" (quoted in Lloyd 2006, 11). However, there have been competing views about whether the people are up to the task of informing themselves to be capable democratic citizens. In fact, much of the evidence points to the deficiencies of citizens and to the drastic shortcomings of the media system to provide the "means to acquire" the necessary information for democracy to succeed. The characterizations are blunt: We have "democracy without citizens" (Entman 1996); America's uninformed citizens are our "dirty little secret" (Blumberg 1990, quoted in Delli Carpini and Keeter 1996, 23); the structure of the media system and its current form of news coverage get in the way of Americans doing their job as citizens (Fallows 1996; McChesney 2012).

Yet, in the face of these difficulties, the United States has been a stable democracy for more than two centuries and that has led some scholars to refer to the "paradox of modern democracy" (Delli Carpini and Keeter 1996, 22). They point to the information shortcuts that Americans use to inform their decisions. These "shortcuts—or heuristics—involve distancing oneself from the raw data by depending of someone else's synthesis of a particular issue or candidate" (51). As a result, the public can navigate through information regarding three broad areas of necessary political knowledge—the rules of the game, the substance of politics, and people and parties (Delli Carpini and Keeter 1996). The information-seeking behavior of the public is circumscribed by the media environment that surrounds it. Citizens cannot, of their own devices, discern the rules of the game, the substance of politics, or people and parties without a mediating system doing the work of gathering the information. That mediating system is my concern here. The news matters. It is the "hard-wiring of our democracy" (Hargreaves and Thomas 2002, 4)—especially in local places; and when it is diminished or absent altogether, its effect is immediate.

The local information environment affects political participation (O'Neill 2010). Absent local news, voters are less likely to turn out (Filla and Johnson

2010). But they are affected differently by different media. Matthew Gentzkow (2006) argues that television, because it is more focused on entertainment than news, reduces the consumption of newspapers and links its introduction into the local media system to lower political knowledge and voter turnout. Jesper Strömbäck and Adam Shehata (2018) show that there is a reciprocal relationship between political interest and watching public service but not commercial news. Danny Hayes and Jennifer Lawless (2015; 2018) connect the decline in local coverage, particularly in US House races, to decreased citizen engagement. Marc Hooghe (2002) and Heejo Keum (2004) argue that the types of programs, entertainment versus news, affects the civic-mindedness of viewers. A cross-national study showed that exposure to news outlets with high levels of political content (such as public television and broadsheet newspapers) contributes most to political knowledge. But that is "contingent" on the person's preexisting level of knowledge (de Vreese and Boomgaarden 2006).

The use of local media has a decided positive effect on community integration, particularly for local television. That community integration is linked to local political interest, knowledge, and participation (McLeod et al. 1996). Further, the use of local television news is associated with the civic duty to keep oneself informed (Poindexter and McCombs 2001).

Against the backdrop of the connection between media and citizenship, Jeffrey Jones (2006) argues that the study of media and politics is flawed by its three central assumptions: that news is the primary and proper sphere of political communication; that the most important function of media is to supply citizens with information; and that political engagement must necessarily be associated with physical activity. He proposes that we should look beyond the "instrumental orientation" of the media to an understanding of how the public integrates its media usage—a cultural view (365).

Whatever cultural media processes are at work, the public does use mass media as a place for political information. And they expect information to be there. Even in this social media–connected world, eight out of ten political conversations happen the old-fashioned way, face-to-face (TVB and Keller Fay Group 2015). That makes sense because the richness of face-to-face interaction is perfectly suited to contested and controversial topics. And the conversation often starts with television. Trust turns to influence as 61 percent of the public (significantly higher than any other news source) say that they refer to local television stories they receive in their daily conversations (TVB and Keller Fay Group 2015). Indeed, "TV, especially local TV, is the biggest content source for political conversations, and thus the key lever for driving political talk" (23).

A voter's decision-making process involves four steps: (1) discovering candidates and issues, (2) gathering information, (3) generating interest, and (4) casting the vote. In each of those steps, television is the dominant source for adults, regardless of party, occupation, gender, ethnicity, and age. For example, the percentage of adults who say that they first learn about candidates and issues from television is more than three times that of adults who cite newspapers (19 percent) and social media (18 percent) as their first touch points. Political ads on television are over three times more likely to spur voters to take action (that is, seek more information about a political candidate or discuss with others) than newspapers or social media. That is also the case for the third step, generating interest and staying informed throughout the election cycle. Finally, television is four times more likely than newspapers or social media to influence the final voting decision (Video Advertising Bureau 2018).

Local television news is the most prominent news source for local voters and people who are civically engaged with their communities—those who vote, volunteer and connect with those around them. An analysis of data from the Pew Research Center provides evidence (fig. 1.2).

Local television news is the only media source that passes the 50 percent threshold for all of the members of the public, whether they are highly active in the community (52 percent) or not active at all (50 percent). Social networking sites are used by just over one-third of highly active community members. Surprisingly, local newspapers are used by less than one-fifth of those citizens. People who always vote are more likely to learn about their communities from local television news; indeed, 63 percent of people who vote regularly get their daily news from local television stations (fig. 1.3).

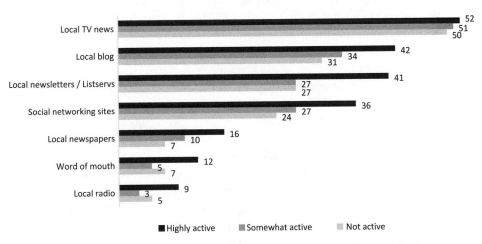

Figure 1.2. Local news habits of those who are highly, somewhat, or not at all active in local politics and groups (in percent). Source: Analysis of Pew Research Center data, "Civic Engagement Strongly Tied to Local News Habits," November 3, 2016 (Barthel et al. 2016).

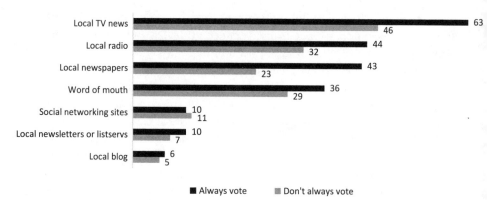

Figure 1.3. Local news habits of those who always or sometimes vote (in percent). Source: Analysis of Pew Research Center data, "Civic Engagement Strongly Tied to Local News Habits," November 3, 2016 (Barthel et al. 2016).

Audience Needs

The media system in the United States is highly competitive and highly commercialized. Media firms must make critical decisions every day about how to achieve and maintain an audience (van der Wurff and Schoenbach 2014, 433). The fundamental tension is whether to see the audience as consumers who are interested in a narrow range of information that satisfies individual demands or as citizens whose informational needs reflect a civic duty to be informed. These orientations have been characterized as citizen demands and civic demands. Citizen demands require information from the media that satisfies individual needs from consumer products to entertainment. Civic demands are informational needs that are geared toward the good of society as a whole. The dilemma is often portrayed as a zero-sum game—that the media and citizens must choose one or the other. However, that is not the case. There is an understanding that the public balances those demands in its expectations for the media (van der Wurff and Schoenbach 2014).

The space between citizen and civic demands is a conundrum for journalists to solve. Christine Schmidt (2018c, 1) proposes that a possible "middle ground," approaching the audience's needs from their perspective by providing information that "speaks to something they need the answer to in order to solve problems or overcome challenges or achieve things in their life." From this perspective, those informational needs can fulfill both citizen (What is the best television on the market? What's playing at the movies?) and civic (What is happening in our local school? What did the mayor/legislator/police chief say about crime?) demands.

That is borne out by research. According to Erik Sass (2014), over 75 percent of Americans think that celebrity gossip and scandal stories receive too much coverage; about half say that entertainment news gets too much attention. On the other hand, about half say that stories relating to humanitarian issues (47 percent), education (47 percent), science (45 percent), government corruption (44 percent), and white-collar crime (42 percent) receive too little coverage. However, even with that criticism, 78 percent say they trusted local television news more than local newspapers, cable TV news, national network news, or national newspapers.

When it comes to political ads on local television, we do know what citizens want. The 2016 Common Content Election Survey (CCES) study, in which Center for Political Communication at the University of Delaware participated, found that 57 percent of the public stated that local newscasts rarely or never examined the political ads that were broadcast. However, 51 percent of the respondents *strongly agreed* that they should examine the ads and almost four in ten (39 percent) *agreed* with the statement. Therefore, almost nine out of ten respondents (88 percent) expressed their desire for local television newscasts to address the political ads that they present. That is an expression of civic demand.

The Danger of Local News Deserts

What happens when television news is no longer a part of the local information ecology or it simply cannot fulfill its civic demand function? What does that landscape look like?

In 2017 Duke professor Philip Napoli conducted an important study entitled *Assessing Local Journalism: News Deserts, Journalism Divides, and the Determinant of the Robustness of Local News*. With the backdrop of the economic challenges that local journalism faces, he and his colleagues looked at news stories in one hundred randomly selected communities in the country. They limited their inquiry to relatively smaller communities—with populations between 20,000 and 300,000—and looked at the local television, print, radio, and online news sources in those markets. Napoli et al. asked two questions: Are some types of communities suffering more than others? Are there particular characteristics of individual communities that are related to the state of their journalism?

Their findings were sobering. Eight communities had *no* news addressing the critical information needs that were identified by the FCC (outlined earlier). Twelve communities had *no original* news stories; that is, there were no stories that originated within the community. Twenty communities had *no local stories* (Napoli et al. 2018). By this calculation, forty communities out of the one hundred labored under a media system that could not fulfill the most basic informational needs of its audience.

But there were other findings that are equally troublesome. Napoli et al. (2018, 2) also found that:

> Only about 17 percent of the news stories provided to a community are truly *local*—that is actually about or having taken place within—the municipality.
>
> Less than half (43 percent) of the news stories provided to a community by local media outlets are original (i.e., are produced by the local media outlet).
>
> Just over half (56 percent) of the news stories provided to a community by local media outlets address a critical information need.

The relationship of the three findings becomes clear if we consider how local news is produced by television stations in the United States and the consolidation that affects that production.

In 2017 the total number of television stations that aired local news programs reached an all-time high—1,072. However, only 703 of those stations actually produced news (Wenger and Papper 2018). The other 369 stations aired news that was produced somewhere else by somebody else who was not in the local community. For the most part, that is only possible if the stations are part of station groups that have news-producing stations. The relationship can be outright ownership or service agreements that bind the stations in scenarios in which one station relinquishes its news production capacity (and just about everything else) to another station in the group. Sometimes those stations are in the same community. In those instances, sometimes the "sharing" of content is a simulcast. That is, the exact same broadcast is aired on two stations in the market at the exact same time (Yanich 2013b). The only difference were the commercials; the station owners sold the same stories twice, to different sets of advertisers.

This consolidation phenomenon occurs much more frequently in smaller markets than in the large metropolitan areas (see chapter 7 for more details). When a station prepares a story, it bears the cost of that production. As in any business, the trick is to realize more revenue than the cost of the production. For stations that are part of a station group, the best way to generate that revenue is to air the story as many times as possible on as many stations as possible, because in each case the station receives revenue through commercials.

Perhaps most concerning of all, even communities that are the county seat (in which government activity occurs) do not see an increase in journalistic production. According to Napoli et al. (2018, 2), "such a pattern would seem to reinforce contemporary concerns about the decline of local government reporting." They conclude that news deserts are prominent in the communities that they studied and the results "seem to exacerbate the concerns about local journalism in the U.S." (14).

The loss of local news in communities is also the concern of journalists, especially when it comes to coverage of city hall. As local television news became more squeezed by profit-maximizing forces, station owners increasingly developed a model of "infotainment" that aims to attract audiences through sensational news (McManus 1994). In so doing, television reporters on the city hall beat perceived a diminishing commitment, lower quality, fewer stories, and less airtime for local government and political coverage (Coulson et al. 2001).

The disconnect between what journalists can and want to do and the structural and organizational impediments that prevent them is clear in Phyliss Kaniss's (1995) examination of the Philadelphia mayoral race in 1991. As stories focused on the race and a search for scandal, the public did not learn about policy or governing. But she makes a telling point (the same one that Napoli made in 2017). The fundamental failing in campaign coverage was not due to the incompetence or personal weaknesses of the reporters: "They failed because of the system of rewards and constraints set up by the news organizations" (365).

Beyond the coverage of city hall, the number of statehouse reporters has declined dramatically. A Pew Research Center study defines these journalists as those who are physically assigned to the capitol. To be sure, most are newspaper reporters (38 percent), but television journalists comprise the next largest group (17 percent). The number of newspaper statehouse reporters declined by 35 percent from 2009 to 2014 (Enda, Matsa, and Boyles 2014). As for local television news, 86 percent of stations do not assign even one reporter—full time or part time—to the statehouse. By definition, these reductions affect the news organization's *capacity* to cover political news (Peterson 2017).

Even when local television stations cover local issues, they focus on crime. In a study of the stations in the Los Angeles market in 2009, crime was the most prominent lead story. The implications for citizen information are clear. We live our lives in local places and the decisions of local officials are especially important. The former communications director of the National Conference of State Legislatures laments the situation: "The public is not being kept aware of important policy decisions that affect their lives" (quoted in Enda, Matsa, and Boyles 2014, 2).

The loss of local news affects the level to which local officials can be held accountable. One area is government finance decisions. Pengjie Gao, Chang

Lee, and Dermot Murphy (2018) found that in municipalities that suffered the closure of its newspaper, the borrowing costs rose from 5 to 11 percent. The increase was not driven by deteriorating economic conditions. According to Gao, Lee, and Murphy (2018, 18), the loss of monitoring produced government inefficiencies:

> Revenue bonds are commonly issued to finance local projects such as schools and hospitals and are backed by the revenues generated by those projects. General obligation bonds, on the other hand, are typically used to finance public works projects such as roadways and parks and are backed by local taxes and fees. Revenue bonds should be subject to greater scrutiny because of the free cash cows that these projects generate, and these bonds are rarely regulated by the state government. A local newspaper provides an ideal monitoring agent for these revenue-generating projects, as mismanaged projects can be exposed by investigative reporters employed by the local newspaper. When a newspaper closes, this monitoring mechanism also ceases to exist, leading to a greater risk that the cash cows generated by these projects will be mismanaged.

Gao, Lee, and Murphy concede that, increasingly, the public will move to online news sources. But they warn that these "paradigm-shifting news outlets do not necessarily provide a good substitute for high-quality, locally-sourced, investigative journalism" (31–32). They quote former *Baltimore Sun* reporter and famous television producer (*The Wire, Tremé*) David Simon's wry comment in 2009 about the focus and interest of online news organizations: "The day I run into a *Huffington Post* reporter at a Baltimore Zoning Board hearing is the day that I will be confident that we've actually reached some sort of equilibrium" (32).

Public health is also affected by local journalism. Health reporter Helen Branswell (2018) writes about Maia Majumder, a computational epidemiology research fellow at HealthMap (a disease detection project run by the Boston Children's Hospital) and the connection to local news. The website uses non-traditional sources to find outbreaks, including local media reports that function as an early warning system much before the official data are available. Such was the case for a massive mumps outbreak in northwestern Arkansas in 2016–2017. Key data were not available from official sources, and it would have been time-consuming to retrieve it. But the local newspaper, the *Northwest Arkansas Democrat-Gazette*, had followed the outbreak closely, reporting that the vaccine refusal rate in that region was higher than anywhere else in the state. That was crucial information for the response to the outbreak.

Majumder is worried about the news deserts in communities and leaving voters behind: "What that means is they lose access to news which is very, very
vital for knowing what's going on in your town. But also from the public health
surveillance point of view, we're losing access to knowing what they need" (6).

With the loss of local coverage, there have been sources vying to fill the
void. First, elected officials provide their own news feeds for public television,
broadcast outlets, or the Internet. California representative and former House
Intelligence Committee Chairman Devin Nunes takes it a good bit further. A
relentless critic of the media and supporter of all things Trump, he set up his
own partisan alternative news site, *The California Republican*. Although it is
classified on Facebook as a media/news company, the small print at the bottom of the page states that it is paid for by the Nunes campaign committee
(Siders 2018).

In addition to the efforts of elected officials, others have attempted to fill
the gap. "For-profit and nonprofit digital news organizations, ideological outlets, and high-priced publications aimed at insiders have popped up all over
the country, often staffed by veteran reporters with experience covering state
government" (Enda, Matsa, and Boyles 2014, 2). However, that effort does not
fill the void left by the overall decline.

Among the digital news sources that have appeared to respond to the
dearth of local news are citizen journalism sites. But if they are to be legitimate substitutions or compliments to traditional media, they must conduct
the type of journalism that, in the words of Frederick Fico et al. (2013, 153),
"informs citizens about local institutions and connects them to their communities." However earnest they are in filling the breach, they are an imperfect
substitute for most newspapers.

Coverage of Local Politics

Apart from the coverage of local issues, in general, local media's attention—or
lack thereof—to local political races affects the politics of the races. You might
think that is intuitively obvious, but, as they say, the devil is in the details.

Geography is important—both for the political jurisdictions and the markets in which the media operate and sell their services. That is particularly so
when it comes to congressional districts and media markets. James Snyder and
David Strömberg (2010) looked at the level of congruence between newspaper
markets and congressional districts and local political coverage. They defined
congruence as the share of the newspaper readership who lived in the congressional district. Then, they followed what they called, "the chain of media
impacts, link by link: congruence increases newspapers' political coverage,

which, in turn, makes voters better informed, which increases monitoring and induces politicians to work harder, which, finally, produces better policies (for their constituencies)" (357). That is how it is supposed to work and based on their research, it did. Snyder and Stromberg found that, as congruence increased, so did the amount of political reporting in the papers—and the effect on the amount of political coverage was significant. But, much more importantly, they also found that the "chain of events" occurred, and it affected both the activity of citizens and that of elected officials: as citizens knew more about their congressional representatives, they monitored their activities and held them accountable for their actions, and they were more inclined to vote. That accountability induced elected officials to act in ways that were clearly responsive to what voters wanted. And the demand for monitoring leads to more political coverage—and so the circle continued. However, there has been a steady decline in the level of journalistic resources dedicated to local politics.

The content of the coverage matters regarding citizens' political knowledge and their participation in politics and voting. And that holds true across nations. Conflict is a major media frame (McManus 1994; de Vreese 2004; Semetko 2000). It has high news value and it attracts an audience. A comparative cross-national study of twenty-seven countries found that using a conflict frame as an evaluation of the European Union (EU) mobilized voters more in those nations than in nations in which the EU was framed in a positive light (Schuck, Vliegenthart, and de Vreese 2016). Further, some argue that conflict signals to the public that something is at stake and that politics is framed as a game with clear winners and losers (Bennett 2016).

According to Johanna Dunaway and Regina Lawrence (2015), the game framing of politics is affected by three classes of contextual variables—the internal news-making context, the media economic market context, and the electoral political context. Although they studied newspapers, their findings are instructive for television. They found that organizational variables matter. Specifically, private independents, and small, local, and privately owned chains produced less game-framing content than large geographically diffuse chains and public shareholder companies. Further, the size and reach of the newspaper affects the coverage as large geographically diffuse firms produce more game-framing content than geographically small chains. They suggest that this may be due to economies of scale in which the large chains do not invest in local coverage. However, they found that a close political race will be covered using the game frame by both types of newspaper chains. Ownership structure does not outweigh that device to cover an exciting race that is made more exciting by continuously following who is up and who is down.

Who gets covered? All members of Congress are not the same when it comes to coverage of the House of Representatives. Brian Schaffner and Pat Sellers (2003) confirm the importance of geography as they focus on the "market-district dyad" which looks at the extent to which a congressional district is located within a newspaper's market. They also found that two types of legislators get more coverage than others—congressional leaders and members of the "out party," the party not controlling the presidency. In each of these cases, the coverage is based on the members' *national* importance and not their local roles. In addition, Jeremy Padgett, Johanna Dunaway and Joshua Darr (2019) looked at how television broadcasters treat members of the US House of Representatives when it comes to giving them access to their airwaves. They found that the broadcasters give the most on-air time to the members of the US House who are the most extremely partisan, thereby reinforcing the notion that the institution is hopelessly polarized. Moderate members do not make the news. The problem with such coverage is that rank-and-file members of Congress lose an important means to communicate with their constituencies. Yes, you could argue that this is less important in our social media age. That is true, but only to a point. Touting your accomplishments through your own social media mechanisms where you control all of the content is very different than being covered by local media. The coverage might even be less favorable than the member would like. At the very least, the coverage signals to the public that the member is an important political actor in local politics.

How does television fit into this story? As mentioned previously, it still commands a large audience. Gregory Martin and Joshua McCrain (2019) looked at local television news to determine if the trend of decreasing attention to local politics was demand or supply-side driven. They did so particularly in this time of local television acquisition by large station groups. They found that the ownership changes had "substantial increases in coverage of national politics at the expense of local politics" (1). So, the changes in the coverage were driven by what the owners wanted to supply.

The preeminence of national coverage at the expense of local issues has been a feature of local television news for some time. Studying newscasts in eleven markets during the 2004 presidential campaign, Martin Kaplan, Ken Goldstein, and Matthew Hale (2005) found that 61 percent of all campaign stories focused on the presidential contest and only one market, Denver, was below the 50 percent mark. Conversely, only 8 percent of the broadcasts had a story that related to a local race—US House, state senate or assembly, among others. Only 12 percent of broadcasts contained a story about a US Senate race. Perhaps more revealing, less than 1 percent of campaign stores contained any critique of candidate ads.

The lack of local coverage and the attendant emphasis on the presidential campaign even have an effect on communities in which social capital is considered to be high. Daniel Stevens et al. (2006) looked at the Minneapolis television market (the thirteenth largest market at the time) during the 2000 campaign. They found that the coverage of the races was highly skewed toward the presidential race with little attention paid to a close US Senate election and virtually no coverage of any other race. That meant that the overwhelming coverage of the campaign was not local but national. That is possible because, with access to network resources and their emphasis on the presidential campaign, it was easier for the stations to stay national rather than local. They also found that the public was annoyed with the coverage and expressed frustration with the brevity and superficiality of the coverage, particularly with the substitution of the reporters' voices rather than that of the candidate. That said, the authors conclude that "civic and political involvement in Minnesota may remain high despite, rather than because of, political coverage by local television news" (61).

This frustration with the local news coverage of political campaigns may have an antecedent in how local newscasts cover the world in general—the "mean world" effect (Allen et al. 2007). Local newscasts' penchant for focusing on crime, disaster, and human peril elevate the audience's sense of danger and vulnerability. That may frame any following stories about news and politics, creating an environment where "there is no truth, nothing is fair and there is no relevance" (510). Further, the public was also frustrated when newscasts tried to clarify points. For example, as broadcasts presented polling results that revealed very different realities—Bush was ahead, Kerry was ahead—they left the audience confused. Focus group participants came to the conclusion that the stations were using the polling numbers "for what they want" (530). In that way, the public saw the media as just another player in the political drama.

Even when local television stations cover local issues, often one topic dominates the reporting—crime. In a study of the stations in the Los Angeles television market in 2009, crime was the most prominent lead story (Kaplan and Hale 2010). That is consistent with my own research when I compared the coverage of crime in relation to the incidence of crime in urban and suburban places (Yanich 2004; 2001).

The Public Interest Obligation

One consideration of what local news covers and does not cover is rooted in its public interest obligation. The government gave broadcasters free use of the electromagnetic spectrum—a public good—in the form of licenses. In return, the license holders acknowledged that they would broadcast to fulfill the "public interest, convenience and necessity." That was the bargain that was struck in the Radio Act of 1927 and the Communications Act of 1934 and reaffirmed in the 1996 Telecommunications Act. Broadcasters have continuously challenged the rule on First Amendment grounds and as unfairly restricting commerce. However, the courts have consistently upheld its importance and its validity (Fowler et al., 2007).

The public interest, however, is an ambiguous and contested notion. When it comes to broadcasting, the FCC is charged with ferreting out how it is met. It uses three principles to regulate the market—diversity, competition, and localism. Of the three principles, localism has been the least studied and is often the most elusive to capture (Napoli 2001; 2003). Yet it is at the heart of the questions that I raise in the book. What could be more important to the citizens of local places than to understand who wants to represent them, what their representatives intend to do, and what they have done?

The most comprehensive study of the information needs of citizens was conducted by the FCC in 2011 and it comes to seemingly opposite views of the role of local television news in this dilemma. First, even as it acknowledges the growth of the Internet, it is unequivocal: "In many ways, local TV news is more important now than ever" (Waldman 2011, 13). Then it offers a more disturbing view of the media: "The current system operates neither as a free market nor as an effectively regulated one; and it does not achieve the public interest goals set out by Congress or the FCC" (25). That is a stark assessment by the very institution that is charged with making sure that the broadcasters operated in "the public interest, convenience, and necessity."

Summary

Local television news remains a dominant source of political information in the United States: (1) Even though it has lost some viewers, it retains a sizable and politically significant audience; (2) there is a lot of local broadcast news on television stations throughout the country, an average of six hours per day; (3) citizens who are the most civically and politically engaged use local television news as their prime source for local political information and (4) where there

is a lack of news—news deserts—civic engagement and political accountability are seriously hampered. Political candidates and advocacy organizations recognize the central role that local television news plays in the
calculus of campaigns. That is why they spend hundreds of millions of dollars to place their ads on those programs. Those political ads are the focus
of the next chapter.

2

A Brief History of Political Advertising

David Axelrod, President Obama's senior advisor, once characterized political ads on local television a "nuclear weapon." During Obama's second campaign, local television gave them greater assurance that their messages would hit the right geographic targets, "it is a national campaign, but it is delivered locally" (quoted in James 2011, 2).

Even though political advertising on television dominates American political campaigns, it is important to remember that the initial reaction to it, by politicians and the public alike, was "hostile, even contemptuous . . . regarding the practice as "antithetical to American democratic political traditions" (Nichols and McChesney 2013, 128). Adlai Stevenson, the Democratic presidential nominee in 1952 and 1956, was aghast: "This is the worst idea I ever heard of . . . the idea that you can merchandise candidates for high office like breakfast cereal . . . is the ultimate indignity to the democratic process" (130).

However, politicians were not the only group that worried about political advertising. Even some of commercial advertising's prominent players did not like the idea. David Ogilvy, founder of Ogilvy and Mather, thought that political advertising, "represented the worst abuse imaginable of the advertising man's skills" (Nichols and McChesney 2013, 134).

That view extended to Ogilvy and Mather's creative director, Robert Spero. He took a leave from the firm to conduct his own analysis of political ads in elections from 1952 to 1976. In *The Duping of America* he reached a fundamental conclusion—that the key distinction between commercial ads and political ads was that the latter had First Amendment protection from fraud and misleading content. Political ads can say whatever they want "without the fear of regulatory reprisal" (Nichols and McChesney 2013, 134). The point that he was making was that political ads routinely contained a level of false and misleading information that commercial advertising could not possibly approach without facing the wrath of the Federal Trade Commission.

In addition to politicians and professional advertising firms who railed against political advertising, there were also newspapers such as the Republican-leaning *New York World Telegram* who expressed concern over the GOP's use of advertising people in congressional campaigns. They ran a large headline saying that "The Hucksters" had taken over the party (Nichols and McChesney 2013, 129).

Oh, how things have changed. We are definitely not in Kansas anymore.

Political ads have been on television for a long time. The 1952 presidential campaign was the first to feature them as Republican candidate, General Dwight D. Eisenhower, evoked memories of World War II in his successful effort to win the presidency. And there have been infamous ads from that time to the present day.

In 1964 Lyndon Johnson's "Daisy" ad portrayed a little girl picking flowers in a meadow as a mushroom cloud rose behind her. It was a graphic and ominous reference to the idea that his Republican opponent, Arizona Senator and retired Air Force General Barry Goldwater, was unfit for office in a nuclear age. The backlash against the ad was such that it was only aired one time.

In 1988 Democratic candidate and Massachusetts Governor Michael Dukakis had a seventeen-point lead over Republican George H. W. Bush. That changed after the Bush campaign aired the "Willie Horton" ad. Horton was a convicted African American man who, while on furlough from a Massachusetts prison, raped a white woman. The ad drew a direct line between that crime and the perception that Dukakis was "soft" on crime. Lee Atwater, the Republican advertising guru who was responsible for the ad, boasted, "By the time this election is over, Willie Horton will be a household name" (West 2017, 2). Bush went on to win 53 to 46 percent. Atwater, before his death of brain cancer in 1991, reportedly apologized for the ad and the racist flames that it stoked (Nichols and McChesney, 2013).

In 2004 Democratic Senator John Kerry was running against incumbent George W. Bush. Kerry was a decorated Vietnam veteran who emphasized that record in his campaign and referred to the men with whom he served as a "band of brothers." That was in contrast to Bush who reportedly was able to evade military combat duty. Enter an unknown independent group—Swift Boat Veterans for Truth. They ran a series of ads that portrayed Kerry as a coward saying that he had betrayed his brothers. The claims were bogus, but Kerry did essentially nothing to repudiate the ads. He thought that the obvious falsity of the ads would be self-evident and that a response would only exacerbate the situation. He was wrong. He lost to Bush in a very tight race.

In 2016 Hillary Clinton ran ads that questioned Donald Trump's fitness for office. They framed the election as a moral choice. The most direct of them used Trump's own derogatory words about women and at the end emphatically states that, "anyone who believes, says, does what he does, is unfit to be president." She hammered again and again in her ads at the notion that Trump was unfit to be president. Another ad, sponsored by Hillary for America, featured children engrossed in watching television as Trump makes his hateful statements. The image fades to black and it is replaced by a single sentence, "Our children are watching" (Dunaway et al. 2019).

These ads are etched in our memories, and they were all part of presidential campaigns. But while most political ads were aired by national television networks through the 1970s, that changed by the 1990s when almost all political advertising had migrated to local broadcast television (Fowler, Franz, and Ridout 2016). That also meant that political ads for local races were now featured on local broadcasts. These ads moved to local broadcasting as the content of ads had become increasingly negative (Fowler, Franz, and Ridout 2016).

Over-the-top ads also made it into down-ballot races. Bridget McCormack was the Democratic nominee in the race for the Michigan Supreme Court in 2012. Five years earlier she volunteered (as other liberal, conservative, Republican, Democrat lawyers did) on a project organized by the Center for Constitutional Rights which sought to obtain civil trials for suspects detained at the prison at Guantanamo Bay, Cuba. The purpose was not to free the prisoners but to provide them with representation that American and international law required. However, in the campaign for the Supreme Court seat, an ad appeared on Michigan television that accused McCormack of being a legal ally of terrorism. It featured the mother of a soldier killed in Afghanistan who said: "My son is a hero and fought to protect us . . . Bridget McCormack volunteered to help free a terrorist. How could you?" (Nichols and McChesney 2013, 126).

There are three essential facts about the ad that characterize our political ad environment—its sponsor, the ad claims, and the response of the stations that aired it. First, the money for the ad did not come from Michigan. It was sponsored by a conservative Washington-based group called the Judicial Crisis Network. They probably did not have a particular objection to McCormack, but they shared the opinion with Michigan conservatives that keeping a conservative majority on the high court was essential (Nichols and McChesney 2013). Second, the claim in the ad—that McCormack wanted to free terrorists—was false on its face. The *New York Times* as well as local papers condemned the ad, pointing out that the volunteers for the group wanted to defend our legal system and to make sure that its protections were applied to all prisoners, as the law required. Third, and this is especially important for my study, is that, despite the false claims in the ads, the ad kept running on Michigan television as the stations did nothing to clarify the message. All the while, the stations collected over $1 million from the Judicial Crisis Network (Nichols and McChesney 2013). They correctly calculated that the McCormack campaign would raise the necessary funds to pay them to air ads that countered the original ad which it did. And the local television stations won again—without having to do any journalism—which brings me to the money, the lifeblood of political advertising. Even in the face of that ad, McCormack won the seat on the court and became its chief Justice in 2019.

Political campaigns in the United States are based on money—a lot of it. The combined total amount for local, state, and national races in 2012 was $9.4 billion; that number rose to $9.8 billion in 2016 (Cassino 2017). If we look at just the presidential and congressional races, the costs keep rising and they account for a very high proportion of the total cost. In the 2000 campaign the total cost (presidential and congressional races) was just over $3 billion. By 2004 it had risen to $4.1 billion; $5.3 billion in 2008, $6.3 billion in 2012, and $6.5 billion in 2016 (Center for Responsive Politics 2018). And most of that went to political advertising. And most political advertising is on television.

The money mattered. In the 2016 election in the House, the average winner spent almost $1.5 million; the loser, just over $354,000. House Speaker Republican Paul Ryan spent the most to retain his seat—almost $13.4 million. In the Senate, the average winner spent about $12.1 million; the average loser spent less than half of that, $5.7 million. The most expensive Senate race was in Pennsylvania, an important battleground state, where incumbent Republican Senator Pat Toomey spent almost $31 million to defeat his Democratic challenger (Center for Responsive Politics 2018).

The Campaign Finance Rules

The money has always been subject to the rules of the game. For my purposes, I go back to the rules that came about in the 1970s when, in 1971, Congress passed a major campaign finance reform bill, the Federal Election Campaign Act (FECA), which it revised in 1974. They were a reaction to the Watergate controversy that resulted in Richard Nixon's resignation from the presidency in August 1974. Although the rules were modified because of legal challenges, those developments were largely complete by 1976 (Fowler, Franz, and Ridout 2016).

The rules were strict and expressly banned candidates from accepting political contributions from corporations and unions. They could have only three sources: individual citizens, party committees, or political action committees (PACs), although candidates can contribute an unlimited amount of their own funds. PACs are comprised of individuals who are affiliated with corporations, unions, or trade associations. They form an association to pool their money and then to distribute it to candidates whom they support. It is important to note that all of the money of PACs comes from the *voluntary* contributions of its members. The contributions were limited in size— for PACs, the limit was $5,000 per election; for individuals, it was $1,000 per election. By 2014, however, the individual contribution limit was raised to $2,600.

In addition to the restrictions on the amount of contributions that a candidate could receive, the reform efforts embodied in FECA also limited the general total amount of spending in an election and the specific amount that candidates could spend in an election campaign. However, those restrictions were wiped away in the case *Buckley v. Valeo*. The United States Supreme Court ruled that election spending was equivalent to election speech and that the First Amendment prohibited Congress from making any law that abridged free speech. To be certain, there is a long-standing and profound debate regarding whether spending money is equivalent to speech (Wright 1975; Sullivan 1996; Smith 1997; Shover et al. 2006; Hellman 2010; Allard 2016). Because of the tenuous ground between money and speech, it was much easier to remove the limits on spending rather than how candidates got the money to spend—the contributions.

The *Buckley* ruling, however, did allow some spending limits to remain— those in voluntary public funding systems. That is a system for the public funding of presidential elections into which candidates can enter. However, once they accept public funding for the presidential campaign and receive a lump sum of money, their expenditures are limited to the amount of that grant. The court reasoned that if the candidates voluntarily opted into the system, they essentially consented to limiting their speech. It is important to note that every presidential candidate opted into the system until 2008, when Barack Obama opted out. Mitt Romney did the same in 2012 (Fowler, Franz, and Ridout 2016). And, of course, in 2016, neither Hillary Clinton nor Donald Trump chose to receive public funding.

The FECA rules had a particularly limiting effect on the amount of independent expenditures that parties could spend on behalf of a candidate that was not coordinated with the campaign. But in 1996 the Supreme Court, in *Colorado Republican Federal Campaign Committee et al. v. Federal Election*

Commission, ruled that such a prohibition was an infringement on the parties' First Amendment rights (Fowler, Franz, and Ridout 2016).

That lifting of the limit was important, but there was a loophole in the campaign finance laws that the parties used to raise and spend *soft money*, which is money raised outside of the regulatory system of campaign finance laws that would ordinarily be prohibited. The parties argued that this *soft money* was used for state and local candidates and for party building, not for federal campaigns and therefore permissible under campaign finance rules. This was contrasted with *hard money* that was raised and subject to the finance rules because it was used to directly fund a federal campaign.

As the courts continued to loosen the campaign finance rules in the 1990s, they made a distinction between *express advocacy* and *issue advocacy*. And that distinction was crucial to the capacity of interest groups to spend money on campaigns. In a nutshell, express advocacy placed the ad squarely under the finance limits. The *Buckley* decision spelled it out: if an ad used terms such as "vote for," "elect," "cast your ballot for," "vote against," "defeat," or "reject," it *expressly* advocated for the voter to take a preferred position. But absent those words, the ad could be considered as expressing advocacy for a position, not a candidate. As such, it could be supported by *soft money* with no limits. Interest groups had found a way to promote their points of view without being encumbered by stringent regulations (Fowler, Franz, and Ridout 2016).

The expanded use of soft money, however, prompted Congress to overhaul campaign finance laws in 2002 with the Bipartisan Campaign Reform Act (BCRA). The act basically removed the parties' use of soft money to get around the strict campaign finance laws. But the parties adjusted; they simply developed and used other ways to raise large amounts of hard money. The most successful of those strategies was donations from individual donors. Once the BCRA rules were implemented, the parties aggressively pursued hard-money individual donors to fill the vacuum left by the loss of soft money. And they were very good at it. For example, in the first campaign after the BCRA went into effect, the presidential election of 2004, the parties increased their contribution total from individuals by 129 percent; and in the midterm election of 2006 by another 82 percent (Fowler, Franz, and Ridout 2016).

Citizens United

The real change in campaign finance rules came in 2010 with the Supreme Court's ruling in *Citizens United v. Federal Election Commission*. The case was brought by an interest group, Citizens United, which produced a highly critical documentary of then-Senator Hillary Clinton that was to be distributed through cable as video on demand for free. The court could have limited its decision only to the *Citizens United* question in which the organization produced television ads for cable and broadcast television announcing the availability of the documentary. The group sought injunctive relief from the restrictions on express advocacy in *Buckley* arguing that a video-on-demand (VOD) documentary should be exempt from the *Buckley* restrictions because its VOD delivery system "has a lower risk of distorting the political process than do television ads" (*Citizens United* 2010, 1). But the Supreme Court did not decide the case narrowly, saying that doing so "was not sustainable under a fair reading of the statute" (16). The court, in a 5-to-4 decision, ruled that the words outlined in *Buckley* that identified express advocacy were unconstitutional and overturned all of the restrictions on interest-group advocacy. In so ruling, the case overturned the restrictions of the BCRA and the search for loopholes was over—in a very big way. They could now raise and spend as much as they could muster in their electioneering activities without limit.

The limitations on contributions and spending contained in the laws that the *Citizens United* ruling dismantled were grounded in the notion that money could corrupt the political process and, therefore, limits were warranted. However, *Citizens United* proposed a very narrow definition of corruption. It was now defined as quid pro quo, a specific amount of money in exchange for a specific act. That rendered the notion of corruption so narrow as to effectively take it off the table. Understood that way, corruption became a relatively rare occurrence. Therefore, the government's legitimate interest in protecting the political system from corruption could not outweigh the First Amendment right of free speech of the groups whose political contributions and spending had been limited. However, political money to acquire political influence is rarely that direct. Justice John Paul Stevens made the point in his dissent:

> At bottom the Court's opinion is thus a rejection of the common sense of the American people, who have recognized a need to prevent corporations from undermining self-government since the founding, and who have fought against the distinct corrupting potential of corporate electioneering since the days of Theodore Roosevelt. It is a strange time to repudiate that common sense. While American democracy is imperfect, few outside the majority of this Court would have thought its flaws included a dearth of corporate money in politics (Nichols and McChesney 2013, 117–118).

The effect of *Citizens United* was thunderous. In order to comply with the ruling, the Federal Elections Commission allowed the creation of super PACs.

These organizations could raise unlimited funds and use that money to expressly advocate for or against candidates without restriction, as long as they did not coordinate their activities with a candidate's campaign. There was another aspect to the ruling—donors to these super PACs had to be identified. There is also a way around that if the organizations formed as a nonprofit 501c group. These *dark money* groups, as they are known, can and do hide their donations from public disclosure and they can do that with unlimited sums. It is important to note that nonprofit 501c groups have been around for a long time and they have proved to be very important in influencing elections. However, the restriction was that political activities could not be their primary purpose (Fowler, Franz, and Ridout 2016).

The effect of *Citizens United* was direct and immediate when it came to outside group spending in political cycles. Across federal elections, the lifting of the ban on using general treasury funds to pay for outside spending led to an increase of 400 percent (in 2014 USD) in independent political advertising between 2010 and 2020 (Abdul-Razaak, Prato, and Wolton 2017). In the presidential election of 2008, just prior to the ruling, outside group spending was at about $338.5 million. In the very next presidential cycle in 2012, it increased about 300 percent to just over $1 billion. In 2016 the total for outside group spending was over $1.4 billion (Statista 2019b). In a study of the decade under the rules of *Citizens United*, Karl Evers-Hillstrom (2020) found that we experienced $4.5 billion in nonparty outside spending, the top ten donors gave $1.2 billion to candidates, parties, and other groups and groups that do not disclose their funders spent $963,000,000. More importantly, we have seen the rise of the modern megadonor, the top 1 percent of whom accounted for seventy-seven of contributions to super PACs. The remaining 23 percent came from the other 99 percent of contributors.

What did all of this potential for political spending mean to private firms? In the days following the ruling, the shareholder value of politically active firms increased as they were now able to anticipate new avenues for political participation. Interestingly, that advantage accrued more to small and medium-sized firms that spend less on lobbying and to firms that operated in heavily regulated industries (Stratmann and Verret 2015). Essentially, *Citizens United* offered a path to influence that could be less expensive than all-out lobbying, but perhaps just as effective.

Whereas *Citizens United* removed the spending limits on organizations, another Supreme Court case did the same for individuals. In *McCutcheon et al. v. Federal Election Commission*, the court by a 5-to-4 decision, removed the aggregate limit that any individual could contribute to political candidates in an election cycle. The court decided that "the right to participate in a democracy through political contributions is protected by the First Amendment, but that right is not absolute" (*McCutcheon* 2014, 1). Congress may regulate campaign contributions to protect against corruption or its appearance. However, the Court ruled that it may not "regulate contributions simply to reduce the money in politics, or to restrict the political participation of some in order to enhance the relative influence of others" (1). Before the ruling, individuals were limited to giving $48,600 combined to all federal candidates and $74,600 combined to all parties and political action committees for a total of $123,200. *McCutcheon* wiped out those limits. There are still limits to what any individual can contribute to an individual campaign—$2,600 or $5,200, if you count the primary and general election. But a person can contribute to as many candidates as she wants.

The real impact of *McCutcheon* is the proliferation of joint fundraising committees (JFCs). These committees allow a contributor to write a very large check to the umbrella group, which then disburses the funds to candidates as it sees fit. The JFC is not a candidate and therefore there is no limit on the amount of money a donor can contribute.

The rules of campaign financing have changed the actions of donors and recipients alike. First, the rules have changed *who* is sponsoring the bulk of the political advertising. Political parties and their soft money spending were dominant until *Citizens United*. Now super PACs and 501c groups are responsible for spending more than the parties on political ads. Erika Fowler, Michael Franz, and Travis Ridout (2016) cite three trends that are the result of the campaign finance rules: the rising cost of campaigns, the rising cost of political ads and elections, and a decrease in transparency.

The cost of campaigns to candidates is on the rise as a result of the increased money that can be used for media, as those limits were undone. Candidates must spend much of their time raising money and, if they are incumbents, they must do that outside of their offices or it would be a violation of the law (Fowler, Franz, and Ridout 2016). In the 2016 election cycle, almost 45 percent of the $9.8 billion that was spent on all media was directed to broadcast television (Cassino 2017). But that also has implications for down-ballot races. In races for the Senate in 2012 and 2014, candidates used an average of 32 percent of their total budgets just to buy political advertising on local television stations (Fowler, Franz, and Ridout 2016).

The second trend is that the cost of ads for parties and interest groups has increased significantly which is all part of the supply and demand of the market. Candidates enjoy the benefit of the *lowest unit rate*. However, that does not apply to interest groups—they pay whatever the market will bear. And local television stations in markets with competitive races understand that the inventory of commercial time, especially on local newscasts, becomes a hot commodity, especially right before election day. Therefore, they command very inflated prices for that commercial time, and they get it (Daunt 2012). Because of *Citizens United*, the gap between what candidates and interest groups pay for ads continues to widen. That may change how donors distribute their contributions between candidates and interest groups. It will certainly change how sponsors make their decisions about political ads buys in the local markets (Fowler, Franz, and Ridout 2016).

The increase in the cost of elections is obvious. Between 2000 and 2016, the total cost of elections (adjusted for inflation) in presidential years increased from $4.4 billion in 2000 to $6.8 billion in 2012 and 2016, an increase of over 150 percent (Center for Responsive Politics 2018). The total for 2016 was close to 2012 because Donald Trump did not spend as much on political ads as expected. He did not have to because he was the recipient of $5 billion of free coverage as the media firms tried to capitalize on the reality-show nature of the campaign.

Midterm elections were also affected by *Citizens United*. The first campaign after *Citizens United* was decided in January 2010 was the midterm election that year. In 2006 the total cost (adjusted for inflation) for congressional races amounted to about $2.8 billion; that jumped to $4.2 billion in 2010, an increase of 150 percent (Center for Responsive Politics 2018). In 2018 the cost of the midterm election jumped to a record high of $5.2 billion as a result of the hyper-partisan contest over who controlled Congress in the age of Trump (Center for Responsive Politics 2019).

The most corrosive aspect of *Citizens United* is how it grossly unbalances the playing field of the election process, not that it was all that balanced before. When considering how citizens make their preferences known by financially supporting a candidate, the ruling produced bizarre and troubling results. With their study of the 2012 election, Blair Bowie and Adam Lioz (2013, 3) revealed some sobering facts:

> The top 32 PAC donors, giving an average of $9.9 million *each*, matched the $313 million that President Obama and Mitt Romney raised from all of their small donors combine—that's 3.7 million people giving less than $200 each.
>
> Nearly 60 percent of Super PAC funding came from 159 donors contributing at least $1 million.
>
> More than 93 percent of the money Super PACS raised came from 3,318 donors with contributions of at least $10,000—*that is .0011 percent of the U.S. population.*

At the Down Ballot level, candidates for the House and Senate raised the majority of the funds from gifts of $1,000 or more.

40 percent of all contributions to Senate candidates came from donors giving, at least, $2,500, from just .02 *percent of the American population*. (Emphasis added)

The third trend that Fowler, Franz, and Ridout (2016) identify is the transparency that surrounds the sponsors of political ads and that is centered on the disclosure of the identity of donors. PACs disclose their donors as required by law. But two groups, super PACS and groups organized as 501c4s, cause some concern. "Super PACS must report contributions and expenditures but they can accept unlimited contributions from groups that are not fully transparent" (37). The second group is nonprofits that are active in politics who organize themselves as 501c4s. Electioneering is not their primary purpose. They do not need to disclose donors; they can use what is called "dark money."

Fowler, Franz, and Ridout looked at advertising disclosure in the 2012 and 2014 election campaigns for president and Congress. They found that "dark money" ads, those that were sponsored by groups who did not disclose donors, were not the majority of interest-group ads in the elections. However, there was a difference between the patterns of the Democratic and Republican ads of full/partial disclosure ads and no disclosure ads. In a nutshell, Republican candidates outpaced the Democrats as the beneficiaries of dark money ads. At the presidential level, about 90 percent of the Democratic group ads were the full/partial disclosure type. For Republicans that proportion was under 60 percent. And that was the only race in which the Republican full/partial disclosure group ads reached a majority (34).

The difference between the disclosure characteristics of the Democratic and Republican group ads was more pronounced at the Congressional level—what I have called the down-ballot races. Over 75 percent of the Democratic House and Senate group ads were in the full/partial disclosure category. In contrast, the majority of Republican group ads for the House and Senate came from dark money, over 60 percent for each. It was almost a direct flip of the ads for Democratic candidates in terms of the identity of the ad sponsors (34).

As Maggie Severns and Derek Willis (2018) argue, there is a strategy that super PACs (both Democratic and Republican) have used to thwart the disclosure of donors. It takes advantage of a blind spot in the law regarding reporting deadlines and works this way: "Start a super PAC after a deadline for reporting donors and expenses, then raise and spend money before the next report is due. Timed right, a super PAC might get a month or more undercover before being required to reveal its donors" (2). Further, if the super PAC launches just before the election, there is not enough time to disclose donors and voters would not know who was funding the group until *after* the election. In the congressional primaries of the 2016 election, $9 million of super PAC spending occurred in that time period in which disclosure was not required until after the election; in 2018, that figure ballooned to $15.6 million. In total for the 2018 campaign, Democratic and Republican aligned committees spent $21.6 million in seventy-eight congressional races before disclosing who donated the money and in many cases, disclosure occurred after the vote took place.

The effect of nondisclosure—either by manipulating the reporting deadlines or simply using the dark money attributes of super PACS and joint funding committees—is that voters never know who is sponsoring the ubiquitous ads that they see. Ads that are designed to persuade them to support or reject one view or another. Voters should know who is doing the persuading and take that into account when they decide to support, reject, or vote for or against a particular position. To be sure, the ads are perfectly legal, and the argument goes that voters should exercise some judgment about them. That is the point. The sponsors of the ads intentionally hide information from the voter that would be crucial to that judgment. There is research that shows that interest-group ads are effective, but that the disclosure of their donors reduces that effect (Ridout, Franz, and Fowler 2013). That is, with the additional insight into the sponsors of the ads, voters were able to make a more informed evaluation of the ads' claims. It is no wonder, then, that some interest groups work diligently to hide that crucial information.

Local television stations, who reap the overwhelming majority of financial benefits from political ads, can be complicit in keeping information from voters. In 2014 Denver station KMGH had a contract with Target Enterprises to air 1,326 political ads during the midterm campaign. The cost was $740,000, representing the largest contract the station had negotiated. The disclosure rules adopted in 2012 require that stations provide information about the contract to the public online. However, the contract was removed from public view when a reporter tried to learn who was paying for the ads (Fenton 2014).

Target Enterprises, which describes itself as a "Republican-oriented media placement company," was one of the most adamant opponents of the efforts by the FCC and political accountability groups to provide information to the public about who was buying the ads (Bienstock 2012, 2). So, its buy in Denver was, according to *Colorado Independent* reporter Sandra Fish, "eye-popping not only for its size . . . but also for its lack of disclosure" (quoted in Fenton 2014, 2). Target even substituted its own disclosure form (rather than the form created by the National Association of Broadcasters) that left out legally required information, such as who was paying for the ads. The form listed the product description as "undisclosed" and the advertiser as "Various B," making it seem that the buy was divided among several groups (Fenton 2014, 2). In fact, the information was not only misleading, it was false. A spokesperson for the station, when challenged about the lack of detail, responded in an email, "I am not identifying the purchaser of the $740K ads as they are not candidates and are not of national importance" (2). That response was perfectly predictable. There is no future in biting the hand that feeds you.

The Effect of *Citizens United* at the Down-Ballot Level

Although the ruling in the *Citizens United* case was directed at federal campaigns, it had a major effect on the campaign finance regulation in states. In his dissent, Justice Stevens issued a scolding, "The Court operates with a sledge hammer rather than a scalpel when it strikes down [BCRA regulation on outside spending]. It compounds the offense by implicitly striking down a great many state laws as well" (Abdul-Razaak, Prato, and Wolton 2017, 8). Prior to *Citizens United*, twenty-three states had bans on the outside spending of corporations and unions. The ruling came down in January 2010. By November of that year all states, with the possible exception of New Hampshire, had adapted to the new regulation. They had either been repealed or they were held to be unconstitutional (Abdul-Razaak, Prato, and Wolton 2017).

Justice Stevens's concerns were well founded. Chisun Lee, Brent Ferguson and David Early (2014) of the Brennan Center for Justice did an extensive examination of the political spending environment at the state level. They found that, "at the state level, it is possible for a single funder to dominate the discourse and the machinery of politics in a way not seen at the federal level." They offer many examples, but one stands out, if only for the blunt acknowledgment of the power of money in local politics. Rex Sinquefield is from Missouri and he made a fortune in index funds. He was giving a speech to fellow business school alumni when he offered direct advice, "If you get involved at the local level with the route I described, you will be amazed at how much influence you can have" (5). His audience would do well to heed his advice. He poured large sums into Missouri's state politics to the point that he was characterized as the state's "largest political donor . . . perhaps the most influential private citizen in the state . . . a new American oligarch" (5). The Brennan report found that since the *Citizens United* ruling, outside money "has flooded elections at all levels . . . and transformed the legal landscape of elections up and down the ticket" (5). Outside spending increased four to twenty times for governor's races in 2014 that were similarly competitive in 2010.

Outside spending for political advertising increased in thirty states in 2014 over 2010. Groups took advantage of the January 2010 ruling with great speed. By election day that year, outside spending had already increased by 80 percent over the levels of 2006.

The Brennan Report identified major attributes of this outside spending process that underlies its success in significantly influencing state elections. First, candidate-specific outside groups are the quintessential collaboration vehicle. They are formed to support the election of one candidate only and they are often staffed by the candidate's former advisors. Second, candidates solicit huge sums for outside groups that support them. Third, candidates coordinate with supportive outside groups on their own messaging. Fourth, candidates and supportive outside spenders use the same consultants (Lee, Ferguson, and Earley 2014).

Let's look at the implications of these factors. Taken together, they provide a veritable playbook for how to influence elections with not even a wink toward the restrictions on collaboration under which the groups and candidates should function. The groups have preferred candidates, policies and outcomes that they want to see in the political process. They organize and fund themselves to ensure these outcomes. And they spend a lot of money doing it. Their behavior demonstrates that it is untenable at best, naïve at worst, to think that there would not be collaboration between them.

The increase in outside spending has differential effects at the state level. In an examination of state legislative races in all fifty states, researchers found that the *Citizens United* ruling was associated with an increase in Republicans' election probabilities in state house races by 4 percent and 10 or more percent in several states. Further, they linked that specifically to the increased spending by corporations (Klumpp, Mialon, and Williams 2016). The increased spending also increased the reelection chances of Republican incumbents while reducing the number of Democratic candidates" (6). Other research reached a similar conclusion—that the effect of the *Citizens United* ruling increased the share of Republican seats in state legislatures, and it was stronger in states where labor interests were substantially weaker than corporate interests. However, it was weaker when there were stronger labor interests (Abdul-Razaak, Prato, and Wolton 2017).

The Rules for Airing Political Ads

The stations in my study received over $220 million during the sixty-four-day campaign period to air political advertisements. There are very specific rules about how that is to be done. First, that sixty-four-day period almost perfectly coincided with the sixty-day period before a general election within which stations were required to charge candidates the *lowest unit rate* for commercial time that they offer to advertisers. That rule does not apply to interest groups. PACs and super PACs are charged whatever the stations can extract from them, given that the inventory of commercial time becomes a scarce commodity as the election date approaches.

Television stations are restricted by law from censoring political ads if they are "uses." A "use" is defined as an ad that is "sponsored by a legally qualified candidate or the candidate's campaign committee, that includes a recognizable likeness of the candidate" (Montero 2014). Without the power to censor or reject a "use" ad, the broadcaster faces no liability for the ad's content. But the censoring prohibition only applies to "use" ads. The ads from entities other than candidates enjoy no such prohibition. Television stations can censor, or even legally reject, ads that are sponsored by PACs, labor unions and other advocacy groups because of their content. However, even though broadcasters may be liable for the content of these ads, they rarely reject them because they do not want to be seen as the "arbiter of what ads are truthful enough to be run and which should be rejected. In the political world, truth is often in the eyes of the beholder" (Oxenford 2012, 1). Therefore, determining whether the ad is "truthful" is a difficult task and broadcasters are not inclined to reject ads, preferring instead to leave it to the "marketplace" to produce a competing version of the issue. Perhaps, of course, it could be an ad that the broadcaster would gladly present on air—for a price.

There is a question regarding the liability of stations if the political "use" ads of candidates are streamed as part of the stations' presentation of the ads. Section 315 of the Communications Act only applies to over-the-air broadcasts of radio and television. As a result, "[as with] third-party, non-use political ads, stations are not prohibited from censoring the on-line version of any advertisement" (Montero 2014, 2). That means that stations could be sued if what they streamed is knowingly and verifiably libelous, even though it is the exact same content that was broadcast.

It is important to note that most of the FCC's political rules that apply to Federal offices also apply to state and local (down-ballot) electoral races. But there is one very important exception—the right of reasonable access is reserved solely for Federal candidates. That guarantees that Federal candidates can demand access to all of the advertising time that is available on a station (Oxenford 2019). The rule does not mean that Federal candidates can demand as much time as they want; only that stations must sell them a reasonable amount of time throughout the dayparts and advertising classes that they have to offer. That is not the case for down-ballot candidates. In fact, the stations do not have to sell them any advertising time at all. If they do sell that time to down-ballot candidates, all of the other political rules apply (Oxenford 2019). Of course, the stations *do* sell advertising time to down-ballot candidates. That is a source of revenue that has become overwhelmingly important to television stations ever since the *Citizens United* ruling.

One of those rules is the lowest unit charge. This rule guarantees that, in the period before an election—forty-five days for a primary election and sixty days before a general election—candidates must be charged the lowest rate for any unit of advertising time in any of the advertising classes that the station offers. This rate is available only to candidates, not to third parties such as PACs or citizen groups (Kirkpatrick 2018).

Stations most often do not have only one lowest unit charge. That charge varies by the classes of advertising time, and those classes are differentiated by the likelihood of the ad being preempted by one of a higher class. For example, suppose a station offers three advertising classes. Ads in Class 1 cost $1,125, and they are fixed and cannot be preempted. Class 2 ads cost $750 and they can be preempted with prior notification; Class 3 ads cost $500 and they can be preempted immediately (Fuhrman 2019). The FCC rules state that candidates must be charged the lowest unit cost.

All ads, political ads included, can be preempted. Therefore, political ad buyers must make the calculation, like any advertiser, regarding the cost of guaranteeing that the ad is aired (eliminating the chance of preemption) versus the savings of the risking preemption. Although political candidates are guaranteed the lowest unit charge in each of the classes, they are subject to the same preemption calculus that worries all advertisers. As a result, political ad buyers have the incentive to purchase higher classes of ads to minimize or eliminate the risk of preemption.

Add to that another incentive. Political ad buyers are often compensated based on a percentage of the total ad buys that they make on behalf of the candidate. The more money they spend on ads the higher their compensation. Justifying the more expensive ad spend as a hedge against preemption is a perfect argument to make to any political candidate.

The Effects of Political Ads

The effectiveness of political campaign ads has been debated for a long time. Do they inform? Do they persuade? Do they mobilize or demobilize voters? Are they good or bad for the political system? Scholars have considered these issues over decades and their conclusions are by no means consistent. That being said, the candidates and interest groups who vie for our attention spend billions of dollars every election cycle in the hope that the political ads they sponsor will have the effect they desire. John Wanamaker, the venerable merchant and founder of the Wanamaker store chain, famously gave us some guidance when he said that, "half the money I spend on advertising is wasted; trouble is, I don't know which half" (AdAge 1999). The theory and the practice have got to meet somewhere.

In *The Persuasive Power of Political Advertising*, Travis Ridout and Michael Franz (2011) contemplate where that meeting might take place. They argue that there are two ways that political advertising can influence a person's vote or who wins an election. The first and most direct is that political advertising can influence voters' evaluations of political candidates. The second way is less direct and suggests that political advertising can encourage or discourage the supporters of one candidate from voting on Election Day. Although the two processes are not entirely separate from each other, they focus on the first approach. They argue that political ads "do matter," but that is contingent on three factors: the campaign context in which the ads were aired; the characteristics of the ads; and the receiver of the messages (5). Further, understanding how ads persuade is more than an academic exercise. If ads persuade by *manipulating*, convincing voters to vote for a candidate who might not act in their best interests, it does not serve the democratic process well. If, on the other hand, ads persuade by *informing*—by providing information to citizens so they can make informed voting decisions—that aids the body politic.

But, what about manipulation as a persuasion tool? I have always been struck by Alexander Hamilton's admonition in the *Federalist Papers*, written in 1788. It was particularly prescient in the 2016 campaign. He argued for a balance between the ability of a government to act on behalf of the governed and its obligation to observe the public will. But he warned us about how the public might be manipulated "by the arts of men, who flatter their prejudices to betray their interests" (quoted in Garzik 2004).

Manipulative political ads can, indeed, persuade voters to vote against their interests or choose a candidate who is inconsistent with their political views. Aggregation theory rests on the notion that irrational choices are randomly distributed in the public's voting behavior and they will balance each other out. However, in testing that proposition, Sean Richey (2013) found that these "irrational" choices are not as random in elections as the theory would suggest. In fact, in a study of the 2000 and 2004 presidential elections, he found that they skewed toward Republican candidates by almost five percentage points and he makes the case that manipulation by the campaigns was a primary factor in the process. Whether the irrational choices skew in one direction or another is not my concern here. The fact that manipulative political advertisements are effective enough to produce that result is at the heart of the issue.

Gregory Huber and Kevin Arceneaux (2007, 974) characterize advertisements as "propaganda that are successful in causing citizens to shift their expressed preferences toward the sponsoring candidate." The authors come to a stark conclusion, "advertising does little to inform, next to nothing to mobilize, and a great deal to persuade potential voters" (975).

Campaign Context

The campaign context refers to such factors as the office at stake (president, Senate, House, governor, etc.), the stage of the campaign, the status of the candidate (incumbent, challenger, open seat), and the competitiveness of the race (Ridout and Franz 2011). For example, candidates for the presidency are already well known to the public and there are many sources of information about them beyond their political advertisements. That was particularly the case in the 2016 campaign. Both Hillary Clinton and Donald Trump were famous personalities in the country. There was information about them— some true, some false—everywhere a voter turned. Although both used political ads to advance their messages, Clinton used the mechanism much more than Trump. But, as I mentioned, Trump had the advantage of billions of dollars of free coverage by the media.

My concern in the book is the campaign environment at the down-ballot level. One of the imbalances that I found in my research was that the overwhelming majority of the political ads and the political ad money was directed at the down-ballot races—about two-thirds for each. These races, for the most part, have candidates who are not that well known to the voters. Therefore, political advertisements become a crucial communication mechanism. In fact, because of the campaign information environment, political advertising is more effective for House and Senate races than at the presidential level. Prominent political ad scholar Darrell West (2010, 174) states: "In presidential campaigns, voters may be influenced by news coverage, and objective economic and international events. These forces restrain the power of advertisements and empower a variety of alternative forces. In congressional contests, some of these constraining factors are absent, making advertisements potentially more important. If candidates have the money to advertise in a congressional contest, it can be a very powerful force for electoral success."

His observation is confirmed by Michael Jones and Paul Jorgensen (2012). They found that in congressional elections, if a candidate can "flood and frankly overwhelm ad space," it increases their market share of that space and that will benefit their share in a two-party vote (182). And that advantage was consistent when controlling for incumbency, quality challengers, expenditures, and total advertisement airings.

The calculus is straightforward. The ad space is a finite resource—there are just so many commercial slots that are available. It is a zero-sum game—a candidate who buys the spot denies that spot to her opponent. At the down-ballot level, with the generally lower level of political information available to voters, the strategic and tactical decisions about the deployment of political ads makes all the difference.

The Tone of Political Ads

The enduring debate about the tone of political ads has always centered on negative versus positive messages. Before we even get to that, there is strong evidence that ads that appeal to our emotions, either positive or negative, have a significant effect on our voting behavior. And that appeal comes not only from the narrative of the ad but from the sound/music and the images that are used to convey the message. This aspect of political ads is especially salient to me as a musician. Perhaps that makes me unreasonably aware of that feature. Who among us of a certain age would not be able to recognize the brilliant, ominous, and effective two-note warning of imminent danger in the movie *Jaws*? Yes, I know—you just sang it in your head.

Ted Brader (2005; 2006) looked at how emotional appeals work in political ads. He examined *affective intelligence* and found that two systems—enthusiasm/satisfaction and depression/frustration—color the influence of political ads. The difference is that each cue evokes different responses on the part of the voter. Positive political information cues enduring political habits such as partisanship, prejudices, and social identity to decode the information. On the other hand, negative cues interrupt those enduring habits making us pay attention to other points of view; "cueing enthusiasm motivates participation and activates existing loyalties while cueing fear stimulates vigilance, increases reliance on contemporary evaluations and facilitates persuasion" (Brader 2005, 388). He reaches three major findings regarding the impact of emotion in political advertising: the images and music in political ads can manipulate emotions and, in doing so, affect the behavior of voters; the notion that positive ads lead to voters liking and candidate or negative ads doing the opposite must take into account the specific psychological theories that underlie specific emotions; emotional ads "do not just simply sway voters, but change the way voters make choices" (402).

For me, his most compelling observation about the power of emotion in music and images in political ads is that it changes the way in which we process political information—not only that we receive it, but that it changes our behavior. And, I imagine, most of us do not recognize the extent to which we are being manipulated in that manner.

Much has been written about the relative effect of positive and negative ads. There is a conceptual disconnect between how citizens define negativity and how researchers understand the term, and this disconnect is important in understanding political participation. Keena Lipsitz and John Geer (2017) found that citizens' perception of negativity is a much stronger predictor of participation than the researchers' view of negativity. That is because citizens made the nuanced observation about negativity as unfairness rather than simply negative characterizations of a candidate. The ad could be negative, but it could also be fair. To citizens, that was the overriding factor.

The evaluation regarding the type of negativity that appears in ads makes a difference in voting behavior. Looking at campaigns for the US Senate, Kim Khan and Patrick Kenney (1999, 877) found that the public distinguishes between, "useful negative information presented in an appropriate manner and irrelevant and harsh mudslinging." The mudslinging had differential effects across voter types. The partisans, those interested in politics, and habitual and sophisticated voters were rarely affected by the tone of the campaign. They were not "demobilized by mudslinging" (885). On the other hand, independents, people with little interest in campaigns, and political novices were much more susceptible to the mudslinging tone of the campaign and much more likely not to vote. Given the disadvantages of mudslinging for candidates, they are better served to have interest groups do most of the slinging on their behalf (Dowling and Wichowsky 2015).

But even if negativity has the potential to produce a backlash toward the candidate who engages in it, nonincumbents can benefit from the approach as candidates must constantly recalibrate their campaign strategies (Blackwell 2013). Conversely, generally promotional advertising and appeals to enthusiasm never resulted in a backlash (Ridout and Franz 2011). Moving between negative and positive strategies is a dynamic process and reading when and how to employ one or the other or both is a crucial aspect of campaigning for elective office (Lovett and Shachar 2011; Malloy and Pearson-Merkowitz 2016). Further, there is evidence that the media engages in ad amplification as they cover the ads themselves. Not surprisingly, the media coverage is skewed toward negative political ads (Ridout and Smith 2008). That's why political campaign consultants are paid the huge sums of money that they demand.

Citizens also make separate evaluations of the tone (positive or negative) of the campaign from the quality of the information that the campaign provides (Sides, Lipsitz and Grossmann 2010). Perhaps, given these nuanced judgments, negative campaigning is not an effective way of winning votes, nor does it depress turnout (Jackson, Mondak, and Huckfeldt 2009; Freedman and Goldstein 1999). But it does produce "lower feelings of political efficacy, trust in government and possibly the overall public mood" (Lau, Sigelman, and Rovner 2007, 1176). Negative advertising combined with a high-choice ideologically diverse media environment does increase political polarization (Lau et al. 2017). Indeed, negative advertising may even be informative as it may temper the effect of self-promotional positive ads that, by design, provide a specific portrait of the candidate (Geer and Vavreck 2014).

The notion of motivated reasoning says that once a voter has developed an evaluation of a candidate, the voter may be "motivated" toward maintaining rather than challenging that position. But motivated reasoners do employ fact-checking, and the claims of negative ads are checked more often than those of positive ads (Redlawsk and Mattes 2017). Fact-checks that challenge the claims of negative ads are more powerful than those that do so for positive advertisements (Fridkin, Kenney, and Wintersieck 2015).

The general idea that negative advertising depresses voter turnout should be considered in terms of timing. According to Yanna Krupnikov (2011, 797), negativity reinforces demobilization only when two conditions are met: "(1) a person is exposed to negativity after selecting a preferred candidate and (2) the negativity is about the preferred candidate." So, negativity works late in the campaign after a voter "decides" whom to support. However, that support is malleable and negative information about the person's "choice" can discourage the vote altogether.

Summary

Political advertisements on television are full of information that contributes to a more participatory citizenship and they are particularly useful as "political vitamins"—as part of a larger informational diet (Freedman, Franz, and Goldstein 2004, 735). They provide information not only about candidates but also about issues that voters want to address, and candidates must acknowledge (Sigelman and Buell 2004; Kaplan, Park, and Ridout, 2006). However, political advertisements on television are a shotgun tactic rather than a rifle shot (Ridout and Franz 2011). Included among the audience are those for whom the information is wasted, as Mr. Wanamaker observed, and those for whom the information is useful. Even though usefulness can be circumscribed, political advertising on television influences voter choice at the ballot box and that is true despite the rise of the Internet. It is especially true in competitive races, and it is persuasive with lower knowledge voters because the messages are short and to the point (Ridout and Franz 2011). That makes sense, because citizens are "cognitive misers" and they limit the amount of political information they can absorb (Valentino, Hutchings, and Williams 2004, 341). So, the short blasts of political ads are a perfect shortcut in the information-gathering process. Political ads have a strong but short-lived effect (Gerber et al. 2011). That is why over 200,500 political ads were presented during the sixty-four-day campaign on the stations that are the focus of this study.

Political advertisements are the product of the media-and-money election complex and they conform to the processes of all advertising—that repetition works. People are inclined to believe what they have seen before, and although repetition does not guarantee success, it increases the odds considerably (Nichols and McChesney 2013). Legendary advertising executive Rosser Reeves put it bluntly: "I think of a man in a voting booth who hesitates between two levers as if he were pausing between competing tubes of toothpaste in a drug store. The brand that has made the highest penetration in his brain will win his choice" (quoted in Nichols and McChesney 2013, 141). He said that in 1948. It is abundantly true today. And, "television provides a superpowerful mechanism to penetrate the brain" (141).

In the next chapter, I explain my research methods and provide profiles of the ten television markets that were the focus of my study.

3
Research Method and Market Profiles

I used two primary methods in my research: content analysis and secondary data analysis. Content analysis produces a systematic and objective description of information content (Riffe, Lacy, and Fico 2014). It has been used extensively over time to examine local television news (Alexander and Brown 2004; Chermak, 1995; Gilliam and Iyengar 2000; Graber 2001; Hale, Fowler, and Goldstein 2007; Yanich 2001).

The second method was an analysis of a secondary database that was provided by Kantar Media. The database was specifically constructed to address the questions that I pose in the book. All of the findings regarding political ads are based on my analysis of the Kantar Media data.

Research Questions

My central concern here is a comparison of the political ads and political stories that appeared on the newscasts of thirty-nine stations, especially those in the markets in key battleground states, including Pennsylvania, Nevada, Ohio, and Florida. I compared those stories and political ads across the presidential and down-ballot races, focusing on the following research questions:

(1) What was the distribution of political ads on the network-affiliated local television stations in the ten markets during the campaign period?

(2) What were the characteristics of the political ads such as race (presidential versus down ballot), sponsor, tone, issue emphasis, and cost?

(3) Were there political news stories referring to the campaign presented on the local newscasts? If so, what did they cover?

(4) Were the issues presented in the political ads covered by the local newscasts during the campaign period? If so, which issues were covered?

The Campaign Period

Election campaigns have become increasingly longer in the United States. Yet, the time between Labor Day and Election Day is regarded as the most intense period of the campaign. The conventions are over, the slate is set, candidates are on nonstop schedules, political ads cover the airways—it's time to get busy. This is the time when campaign strategies, messages, and tactics will be on full display. As a result, I identified the period between September 5 (Labor Day) to November 7 (the day before the election) as the focus of the work.

Further, this period is consistent with the *lowest unit rate* rule that governs the cost of political advertising to candidates in US elections. It was established in 1971 in the Federal Election Campaign Act (FECA). The rule states that the candidate must be charged the least expensive rate that the broadcaster offers for the requested airtime. The period in which that rule is in effect is sixty days prior to a general election and forty-five days prior to a primary election. The period from September 5 to November 7 was sixty-four days.

The lowest unit rate only applies to candidates. It does not apply to political action committees or any other interest group that buys time for political advertising from the station. They pay whatever the market will bear given the scarcity of available broadcast ad time.

The Television Markets

Access to the content of local newscasts was possible through a special arrangement with Internet Archive, a San Francisco–based nonprofit digital library with whom I collaborated for a previous research project. One of the archives that Internet Archive created focuses on local television news. Through the arrangement, Internet Archive provided streaming access to the complete local news broadcasts that formed the content database for the research. Our coding team accessed the broadcasts online and watched them exactly as they were broadcast over the air. We saw exactly what the audiences saw in each of the markets for each of the newscasts.

There are 210 television markets in the United States ranked by size of the market as measured by the number of television households. For the 2016 presidential campaign, Internet Archive identified ten television markets across the country in which to capture the local newscasts of the stations throughout the campaign.

The television markets that I studied were, in rank order of their size: Philadelphia (#4), San Francisco (#6), Tampa-St. Petersburg (#11), Phoenix (#12), Denver (#17), Cleveland-Akron (#18), Raleigh-Durham (#25), Milwaukee (#35), Las Vegas (#40), and Cedar Rapids-Waterloo (#90). These rankings are based on Nielsen's National Television Household Universe Estimates for the 2016–2017 television season in which the number of television households was 118.4 million (Nielsen 2016). The combined markets in the research account for 15,347,230 (13 percent) of US television households and over forty-two million people (about 13 percent of the US population). Nine of the ten markets—with the exception of San Francisco—were in battleground states during the 2016 election (Mahtesian 2016).

We had extensive discussions with the Internet Archive team about the choice of the markets to include in the sample. Of course, battleground states were the most important to consider. Beyond that, as in all research, the availability of data affects what is included. The key criterion was having broadcast data for each market from September 5 to November 7. As a result, we gathered data from all of the battleground states for which IA had the necessary data. This included nine of the eleven battleground states in the 2016 election—Florida, Arizona, Nevada, Colorado, Iowa, Wisconsin, Pennsylvania, Virginia, and North Carolina (Mahtesian 2016). The tenth state in the sample was California—not a battleground state.

The importance of the battleground states was emphasized by the attention that the presidential candidates directed to them. The candidates did not see all of the states as equal in terms of the resources they dedicated to persuading those voters. For example, 94 percent (375 out of 399) of general election campaign events occurred in twelve states (National Popular Vote 2016). However, the nine states that were part of this research accounted for over three-fourths (77 percent, 309 out of 399) of those presidential campaign events (National Popular Vote 2016).

Only three of the states (Florida, Pennsylvania, and Nevada) had a relatively even number of campaign events between the Democratic and Republican candidates (table 3.1). In the other states, one party or the other had an advantage. In fact, Republicans had the advantage overall, with 179 events compared to the Democrats' 130 events.

Table 3.1. Presidential Campaign Events in Nine Battleground States, 2016

State	Events	Democratic Events	Republican Events	Electoral Votes
Florida	71	36	35	29
North Carolina	55	24	31	15
Pennsylvania	54	26	28	20
Ohio	48	18	30	18
Iowa	21	7	14	6
Colorado	19	3	16	9
Nevada	17	8	9	6
Wisconsin	14	5	9	10
Arizona	10	3	7	11

Source: National Popular Vote, based on data from FairVote, 2016

The Television Stations

The stations whose broadcasts were included in this research comprised all of the network affiliated stations (ABC, CBS, Fox, and NBC) in the television markets that delivered a daily newscast to the viewers. There was one exception to that arrangement. Due to a technical difficulty, the CBS-affiliated station in Tampa (WTSP) was not included in the sample of stations. As a result, we coded the broadcast content of thirty-nine stations. For a complete list of the stations and their ownership characteristics see chapter 4.

The Broadcasts

The sample of broadcasts for this research covered the period from Monday, September 5 through Monday, November 7, 2016 (the day before the election)—nine weeks plus one day (November 7) for a total of sixty-four days.

Each week (Monday through Sunday) and each market were treated as a separate entity. Therefore, I drew a random sample of sixteen broadcasts for each week in each television market. I applied the same 16 broadcast random sample approach to each market on November 7. This process assured an equal representation of broadcasts across markets and across the campaign period.

This approach yielded a possible total of 1,600 broadcasts as the basis for the content analysis (160 broadcasts × ten markets). However, the total number of broadcasts for the project was 1,552. That was due to a technical problem that Internet Archive experienced in the capture of broadcasts in Raleigh, North Carolina, for the last three weeks of the election period. Consequently, the total number of broadcasts for the Raleigh market was 112.

The broadcasts consisted of 1,103 thirty-minute (71 percent) and 449 sixty-minute (29 percent) programs, accounting for one thousand hours of coded content. Across all of the markets I studied, the broadcasts for the project accounted for just over 8 percent of the newscasts that occurred during the campaign period. Through special arrangement, Internet Archive streamed the local television newscasts from those markets to our coders at the University of Delaware during the campaign period.

Units of Observation

For the content analysis, there were two separate units of observation and, as a result, the coding was done in a necessary sequence. The coding of the broadcasts was accomplished by a team of undergraduate and graduate students at the University of Delaware. We first coded the individual units that comprised the broadcasts. This process was used to initially identify the elements of the broadcasts and to specify the political stories. We could then apply a separate coding scheme to the political stories.

The content of the broadcasts in the sample was coded by eleven undergraduate and graduate students over a five-month span and after a training period of six weeks. Three separate tests of inter-coder reliability were conducted during the training phase as the coders learned the coding scheme. A final test of inter-coder reliability was applied at the end of the training period. That test yielded inter-coder reliability scores between .86 and .90 using Krippendorf's Alpha, Cohen's Kappa, and Fleiss's Kappa for the critical variables in the coding scheme. The political stories were coded by three coders and the inter-coder reliability test revealed scores of .82 on all three indexes. The scores for each of the variables met the generally accepted criterion (above .75) for excellent agreement (Banerjee et al. 1999).

The coding revealed 58,873 broadcast units that comprised the newscasts consisting of stories (29,765), commercials (11,991), political ads (10,229), and sports/weather segments (6,888)). The category of stories was comprised of human interest (8,967), crime (6,374), public issues other than crime (6,254), fire/accidents/disasters (3,250), and international stories, including Afghanistan/Iraq/Iran/Syria (1,075).

The Political Ad Data

The data for the political ads that were aired in the project markets were derived from Kantar Media, a research firm that monitors advertising, among other services. The database was specifically designed to meet the needs of the project; it was purchased from Kantar Media and included data of the stations in each of the ten markets in the research for the period from September 5 through November 7.

The Kantar data used the individual political ad as the unit of analysis and showed that during the research period, 200,511 ads were presented on the stations in the markets that comprise the project. The variables for each ad that Kantar provided were: a link to the ad; the name of the sponsor; race to which the ad was addressed; the state and the television market in which the ad appeared; the station, network affiliation, the specific name of the program on which the ad appeared; the type of program (local television news, talk, news forum, slice of life, entertainment, news other, sports, other); the date and the exact time that the ad was aired; the length of the ad (in seconds); the daypart for Monday through Friday for which it specified precise time periods (early morning, daytime, early fringe, early news, prime access, prime time, late news, late fringe); the estimated cost of the ad; the type of ad (candidate, candidate and party, issue-election, party); party affiliation (Democrat, Republican, Libertarian, other); the election for which the ad was aired (general, primary-Democrat, primary-Republican); the election level (federal, state); the specific issue addressed in the ad (where applicable); the race (US president, US House, US Senate, governor); the tone of the ad (negative, positive, contrast).

I used this data to construct variables in the database that were central to the analysis. From this data, I was able to create political ad profiles for the ten markets and the thirty-nine stations in the sample. The data formed the basis of the political ad analysis.

Television Market Profiles

The Nielsen Company identifies 210 television markets in the United States. They call them designated market areas (DMAs). Nielsen assigns a rank to each market based on the number of television households that it comprises. I used that definition of market for this research.

I developed profiles of each market along several dimensions to illustrate their characteristics. They include socioeconomic, sociodemographic, and media-system factors. For purposes of clarity, where there are several cities in the market, I refer to it by the dominant city. The profiles show that there are significant differences among them. The data sources for the profiles are BIA/Kelsey, County Health Rankings and Roadmaps from the University of Wisconsin Population Health Institute, Applied Geographic Solutions, Inc. (AGS), which used FBI Uniform Crime Reports, and the Opportunity Index. The BIA/Kelsey data was reported at the television market level. The Wisconsin Population Health Institute and AGS data and the Opportunity Index were reported at the county level. Therefore, in order to construct an overall television market indicator, I identified each county in the market and recorded the data point of interest (such as crime, population, number of television stations, average household income, unemployment level). I then constructed the overall market indicator for that characteristic by weighting the data point by the proportion of the overall market population that the county represented.

Market Size, Population, Economic Factors

There were 118.4 million television households in the United States in 2016 and each household is assigned to one television market (Nielsen 2016). Each market is rated (from 1 to 210) based on the number of television households that it contains. The markets that I studied varied greatly in size—from Philadelphia at number 4, with almost three million television households and almost eight million people, to Cedar Rapids at number 90, with only 346,000 TV households and just under one million people (table 3.2).

The markets varied in overall population, but they were also quite different in their racial and ethnic composition. Cedar Rapids had the most homogeneous population—90 percent of its residents were white. On the other hand, two markets, San Francisco and Las Vegas were much more racially diverse with white populations below 50 percent and Asian and Hispanic residents accounting for significant proportions of the overall picture. Even for the markets in between, in which whites accounted for substantially more than half of the population, African Americans accounted for the second most prominent group in three markets—Philadelphia (19 percent), Raleigh (28 percent), and Milwaukee (14 percent).

The median household income ranged from a high of $171,083 in San Francisco to just over half of that in Tampa at $89,874. Much more striking is the income ratio which measures the distribution of income across the population. The 80/20 rule is a measure of income inequality describing the disparity in income between the household at the 80th percentile of income and the household at the 20th percentile (University of Wisconsin Population Health

Table 3.2. Market Profiles

Market	DMA (Rank #)	TV Households	Population	White (%)	Black (%)	Asian (%)	Hispanic (%)	Median Household Income ($)	Income Ratio*
Philadelphia	4	2,917,920	7,837,361	64	19	6	11	123,217	1.8
San Francisco	6	2,484,690	7,737,226	43	6	26	24	171,083	1.3
Tampa	11	1,859,820	4,680,634	69	11	3	17	89,874	1.0
Phoenix	12	1,848,850	5,326,760	58	5	4	30	93,236	1.0
Denver	17	1,576,090	4,138,622	71	4	4	20	115,457	5.5
Cleveland	18	1,493,160	3,711,846	79	15	2	4	96,115	1.5
Raleigh	25	1,131,460	3,105,296	57	28	4	10	97,015	2.4
Milwaukee	35	882,210	2,347,855	73	14	3	10	104,668	2.4
Las Vegas	40	833,910	2,250,246	48	11	11	30	93,540	0.4
Cedar Rapids	90	346,120	966,154	90	4	2	3	100,838	1.3

* Income ratio = ratio of income at the 80th percentile to income at the 20th percentile.
Sources: BIA/Kelsey; County Health Rankings and Roadmaps, University of Wisconsin Population Health Institute, 2016

Institute 2016). That means that for households at the 80th percentile, only 20 percent of households have *higher* incomes. Conversely, for households at the 20th percentile, only 20 percent of the households have *lower* incomes.

Let's look at two numbers that stand out which represent very different pictures of income distribution. First, Las Vegas. The income ratio is 0.4 which says that the wealthiest fifth of households (those at the 80th percentile) have incomes that are under 50 percent higher than those at the 20th percentile. At the other end of the spectrum is Denver where the households at the 80th percentile have incomes that are five and half times higher (550 percent) than those at the 20th percentile. The distributions are skewed, but in opposite directions.

In Raleigh and Milwaukee, the wealthiest fifth of households, with income ratios of 2.4, outdo their lower income neighbors by almost 250 percent. In Philadelphia, at 1.8, the difference is almost 200 percent. Tampa and Cedar Rapids, each with a ratio of 1.0, show that that the wealthiest fifth of the households have incomes 100 percent more than those in the lower income range. In short, distribution of income in the markets varied greatly.

The Opportunity Index

The sociodemographic and socioeconomic information gives us important information about the markets. It does matter how large their populations are and how they are distributed by race and ethnicity and how much money households have at their disposal. Another way to look at the manifestations of those conditions is to understand the opportunities that arise. The Opportunity Index is one such multidimensional measure (Opportunity Nation 2016). It includes indicators within three dimensions of community well-being: economy, education, and community. The Opportunity Index uses data from various sources such as the US Census Bureau, the US Bureau of Labor Statistics, and the US Department of Justice, among others, to develop a score for each of the dimensions on a ten-point scale. The county-level Opportunity Index is comprised of fourteen indicators. The factors in the economy dimension are jobs, wages, poverty, income inequality (the 80/20 rule discussed earlier), access to banking services, affordable housing, and Internet access. The factors in the education dimension are preschool enrollment, high school graduation, and postsecondary completion. The community dimension included: youth economic and academic inclusion, community safety, access to health care, and access to healthy food. The overall Opportunity Index was calculated giving each dimension equal weight.

Table 3.3. Opportunity Index

Market	Opportunity Index	Economic Score	Education Score	Community Score
Philadelphia	55.0	57.3	55.5	52.0
San Francisco	58.7	60.0	63.3	53.0
Tampa	46.5	54.5	44.4	40.7
Phoenix	44.1	52.0	43.5	36.5
Denver	52.2	59.3	51.1	45.7
Cleveland	52.2	55.4	52.0	49.1
Raleigh	50.4	55.6	52.4	43.9
Milwaukee	15.9	17.2	16.2	14.4
Las Vegas	37.1	50.5	28.9	32.1
Cedar Rapids	56.7	63.5	63.6	60.4
National Average	52.4	52.9	54.4	46.8

Source: Opportunity Nation, 2016; range is 1–100

I developed the Opportunity Index for the television markets in each of the dimensions as well as an overall index. The national average of the Opportunity Index was 52.4 (on a scale of 1–100), and only three of the markets, San Francisco at 58.7, the highest among the markets, Cedar Rapids at 56.7 and Philadelphia at 55 exceeded that score (table 3.3). At the other end of the spectrum, Milwaukee's Opportunity Index was 15.9 and Las Vegas was the second lowest at 37.1.

A closer look at the dimension scores reveals that, in general, the economic scores are relatively higher than those of the other dimensions within each market. For example, in Las Vegas there is a difference of over 21 points between the economic and education scores and another 18 points between that and the community score. The important point here is that, like with the socio-demographic factors, the citizens of the markets experienced different levels of opportunity, as measured by the index.

Television Stations

I looked at the activity of the network-affiliated stations (ABC, CBS, Fox, NBC) in the markets (and one CW station in Raleigh). Their service is defined as "main" by BIA/Kelsey (2018). However, there were other full-power stations in the markets, and their service is defined as "public" by BIA/Kelsey. The number of "main" service stations in the markets varied, but generally, as we might expect, there were more stations in the larger markets. Philadelphia and San Francisco each had seventeen main service stations (table 3.4). Cedar Rapids, the smallest of the markets in this research, had only seven "main" service stations.

The stations that were included in the research were chosen because they derived the overwhelming majority of the advertising revenue in each market. Across all of the markets, the average proportion of that revenue during the 2016 campaign period was 78 percent. The range was from 98 percent in Cedar Rapids to 58 percent in Tampa (remember, the Tampa revenue is only for three stations). A technical glitch resulted in missing the content of the CBS-affiliated station, WTVD.

The capacity of any station to produce news is greatly dependent on the size of its news staff. There was wide variation among the markets regarding the number of news staff for the stations that were examined in this research (project stations). Denver had the highest number of news staff at 191. That was only slightly below San Francisco's 193 news staff for the project stations.

Although news staff is not the only resource that is used to produce newscasts, it is arguably the most important. However, that did not neatly translate into the number of newscasts that the stations presented each week during the period that I studied. The project stations in Las Vegas presented 241 newscasts per week—the most of any market—with just 91 news staff. That was

Table 3.4. Markets and Stations

Market	Main Service Stations*	News Staff for Project Stations**	Broadcasts/ Week for Project Stations	Market Revenue of Project Stations* (%)
Philadelphia	17	160	218	81
San Francisco	17	193	195	74
Tampa	12	87	220	58
Phoenix	14	124	201	61
Denver	15	191	216	80
Cleveland	12	131	208	86
Raleigh	9	89	133	65
Milwaukee	10	153	218	95
Las Vegas	9	91	241	85
Cedar Rapids	7	65	121	98
All markets average	12	128	197	78

* Source: BIA/Kelsey, 2018
** Source: News Measures Research Project, 2017

followed by Tampa with 220 newscasts per week with just 87 total news staff. At the low end of the spectrum, Cedar Rapids, with just 65 news staff produced 121 broadcasts per week. Conversely, Denver with a news staff of 191 (the highest number by far) produced 216 newscasts per week.

These data tell us that, at least by the metric of the number of newscasts, the station managers used their news staff in very different ways. Just compare Denver and Tampa—they produced about the same number of weekly newscasts, but the news staff of the Tampa stations was less than half of that in Denver.

Television Stations, Affiliation, Ownership

All of the station groups that owned the project stations were ranked within the top 27 television markets in the United States in 2015 based on estimated spot revenue (Miller 2016). The range in their revenue was very large (table 3.5). For example, Fox Television Stations had estimated spot revenue in 2015 of over $1.6 billion and controlled four stations in four different markets. At the other end of the spectrum, Capitol Broadcasting (# 27), had estimated spot revenues of about $67,000,000. It controlled just two stations, but they were in the same

Table 3.5. Station Groups

Rank	Group	2015 Spot Revenue ($)	Stations	Markets
1	Fox	1,646,750,000	4	4
2	CBS	1,570,050,000	3	3
3	Nexstar	1,421,650,000	3	3
4	Sinclair	1,398,425,000	4	3
5	Comcast/NBCU	1,289,250,000	2	2
6	Tegna	1,276,700,000	3	3
7	Tribune	1,209,200,000	3	3
8	ABC/Disney	1,064,500,000	2	2
9	Hearst	747,100,000	1	1
10	Raycom	746,400,000	1	1
12	Scripps	617,350,000	6	6
13	Gray	535,250,000	1	1
15	Meredith	403,350,000	2	2
21	Quincy	107,075,000	1	1
24	Weigel	83,000,000	1	1
27	Capitol Broadcasting	66,950,000	2	1

Source: Miller (2016), TVNewsCheck.com

market (Raleigh). Likewise, Sinclair Broadcasting Group (revenues of about $1.4 billion) controlled four stations in three markets. The station group that controlled the largest number of stations was Scripps, with revenues of just over $617,000,000, with six stations in six markets.

The stations that I examined in the research had a variety of owners or controlling entities which resulted in various ownership profiles within the markets. There were only two markets in which there was a measure of consolidation regarding the project stations. In Raleigh, Capitol Broadcasting owned and operated both WRAL and WRAZ. Likewise, in Cedar Rapids, Sinclair owned KGAN, but it also controlled the programing of KFXA through a local marketing agreement with its owner, Second Generation of Iowa, Ltd. (table 3.6). In the other eight markets, the stations were owned or operated by separate entities. Therefore, the majority content that I examined reflected markets that were not consolidated. That said, the stations were still controlled by entities that were among the largest station groups with television stations in many other markets.

In Philadelphia and San Francisco, the stations were owned and operated by the networks themselves (table 3.6). Fox Television Stations also directly controlled its affiliated stations in Tampa and Phoenix. CBS directly controlled its affiliate in Denver. The ownership group that controlled the most stations across the markets was Scripps (the twelfth-largest station group), which has thirty-three stations in twenty-four television markets. They were present in six of the ten markets: Tampa, Phoenix, Denver, Cleveland, Milwaukee and Las Vegas.

Summary

The methods that I used were those that the research questions demanded. The only way to understand the content of the broadcasts was to systematically and rigorously look at them. Likewise, the only way to understand the political ads that appeared in the markets in the study was to develop a database that specified the attributes that would reveal their content and their broadcast characteristics (when they were aired, on what program, in which markets, and so on). The following three chapters present my findings.

Table 3.6. Markets and Project Stations

Market	Station	Network Affiliation	Owner/Operator
Philadelphia	KYW	CBS	CBS Television Stations
	WCAU	NBC	NBC Universal
	WPVI	ABC	ABC Inc
	WTXF	FOX	Fox Television Stations
San Francisco	KGO	ABC	ABC Inc
	KNTV	NBC	NBC Universal
	KPIX	CBS	CBS Television Stations
	KTVU	FOX	Fox Television Stations
Tampa	WFLA	NBC	Nexstar
	WFTS	ABC	Scripps
	WTVT	FOX	Fox Television Stations
Phoenix	KNXV	ABC	Scripps
	KPHO	CBS	Meredith
	KPNX	NBC	Tegna
	KSAZ	FOX	Fox Television Stations
Denver	KCNC	CBS	CBS Television Stations
	KDVR	Fox	Tribune
	KMGH	ABC	Scripps
	KUSA	NBC	Tegna
Cleveland	WEWS	ABC	Scripps
	WJW	FOX	Tribune
	WKYC	NBC	Tegna
	WOIO	CBS	Raycom
Raleigh	WLFL	CW	Sinclair
	WNCN	CBS	Nexstar
	WRAL	NBC	Capital Broadcasting Co.
	WRAZ	FOX	Capital Broadcasting Co.
Milwaukee	WDJT	CBS	Weigel Broadcasting
	WISN	ABC	Hearst
	WITI	FOX	Tribune
	WTMJ	NBC	Scripps
Las Vegas	KLAS	CBS	Nexstar
	KSNV	NBC	Sinclair
	KTNV	ABC	Scripps
	KVVU	FOX	Meredith
Cedar Rapids	KCRG	ABC	Gray Television
	KFXA	FOX	Sinclair, LMA w. KGAN
	KGAN	CBS	Sinclair
	KWWL	NBC	Quincy Media

4
Political Ads

This chapter provides an overall picture of the political ads across the markets. I will address the individual markets in chapter 6.

My findings are based on my analysis of the political ads database provided by Kantar Media for the purposes of this project. The data covers the campaign period from September 5 through November 7, 2016, for the ten television markets that I examined. The findings are based on a comparison of the political ads activity across the presidential and down-ballot (DB) races. The DB races included US Senate, US House, and governor contests in the states in which the markets were located. Of course, both the Senate and governor's races were statewide. House races were not. Therefore, I identified the US House districts whose boundaries were part of the counties that comprised each television market and I included their political ads as part of the DB races.

Quantity and Money

The most prominent finding that jumps out of the data is that the DB races got the lion's share of the money and the ads. In the sixty-four days during the campaign period, the local televisions stations in the ten markets in the study showed their audiences 200,511 political ads—almost 3,200 per day. But they were not evenly distributed between the presidential and DB races. Almost seven out of ten ads (69 percent, or 138,662 ads) were directed at the DB races whereas just under one-third (31 percent, or 61,849 ads) referred to the presidential race (fig. 4.1).

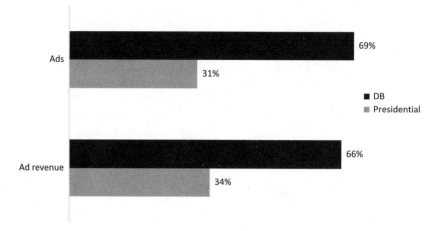

Figure 4.1. Distribution of political ads and revenue by race.

That difference was also reflected in the money that was spent on the ads. The stations received a total of $220,501,650 to air those ads during the campaign period. A very large proportion of that money—just under two-thirds, $145,234,490—went to ads for DB races; the remainder (34 percent), $75,267,160, paid for the airing of presidential ads. In other words, the station revenue for DB ads almost doubled that for the presidential race.

Both the number and cost of the ads represented a significant investment by political ad sponsors in the local television stations in the markets. And remember, the volume of ads and the revenue that the stations derived from them only represents a sixty-four-day period, albeit the most intense time of the campaign. The DB races were the overwhelming focus of political ads.

Distribution over Time

As we might expect, the distribution of the political ads varied over the campaign period. But it followed a logical pattern. There were more ads in the last week of the campaign than in the first week. With nine weeks to go to Election Day, the stations aired just over 13,000 political ads in that week. There was a steady increase in that number as Election Day drew closer and in the last week of the campaign, the stations presented 42,235 political ads. For this analysis, I included November 7, the day before the election, in the last week.

The pattern of the presentation of the ads over the campaign period was somewhat different for the DB and presidential races. For the DB races, there

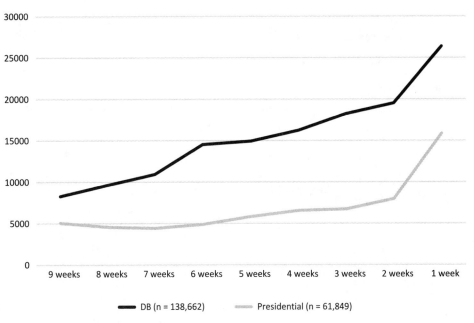

Figure 4.2. Total number of ads each week by race.

was a steady increase throughout the period (fig. 4.2). That was particularly so
in the last two weeks of the campaign. However, the number of weekly ads for
the presidential race stayed relatively level during the first seven weeks of the
campaign, spiking only in the last two weeks in a mirror of the DB ads.

Ads by Race Across the Markets

As the distribution of the total number of ads was not evenly distributed
between the presidential and DB races, there was much variation across the
ten markets regarding that same comparison. In all of the markets except
Cleveland (shown in light gray in fig. 4.3), there were more DB ads than presidential ads, and the differences between the races were significant.

The overwhelming market leader in the number of ads that were aired for
both races was Las Vegas (46,590 ads). But there were many more DB ads
(36,268) to presidential ads (10,322). The ratio was 3.5:1. The audience in Philadelphia also saw a significant number of ads (34,872) with a DB to presidential ratio of 2.9:1. The market in which the audience saw the fewest number of
total ads was San Francisco (2,338), but, again, there were many more DB ads
(1,587) to presidential ads (751) with a ratio of 2.1:1.

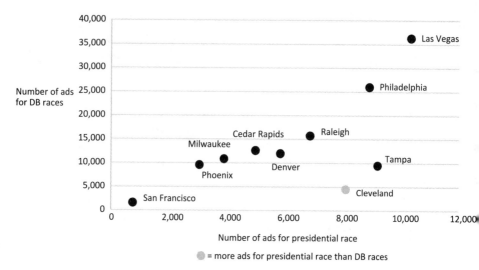

Figure 4.3. Number of ads shown in down-ballot versus presidential races by market.

The larger point to be made is that in nine of the ten markets, there were more ads presented for the DB races than the presidential race. That difference was substantial except for Tampa where the number of the ads devoted to each race was about even (although there were still more DB ads). Among the other eight markets, DB ads at least doubled or more than tripled presidential ads. DB ads overwhelmingly carried the political advertising message in those markets.

For purposes of clarity, in my analysis the markets will be presented in rank order based on the total number of political ads that were shown during the campaign period. That order is: (1) Las Vegas, 46,590 ads; (2) Philadelphia, 34,872 ads; (3) Raleigh, 22,554 ads; (4) Tampa, 18,682 ads; (5) Cedar Rapids, 17,840 ads; (6) Denver, 17,597 ads; (7) Milwaukee, 14,788 ads; (8) Phoenix, 12,639 ads; (9) Cleveland, 12,611 ads; (10) San Francisco, 2,338 ads.

Money Spent Across the Markets

As we might expect, the volume of political ads in a market dictated the amount of revenue that the local television stations received during the campaign period. However, the difference in the proportion of revenue between the DB and presidential races varied significantly across the markets. There was also significant variation of the average cost of a political ad across the

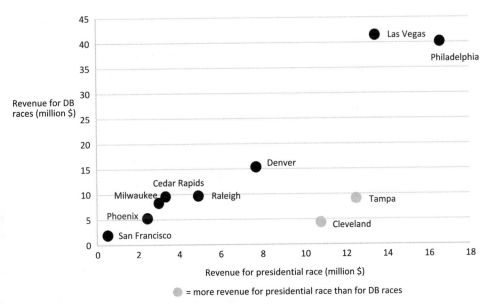

Figure 4.4. Market revenue in down-ballot and presidential races.

markets. Philadelphia was the most expensive at $1,628; Denver was second at $1,311; followed by Cleveland at $1,202; Las Vegas at $1,180; Tampa at $1,154; San Francisco at $1,050; Phoenix at $894; Milwaukee at $871; Raleigh at $647, and Cedar Rapids at $433.

The stations in Las Vegas aired over 46,500 political ads during the campaign period—the most of any market. As a result, its stations realized almost $55 million in revenue, but the DB races garnered over 75 percent of that money, $41.5 million, a ratio of 3:1 over the presidential race (fig. 4.4).

Philadelphia was another market in which political ad activity covered the airwaves. And although there were more total ads aired than in Las Vegas, the stations in the Philadelphia market enjoyed the highest revenue—almost $57 million. That was because ad time on the Philadelphia stations, the number 4 market in the country, was more expensive than Las Vegas (number 40). But the revenue pattern mirrored Las Vegas. The DB races captured 71 percent of the money—over $40 million to about $16.5 million for the presidential race. That ratio was 2.5:1.

The stations in Las Vegas and Philadelphia received a significant amount of money during the campaign period. The other markets in the study clustered at lower revenue levels, but they were still substantial sums. The stations in Denver brought in a total of just over $23 million—over $15 million to the DB races.

In only two markets, Tampa and Cleveland, did presidential ad spending surpass the DB races. Of the $21.5 million in Tampa, the presidential race received about $12.5 million. In Cleveland, the presidential race received almost $10.8 million of the total of about $15.1 million.

As Las Vegas and Philadelphia represented the highest number of ads and in revenue, San Francisco was at the other end of the spectrum. It had the fewest number of ads (2,338) and the least political ads revenue (about $2.5 million). However, it was distinguished in the proportion of the money between the races. Over $1.9 million was spent on the local races—a ratio of almost 4:1. That was higher than any other market.

Ads by Program Type

The political ad sponsors had an overwhelming preference regarding the type of program for the placement of their ads—local television newscasts. Across all markets, over half of the political ads (about 51 percent, or 101,246 ads) appeared on local newscasts. That almost doubled the next category of programing—other news, which included talk shows, news forums, cable (about 26 percent, or 52,757 ads). The remaining political ads were placed on non-news programming which included entertainment and sports (about 23 percent, or 46,508 ads).

That distribution across program types was consistent between the DB and presidential races. Political ad sponsors overwhelmingly preferred local television news (fig. 4.5). It is important to note that, although the proportion of ads across program types by race is quite similar, the bars in the graph represent

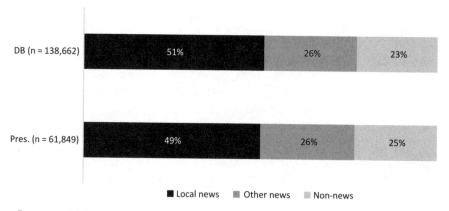

Figure 4.5. Ads by program type by race.

very different total numbers of ads. To wit: DB races accounted for 138,662 ads compared to 61,849 for the presidential race.

Program Type by Market

The parity of political ads for program type across the DB and presidential races was reflected within the markets. However, there were different proportions across the markets.

For example, in the two markets that saw an overwhelming number of ads compared to the others, Las Vegas and Philadelphia, the proportion of ads on local television news was almost six out ten and about 50 percent, for both the DB and presidential races (fig. 4.6). The two markets accounted for over 81,000 ads, and there were hotly contested local races. Political ads sponsors relied heavily on local television news to deliver their message.

San Francisco was at the other end of the spectrum regarding the number of ads (including those that referred to ballot initiatives) its citizens saw (a total of 2,338). However, local television news was overwhelmingly used as the vehicle to deliver them. For the DB races, almost two-thirds of the ads were placed on local television. That was even higher (almost three-fourths) for the presidential race (fig. 4.6).

There were two markets, Raleigh and Cedar Rapids, where local television newscasts were used for just over one-third of the ads for both the DB and presidential races (fig. 4.6). And, unlike the other markets, non-news programs came in a very close second (or higher) as the preferred program type by political ad sponsors for both the DB (35 percent and 37 percent, respectively) and presidential races (33 percent and 36 percent, respectively).

Ads by Time of Day Aired

In addition to making decisions about what type of program they prefer for their ads, sponsors also make decisions about when during the broadcast day they want their ads to appear. The ads are an expensive method to reach voters and the sponsors strive to get the most for their money. That means that they want to reach the members of the audience whom they can persuade. Television programs have different audiences, and they watch at various times during the day. So, when an ad appears can affect its effectiveness. Remarkably, the overall distribution of the ads across the day was virtually identical for both the DB and presidential races. Therefore, I show the findings for all ads across the day.

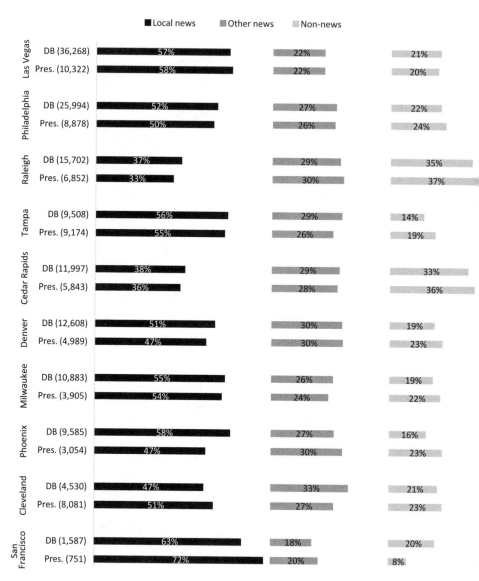

Figure 4.6. Proportion of ads by program type by race by market.

The sponsors leaned heavily on the early morning hours (between 5 AM and 9 AM)—almost 39,000 DB ads and another 16,000 presidential ads, about 27 percent (fig. 4.7). But another fifth (21 percent) were presented in the period between 9 AM and 4 PM—over 29,000 DB and over 13,500 presidential ads. So, by four o'clock in the afternoon, almost half of the political ads were aired. If

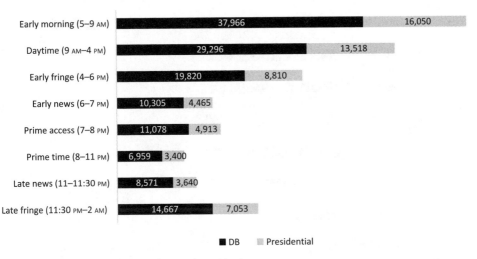

Figure 4.7. Total number of ads (200,511) aired by daypart.

you add the two-hour period just before early news (early fringe), the proportion jumps to 62 percent. Interestingly, the prime-time slot (between 8 and 11 PM), had the fewest number of ads. The late news slot (only 30 minutes in length) accounts for almost 6 percent of the ads, indicating the importance that sponsors placed on those news programs.

To be sure, the time periods that I report here are not all equal in length. They reflect the segments of the day that Kantar Media describes. However, I wanted to compare the segments more evenly—to standardize the comparison. Therefore, I calculated the average number of ads that appeared *hourly* in each segment. The caution with this approach is that it distributes the ads evenly throughout the time slot. I do not know if that was the case. It probably was not. However, with that caveat, it does give us a more nuanced view of the importance of the segments to political ads sponsors. By this calculation, the late news time slot (11 to 11:30 PM) accounted for over 24,000 ads if it were an hour in length, more ads than any other (fig. 4.8). Likewise, the second most popular segment for political ads was prime access (7 to 8 PM) at almost 16,000 ads per hour. After those two, in descending rank order of the number of ads per hour, the popularity of the segments was early news (6 to 7 PM) at 14,770 ads; early fringe (4 to 6 PM) with 14,315 ads; early morning (5 to 9 AM) with 13,504 ads; late fringe (11:30 PM to 2 AM) with 8,688 ads; daytime (9 AM to 4 PM) at 6,116 ads; and lastly, primetime (8 to 11 PM) with 3,453 ads.

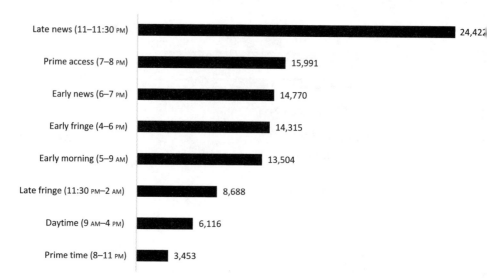

Figure 4.8. Number of ads per hour by daypart.

Ads by Sponsors

The decisions regarding the message, placement, and tone of political ads were made by sponsors who fell into three categories—the candidate only, a combination of the candidate and party, and interest group, which included political action committees. Before I address the races in the ten markets I studied, it is important to note that, at the national level throughout the entire campaign, Hillary Clinton/pro-Clinton groups sponsored 75 percent of the ads compared to that same combination for Donald Trump at 25 percent (Beckel 2016). Clinton also enjoyed an advantage in the number of ads within the ten markets that I studied through the sixty-four-day campaign period. Not including pro-candidate groups, candidate Clinton sponsored about twice as many ads as candidate Trump (28,930 to 14,604 ads, respectively, out of about 62,000 total ads in the markets for the presidential race).

By far, the most prominent sponsors of ads were the candidates themselves. They accounted for almost half of the ads (97,560). Interest groups came in second, sponsoring just under 30 percent of ads (57,569). The remainder of the ads, just under 25 percent, was presented by sponsors identified as a combination of the candidate and the political party to which they belonged (45,382).

The distribution of sponsors by race was very different. For the DB races, candidate ads were the most prominent—almost four in ten (fig. 4.9). Candidate

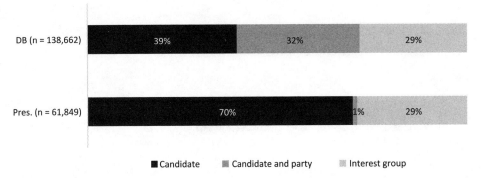

Figure 4.9. Sponsor by race.

and party ads and interest group ads were relatively evenly distributed at 32 percent and 29 percent, respectively.

For the presidential race, the ads were significantly the province of the candidate (70 percent) and interest group (29 percent). Ads sponsored by the candidate and party were extremely rare (1 percent).

The Tone of the Ads

Political ads carry a message that is used to advance a candidate's position, to
question an opponent's capability or positions on a given issue or to support or
oppose a particular idea. As such, they can be characterized as three types—
positive, contrast, and negative. In essence, the ads perform a function (Benoit
2000). Both positive and negative ads convey one sentiment and it is clear to
the viewer that it is either in support of or in opposition to a candidate or a
position. We have all seen the features of each. Positive ads have images that
represent the best side of candidates and issues, accompanied by musical
themes that cue the viewer to react (Brader 2005; 2006). Contrast ads offer
more precisely what they say—a contrast between the views of the candidate
and the opponent or between views regarding an issue.

For both the DB and presidential races the overall distribution of the ads
by tone was remarkably consistent (fig. 4.10). In both races almost 60 percent
of ads were negative. Just 26 percent of the presidential ads were contrast ads
as opposed to 22 percent in the DB races. The rarest of ads were positive, 20
percent and 16 percent for the DB and presidential races, respectively. This
bears out the perception that negative ads were the order of the day.

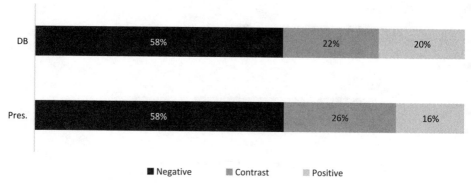

Figure 4.10. Tone by race.

Ads by Tone, Sponsor, and Race

Comparing the sponsors and the tone of ads revealed some similarities and striking differences between the DB and presidential races. The burden of a negative, contrasting, or positive message was not borne equally among the sponsors in the races. For both the DB and presidential races, the candidate-sponsored ads used all three tones. However, there was a striking difference in that distribution between the DB and presidential races. About 43 percent of candidate-sponsored DB ads struck a positive tone, with about 23 percent going negative (fig. 4.11). For the presidential race, that distribution was almost the exact opposite. About 46 percent of the ads were negative and only 22 percent were positive. Clearly, the tactics for the candidate sponsors were different for the races.

There was a significant difference in the tones of the ads that were sponsored by the candidate and party and interest group across the races. For the DB races, the overall distribution of the tone of ads was decidedly negative. Two types of sponsors overwhelmingly focused on negative ads—84 percent for interest groups and 78 percent for candidate and party (fig. 4.11). And those two groups accounted for over 60 percent of the ads for those races (see fig. 4.9). Therefore, negative ads were the order of the day.

For the presidential race, the negative ads were overwhelmingly presented by interest group—almost nine out of ten of their ads were that tone. Further, unlike the DB races, the plurality of candidate-sponsored ads (46 percent) were negative with the smallest proportion being positive in tone (21 percent). The candidate and party sponsor's ads revealed the biggest difference between the races. About three-fourths of those ads were positive in the presidential race. However, candidate and party–sponsored ads only accounted for about 1

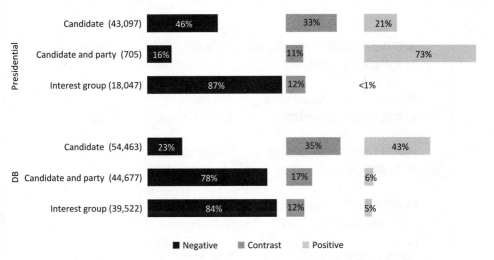

Figure 4.11. Tone by sponsor by race. (Percentages may not total 100 due to rounding.)

percent (705 ads) of the total number of presidential ads. So, even though they were positive, they represented a very small fraction of the ads that viewers saw.

Ads by Tone and Market

Negative political ads were the most prominent type in both political races. But how did that play out in the markets? In Las Vegas and Philadelphia, the markets that saw volumes of ads that far outstripped the others (46,590 and 34,872 ads, respectively), both races were dominated by negative ads. In Las Vegas, the proportion of negative ads was over 70 percent for DB races and over 50 percent for the presidential campaign (fig. 4.12). In Philadelphia, negative ads comprised about 60 percent of both races. Raleigh (22,554 ads) and Tampa (18,682 ads) saw a similar distribution to Philadelphia.

There were significant differences between the races in the markets that aired relatively fewer ads. In Milwaukee (14,788 ads), Phoenix (12,639 ads), Cleveland (12,611 ads) and San Francisco (2,338 ads), there were more negative ads than any others in the presidential race. In fact, the differences in Phoenix and San Francisco between the races jumped out—about 70 percent of the presidential ads were negative compared to 34 percent for the DB campaigns. However, in San Francisco, 100 percent of the presidential political ads were negative compared to about 30 percent for the DB races. To be sure, that market saw the fewest ads, by far, and it is important to note that all of those negative ads were sponsored by PACs.

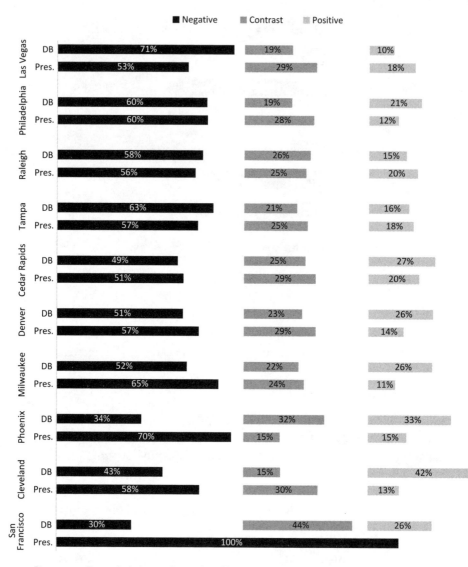

Figure 4.12. Tone of ads by race by market. (Percentages may not total 100 due to rounding.)

Issue Ads

In addition to conveying the negative, contrasting, and positive aspects of candidates, political ads address policy issues. Their function is equivalent to those that depict candidates—to persuade the public about the merits or demerits of policy positions that are important to the sponsors. The prominence of policy political ads was seen in the analysis. Out of the 200,511 political ads that were aired in the ten markets that I studied, 163,574 (82 percent) were directed at a policy issue. That is a significant proportion. And, overall, the very large majority of them, 115,120 ads (70 percent) were presented in the DB races.

Based on my analysis of the Kantar Media data, I identified seventeen policy areas that the ads addressed. The question is, how were they delivered across the DB and presidential races? There was a statistically significant difference (p < .05). Campaign finance reform, taxes, and women's rights were the most prominent issues that were the focus of ads but their distribution between the races was starkly different. Campaign finance reform was the single most important issue as measured by the number of ads (25,439) but the vast majority of them (87 percent) were aired in the presidential race (fig. 4.13). That is understandable, given the views of the public in which overwhelming bipartisan majorities regard the reduction or counterbalancing of the influence of big campaign donors on the federal government as important (Kull 2018).

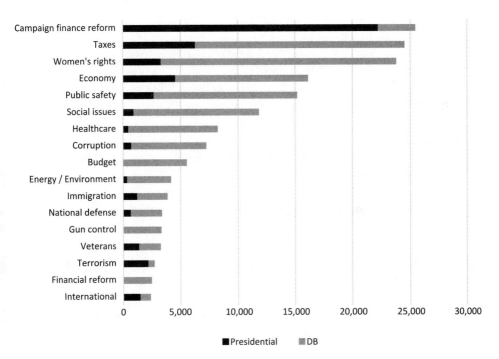

Figure 4.13. Issues addressed by ads across presidential and down-ballot races (in numbers).

Only two other issue ads were most prominent for the presidential race—terrorism and international topics. But, as we see, there were relatively fewer of them that were presented (2,715 and 2,380 ads, respectively). The rest of the issue ads were most prominently presented within the DB races.

After campaign finance reform, taxes (24,515) and women's rights (23,812) were the next two most prominent issues that the ads addressed. In each instance, the vast majority of the political ads were presented in the DB races—75 percent and 86 percent, respectively. That distribution in favor of the DB races over the presidential race was evident in the other issue ads. For example, of the 16,143 ads that addressed the economy, about 72 percent were presented in the DB races. Issue ads that focused on healthcare (8,229 ads) saw 94 percent during the DB races. On average, the DB races saw 85 percent of the issue ads for those topics and for some topics—budget, gun control, and financial reform—100 percent of the ads occurred in the DB races.

Issue Ads by Markets

In each of the markets, there were many more ads for the DB races than for the presidential race. For example, Las Vegas aired just under 30,000 DB ads compared to just over 8,000 ads for the presidential race—a highly skewed distribution. In order to graphically compare the patterns of those issue ads in the market, it was necessary to reduce the skewness by creating a log transformation of the ads data. The following graphs show the results of that transformation. That said, it is important to recognize the differences in the volume of ads for each race. That is provided in each graph.

The most important feature of the graphs is a comparison of the patterns that represent the issue ads for the DB and presidential races. There were only two markets, Las Vegas and Philadelphia, in which there were ads addressing all of the seventeen issues in the races (fig. 4.14). That makes sense because the stations in those markets presented the highest number of political ads and realized the most revenue from that activity than the other markets in the study. In Las Vegas, the DB ads touched on many more issues than those in the presidential race. Further, consistent with the issue ads in general, only campaign finance reform, terrorism, and international issue ads were more prominent in the race for president. In all the other issue areas, the DB races saw more ads.

In Philadelphia, too, many more issues were addressed in ads in the DB races than at the presidential level. For example, issues such as budget, energy/environment, financial reform, gun control, and healthcare were covered in

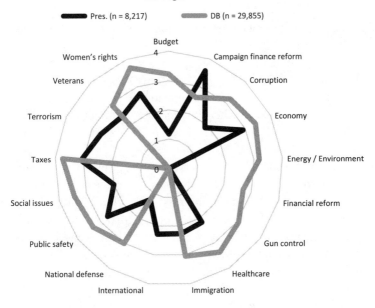

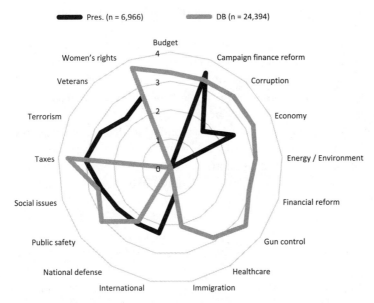

Figure 4.14. Political issue ads in presidential and down-ballot races in Las Vegas (top) and Philadelphia (bottom).

political ads only at the DB level, and the Pennsylvania US Senate race was hotly contested.

The patterns in the Raleigh television market showed that the budget, corruption, healthcare, public safety, and taxes were important issues for the DB races. In Tampa, both races almost equally addressed issues such as corruption, the economy, healthcare, immigration, taxes, and terrorism. That is understandable because, as I indicated previously, Tampa was one of only two markets (Cleveland was the other) in which the number of presidential ads exceeded those of the DB races. However, in Tampa, the number of ads for each race was close to even (fig. 4.15).

In Denver, the issue ads patterns were quite different across the races. Some issues were raised *only* in the DB races—energy/environment, veterans and terrorism; some—economy and taxes—were addressed equally. Interestingly, healthcare was only an issue in the presidential race (fig. 4.16).

In Cedar Rapids, both races looked at the economy and taxes in equal measure, but energy/environment, financial reform, and healthcare only appeared in the DB races (fig. 4.16).

In Phoenix, only ten of the seventeen issues were covered in ads and there was a significant difference between the DB and presidential races. The presidential race focused mainly on campaign finance reform and less so on national defense and women's rights. By contrast, the ads in DB races addressed all of the issues with much attention directed at healthcare, immigration, public safety, social issues, taxes, and women's rights (fig. 4.17).

In Milwaukee, the ads covered thirteen of the issues. There was some consistency between the races for national defense, public safety, taxes, and women's rights. However, campaign finance reform and immigration were the sole province of the presidential race. The DB races covered budget, energy, and environment, and healthcare issues (fig. 4.17).

The Cleveland voters saw ads that addressed thirteen of the seventeen issue areas and it was one of the two markets (the other was Tampa) in which the presidential race enjoyed a majority of them (fig. 4.18). There was some congruence between the races for the economy, public safety, taxes, and women's rights. The presidential ads covered many more of the issues than those for the DB races.

The market in which there was virtually no congruence regarding issue ads was San Francisco. To be sure, the market saw the fewest number of those ads, by far—a total of 1,609, and they only addressed six issues. However, there was absolutely no overlap in the presidential ads (energy, immigration, women's rights) and DB ads (corruption, financial reform, public safety).

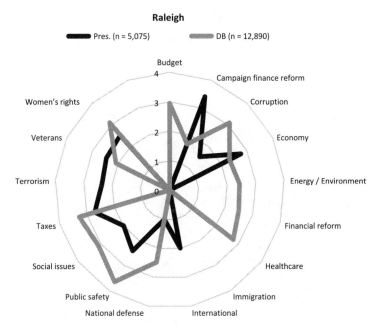

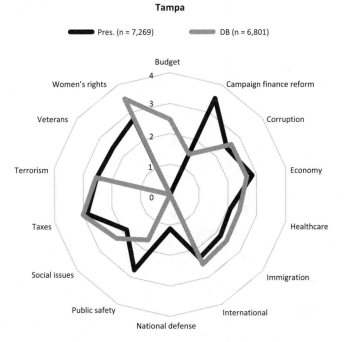

Figure 4.15. Political issue ads in presidential and down-ballot races in Raleigh (*top*) and Tampa (*bottom*).

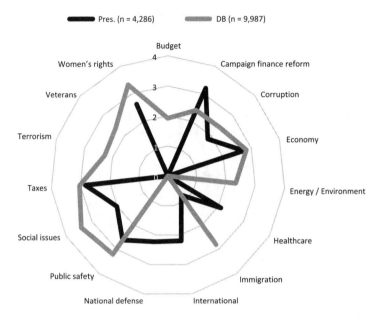

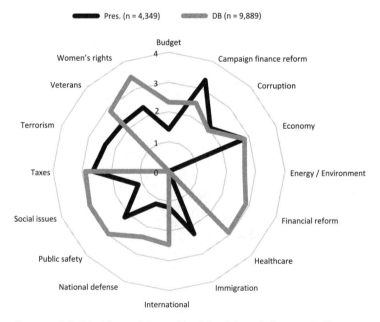

Figure 4.16. Political issue ads in presidential and down-ballot races in Denver (*top*) and Cedar Rapids (*bottom*).

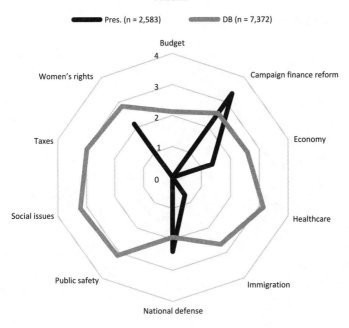

Phoenix

Pres. (n = 2,583)   DB (n = 7,372)

Budget
Campaign finance reform
Economy
Healthcare
Immigration
National defense
Public safety
Social issues
Taxes
Women's rights

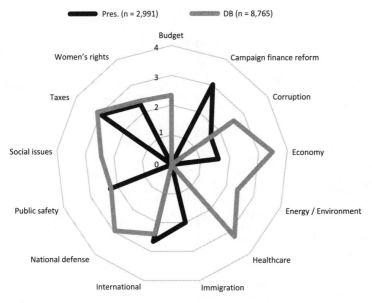

Milwaukee

Pres. (n = 2,991)   DB (n = 8,765)

Budget
Campaign finance reform
Corruption
Economy
Energy / Environment
Healthcare
Immigration
International
National defense
Public safety
Social issues
Taxes
Women's rights

Figure 4.17. Political issue ads in presidential and down-ballot races in Phoenix (*top*) and Milwaukee (*bottom*).

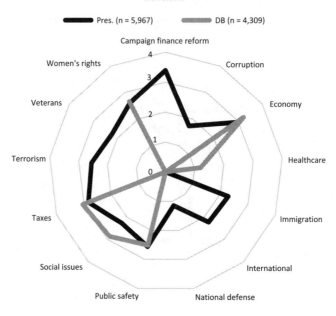

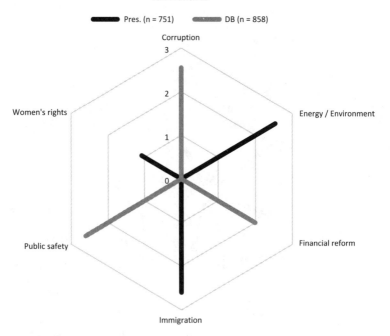

Figure 4.18. Political issue ads in presidential and down-ballot races in Cleveland and San Francisco.

In general, the markets reflected very different treatments of issue ads between the presidential and DB races that, presumably, reflected what the ad sponsors thought would resonate with voters.

Summary

The political ads that were aired during the September 5–November 7 campaign period were numerous (200,511 ads), expensive (over $220,000,000), and overwhelmingly directed at the down-ballot rather than the presidential race both in terms of numbers and the money spent. Their tone was mostly negative, especially those sponsored by interest groups at both the down-ballot and presidential level.

Often, we think that the ads portray the virtues or shortcomings of candidates. Although this is the case, over eight in ten were directed at a policy issue—either by the candidate or, much more often, by an interest group. In each instance, the sponsor wanted to convince viewers, whom they fervently hope will become voters, about the merits of their position or the shortcomings of that of their opponent on issues as varied as, for example, campaign finance reform, women's rights, taxes, and gun control. The message did not present a balanced view of the issue under discussion. That was not its purpose. It was expressly intended to persuade the viewer/voter to agree with the position that the ad sponsors took which is their legal right. The sponsors did not spend all of that money to simply open the floor for discussion.

And that is where I come to the question that I posed at the beginning of the book. The vast majority of the ads were aired on news programs—especially local television newscasts. The stations in the ten markets received over $220 million in a sixty-four-day period. By definition, the political reality that the ads conveyed was bought. With all of the information that political ads convey to citizens, what was the relationship between those ads and the news content of the programs that carried them? I look at that question in the next chapter.

5
Political Stories

This chapter presents an overview of the political stories across the markets (for details on the individual markets, see chapter 6). The findings described in this chapter are based on a content analysis of 1,552 local news broadcasts from the ten markets that were included in my research. The broadcasts covered the campaign period from September 5 through November 7, 2016. The broadcasts were drawn randomly each week in each of the markets. They represent the broadcasts in the markets throughout the campaign period.

Length and Time of the Broadcasts

Newscasts in the ten markets consisted of 30- and 60-minute durations and that was reflected in the sample. There were 1,103 half-hour newscasts (71 percent) and 449 hour-long newscasts (39 percent). They accounted for a total of 55,264 minutes of broadcast time—30,113 on half-hour programs and 25,151 on hour programs.

The newscasts were presented throughout the broadcast day: 686 (44 percent) were aired between 4:30 AM and 12 PM; 424 (27 percent) were presented between 12 PM and 6 PM; 442 (29 percent) were broadcast between 6 PM and 12 AM. That distribution is consistent with the stations' emphasis on achieving a news audience early in the day.

Elements of the Broadcasts

Newscasts are comprised of categories of units which I call *broadcast elements*. Using that construct, I accounted for all of the elements of the newscasts. As a result, I identified nine broadcast elements that, taken together, account for the entire broadcast. They are, in order of their total numbers: (1) commercials, (2) political ads, (3) soft news, (4) sports/weather/traffic segments, (5) crime, (6) public issues, which included all public issues *except* crime, (7) political stories, those directly addressing the campaign, (8) fires and accidents, and (9) international stories, including the war on terror (see table 5.1).

The 1,552 broadcasts that we coded contained 10,229 political ads and 3,845 political stories. Given the random selection process of the broadcasts, they are representative of both the broadcast content and the political ads that appeared in the television markets during the campaign period. These are the ads and stories that form the basis of my comparison between broadcast content and political ads.

Television news programs deal with a finite resource—time. Therefore, the amount of time that a newscast devotes to a particular broadcast element represents its importance in the newscast. To account for this condition, I show the composition of the typical news program as the proportion of newscast time that was devoted to each broadcast element. There was a statistically significant difference between the composition of 30- and 60-minute newscasts ($p < .05$). However, in practical terms, the difference was not very large or substantive. Therefore, I show the elements that comprise both types of broadcasts.

The most striking feature is that almost one-quarter (23 percent) of broadcast time was occupied by commercials (fig. 5.1). That was followed by about one-fifth (21 percent) of sports, weather, and traffic segments. The most prominent type of story was soft news (15 percent), followed by public issues (10 percent), which I define as all public issues *other than* crime. Political ads and

Table 5.1. Broadcast Elements

Element	Total
Commercials	11,992
Political ads	10,229
Soft news	8,967
Sports/weather/traffic	6,888
Crime	6,372
Public issues	6,254
Political stories	3,845
Fires/accidents	3,250
International	1,075
Total	58,872

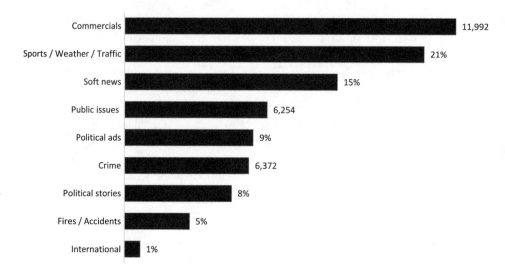

Figure 5.1. Composition of newscasts by broadcast time. (Percentages may not total 100 due to rounding.)

crime weighed in at about the same proportions as political stories (9 percent each). Political stories (defined as referring to the campaign) occupied only 8 percent of the broadcasts. International stories, which included the war on terror, received almost no coverage on local television news. That sparse coverage of international stories is consistent with my research regarding local television news (Yanich 2004).

Political Stories and Ads on the Broadcasts

In very real terms, commercials, sports/weather/traffic segments, and promos are structural features of local newscasts—they are always included. They are not subjected to the daily news selection calculus in which news directors engage. It is a zero-sum game—some stories are in and that puts other stories out. In fact, the professional literature treats them as separate entities from stories (Donald, Maynard, and Spann 2008).

To accommodate that reality, I looked at the distribution of broadcast time among the stories and political ads as a separate part of the newscast because these broadcast categories *are* subject to the zero-sum game of the news selection process. That is, I removed the structural broadcast categories and calculated the amount of the remaining time that was devoted to stories and political ads. For the purposes of my examination, I included political ads in that calculus because they are a different entity than the regular commercials that the stations present and, obviously, they are central to the questions I undertook. I use *total news time* to distinguish this portion of the broadcast from the entire broadcast time (Yanich 2011). Using this metric, the stations combined total of news time was 515 hours. There is a caveat in this calculation. Total news time includes political ads. But broadcasters are obligated to air political ads for federal offices that meet the "use" criterion—an ad sponsored by a legally qualified candidate or the candidate's campaign committee, that includes a likeness of the candidate (Montero 2014). That said, I include the political ads in the discussion about the part of the newscast in which news directors had discretion regarding story type because there was much broadcast time in which that news selection process unfolded.

This view of the composition of the broadcasts revealed very important realities of the news selection process. Regarding story type, soft news was the overwhelming choice of news producers, accounting for over one-quarter of news time (fig. 5.2), almost doubling its proportion when looking at all broadcast categories (see fig. 5.1). Most important for my analysis was the

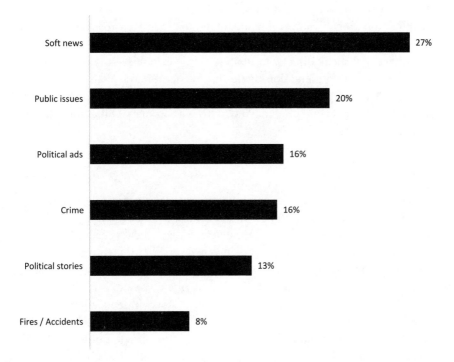

Figure 5.2. Broadcast time for stories and political ads.

difference in the time devoted to political ads and political stories. Political ads occupied more news time than political stories (16 percent and 13 percent, respectively). Remember, political ads were overwhelmingly 30-second spots only. On the other hand, political stories were, on average, the longest of the story types, a median of over 65 seconds.

The median duration of all stories was 33 seconds, but that varied significantly across story type. Fire/accidents stories were the shortest, a median of 28 seconds, followed by crime at a median of 30 seconds). That is understandable, given that most crime and accidents stories deliver quickly recognizable narratives focused on human peril or danger, almost always accompanied by video (Entman 2006; Gilliam 1998; Yanich 2004). The other story types required more explanation in the narrative and the pictures that accompanied it. Political stories were the longest in duration by a significant margin, a median of 43 seconds. Soft news and public issues were the next longest stories, with medians of 32 and 30 seconds, respectively.

Placement and Presentation Mode

The owners and managers of television stations must attend to the financial health of their organizations. The use of resources for the broadcast is crucial to that task. In addition to time (duration), there are two production aspects of the stories that speak directly to that economic calculus—-the placement of the story and the presentation mode that is used to convey its substance. I looked at each of these factors for the political and nonpolitical stories that were presented in each of the markets. This is a summary of the stories across all of the markets.

Story Placement

A complimentary characteristic of time in a broadcast is story placement. Just like the judgment regarding how much time will be devoted to a story, the decision about where to place it in the newscast is critical because the stories of a newscast are viewed by the audience in a series. Unlike print media, the audience cannot skip over the first story to get to the second or third or others. Therefore, each story in the broadcast has two purposes: to inform the audience and to hold that audience for the next story. Indeed, there is some research that suggests that the need to hold an audience has made the news "infotainment" (McManus 1994), and that it is constructed only to sell the audience to advertisers (Hamilton 2004). Consequently, the placement of a story is a crucial factor in the cost calculus of a newscast. In the placement decision, the station explicitly indicates what information it thinks will achieve and hold an audience.

Coupled with duration, the placement of a story sets what news directors call the "pace" of the newscasts. The variable I constructed for story placement was block, defined as the time between the commercial breaks. The first block is the period from the opening of the newscast to the first commercial break. It typically lasts between nine and eleven minutes and it is, by far, the longest period of uninterrupted news in the program. It is the opportunity for the broadcast to capture and hold an audience.

In my analysis, I maintained the content of blocks 1 and 2, but I collapsed the findings for blocks 3 to 6 into a category that I call block 3+.

There was a significant difference in where the stations placed the political and nonpolitical stories ($p < .05$). Almost two-thirds of the political stories appeared in the first block of the newscasts, compared to just 40 percent of nonpolitical stories. Correspondingly, the later blocks saw more nonpolitical stories—only 10 percent of political stories appeared in the second block (fig. 5.3).

In some ways, we would have expected this result. The political campaign was *the* story from September to early November in 2016. There was an intense presidential race along with down-ballot contests that called for coverage. Tweets, charges, countercharges were flying through the air and it would make sense that the stations would direct their attention and resources to cover them. But, as I will show later in this chapter, the nature of that coverage was less probing than we might have expected, given the campaign.

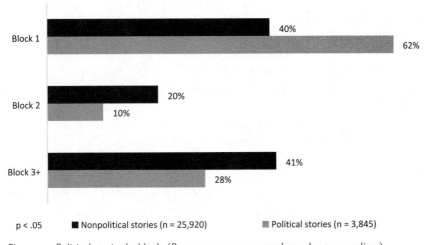

Figure 5.3. Political stories by block. (Percentages may not total 100 due to rounding.)

Presentation Mode

Selection, duration, and placement are all important production aspects of news stories. However, the most cost-sensitive factor in the production of a newscast is the presentation mode of the story. It involves decisions regarding the deployment of the station's most costly resources—personnel. News production is extremely labor-intensive. And there is a lot of news time to fill. On average, the big four affiliates in the local television markets produce about six hours of news per day (Papper 2018). Therefore, the decisions regarding how a news story is presented represents a major economic decision.

By definition, different presentation modes require different expenditures of resources, and the choice of presentation mode for story types reflects the station's judgment regarding which stories can capture and deliver an audience to advertisers. Consequently, the choice of presentation mode in a newscast has major economic implications. I define presentation mode as the system of professional broadcast techniques used to communicate the narrative or the pictures of the stories to an audience. I identified five types of presentation mode: voice-over by anchor, package, anchor-read without video, and voice-over by reporter.

In the voice-over by anchor mode, the story was delivered by the news anchor who provided the narrative as the videotape that was shot for the story was shown on the screen. In my previous research, this presentation mode was the most often used by the stations. The frequency of the use of this mode makes economic sense. The anchor represents the "brand" of the station to the community and, typically, the anchor is the highest paid member of the news staff. Using the anchor in the presentation of as many stories as possible increases the return on that investment.

In the package presentation mode, a news crew (reporter and camera operator) went to the scene of the story, shot video, produced the video for broadcast and the reporter wrote the narrative for the voice-over. The package mode required more time and resources and it was the most expensive method for presenting a story.

A third approach to presenting stories was the reading of the narrative by the anchor without any video being shown on the screen (anchor read without video)—the proverbial talking head. It was the least expensive presentation mode to employ.

The fourth mode that was used involved a voice-over by a reporter. It mirrored the same approach using the anchor. Typically, the anchor would introduce the story and then "toss" the responsibility for the rest of the

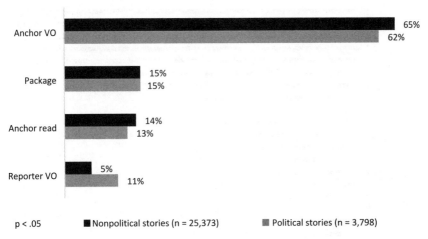

Figure 5.4. Stories by presentation mode. (Percentages may not total 100 due to rounding.)

reporting to a reporter who was, most often, in the studio. The "toss" was often accompanied by a comment that seemed to create more excitement about the upcoming story. The anchor would say something like, "here with the rest of the story, live in the studio, is reporter so-and so."

There was a statistically significant difference in how the news directors presented the political and nonpolitical stories ($p < .05$) (fig. 5.4). We see that the voice-over by anchor was overwhelmingly the most prominent presentation mode that was used for both types of stories (65 percent and 62 percent for nonpolitical and political stories, respectively). And the use of the package and anchor-read modes were virtually the same. However, there was a significant difference in the voice-over by reporter mode as over twice as many political stories were presented that way compared to nonpolitical stories. That may be due to the fact that reporters (rather than anchors) were often used to convey the campaign event stories that comprised the bulk of political stories.

Political Ads Across the Broadcasts

Given the proportion of time that was devoted to political ads on the broadcasts, how did that translate into the *number* of ads that were presented on the newscasts? Of the 1,552 broadcasts that comprised the sample, 77 contained no political ads; those broadcasts occurred early in the campaign period—70 percent of

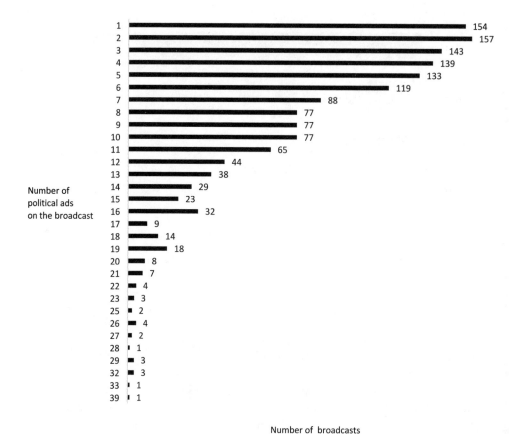

Number of
political ads
on the broadcast

Number of broadcasts

Figure 5.5. Distribution of political ads across broadcasts.

them occurred in the first four weeks. Further, they occurred in all of the television markets. How were the ads distributed across the broadcasts?

The first feature that we see with the distribution of the political ads is the
range—some broadcasts (154) only presented one political ad. Another broadcast presented 39 political ads (fig. 5.5). At first blush, that would seem very
unlikely. However, that broadcast lasted one hour, it was in Las Vegas, and it
occurred on November 7, the day before the election. The Las Vegas market
aired the most political ads among all of the markets. Further, considering
that political ads were only 30 seconds long, they would occupy only 18 minutes of the hour-long broadcast. That is entirely within the usual amount of

time devoted to commercials for that length of broadcast. In that broadcast, political ads largely replaced the regular commercials that were normally part of the newscast.

The tipping point seemed to be about 16 political ads—32 newscasts contained that number of ads. The average number of ads in the broadcasts was 6.6, but the standard deviation was 5.4, which indicated a wide variation in the number of ads across the broadcasts.

The number of political ads per broadcast is an important point. But the volume of ads is not the only feature that dictates the viewers' ad experience. We must remember how they were presented in the newscasts—in bunches, to use a colloquialism. The political ads were shown during the commercial breaks in a sequence, one after the other. So, the ad for one candidate was followed by the ad of another candidate, frequently the opponent, and that was followed by another ad. Therefore, citizens were bombarded with often irreconcilable versions of the same reality.

Political Stories Across the Broadcasts

Just like the political ads, I looked at how the proportion of broadcast time devoted to political stories translated to the *number* of those stories on the broadcasts. Out of the 1,552 broadcasts, 240 contained no political stories at all (about 15 percent). Again, as with the political ads, almost 60 percent of those broadcasts occurred during the first four weeks of the campaign period. In addition, like the political ads, the broadcasts without political stories occurred in all of the ten television markets.

There were 346 broadcasts that contained only one political story and another 352 newscasts presented two political stories. There is a significant decrease in the number of political stories after the first two categories—244 broadcasts presented three political stories and then another decrease to the 155 broadcasts that presented 4 such stories. The tipping point seems to be 5 political stories (there were 90 broadcasts in that category). The average number of stories was 2.4, but the standard deviation was 2.2, indicating a relatively wide range for the number of stories on the broadcasts (fig. 5.6).

Political Stories and Ads by Markets

There was quite a difference between how the stations and the markets used their broadcasts, and it illustrated the different news selection decisions that the stations made. This section lists the markets in the order of the number of

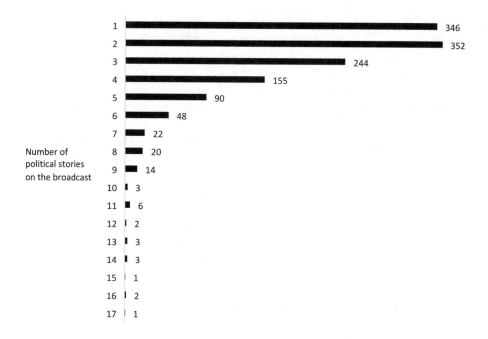

Number of
political stories
on the broadcast

Number of broadcasts

Figure 5.6. Distribution of political stories across broadcasts.

political ads that were aired. The shapes that appear in the graphs below represent the proportion of stories and political ads that comprised the newscasts. I used this approach in order to recognize more easily the differences across the markets—different shapes, different distributions of stories. In describing the graphs, I used the term "story type" to represent the proportions of both the stories *and* political ads to make it easier to convey the findings.

The markets that saw the largest number of political ad airings and the most revenue were Las Vegas and Philadelphia. They were remarkably similar in the proportion of broadcast time that the stories/political ads comprised on their newscasts. For example, soft news occupied the most broadcast time (25 percent and 27 percent, respectively). Then, political ads came in second in each market (23 percent and 19 percent, respectively). Crime was third in both markets. However, the median duration of the stories was very different. In Las Vegas, political stories were the longest (57 seconds) followed by public issues (42 seconds). However, in Philadelphia, political stories had a median of 101 seconds while all of the other story types had medians around 30 seconds (fig. 5.7).

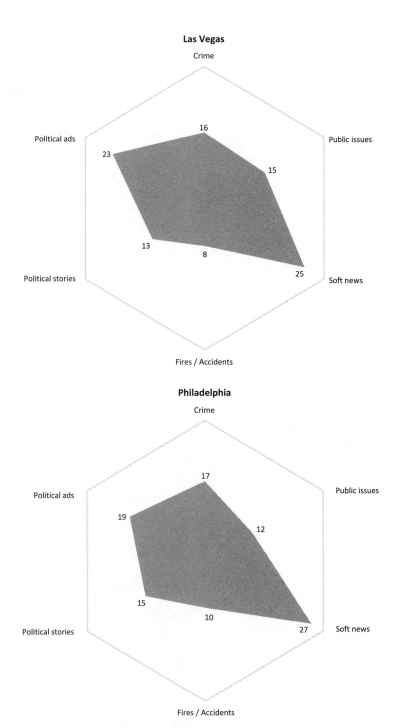

Figure 5.7. Airtime by story type in Las Vegas and Philadelphia (in percent).

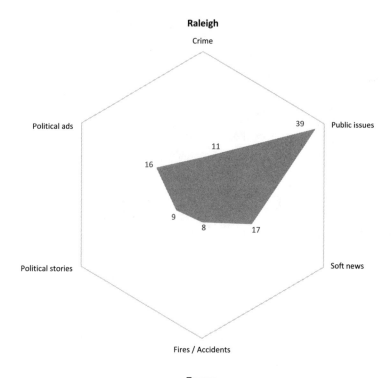

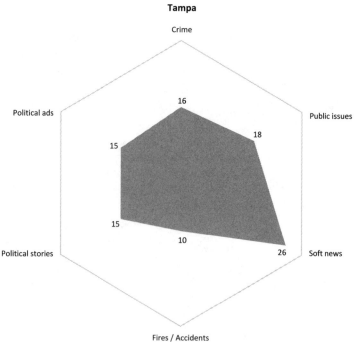

Figure 5.8. Airtime by story type in Raleigh and Tampa (in percent).

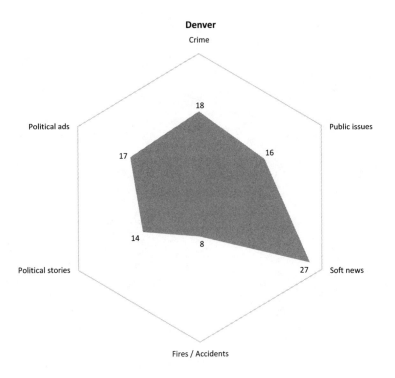

Denver

Crime

18

Public issues 16

Political ads 17

Soft news 27

Political stories 14

Fires / Accidents 8

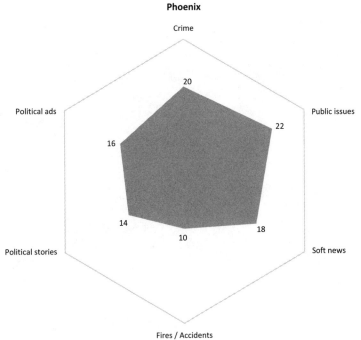

Phoenix

Crime

20

Public issues 22

Political ads 16

Soft news 18

Political stories 14

Fires / Accidents 10

Figure 5.9. Airtime by story type in Denver and Phoenix (in percent).

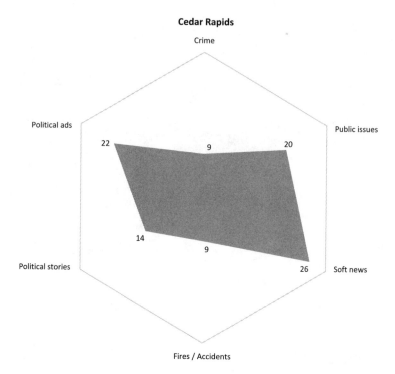

Cedar Rapids

Crime

Political ads — 22 — 9 — 20 — Public issues

Political stories — 14 — 9 — 26 — Soft news

Fires / Accidents

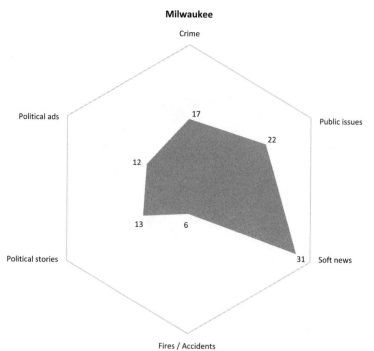

Milwaukee

Crime

Political ads — 17 — 12 — 22 — Public issues

Political stories — 13 — 6 — 31 — Soft news

Fires / Accidents

Figure 5.10. Airtime by story type in Cedar Rapids and Milwaukee (in percent).

The stations in Raleigh dealt with the stories very differently. There was a significant emphasis on public issues. Those stories comprised almost 40 percent of the broadcast time (median of 28 seconds). That was more than double the time directed at soft news (17 percent, median of 33 seconds) and four times the amount of time used for political stories (9 percent, median of 32 seconds). In fact, the stations in Raleigh covered more public issues as a proportion of their newscasts than any other market (fig. 5.8).

In Tampa, the distribution across the story types was much more even and, although soft news occupied over one-quarter of news time (26 percent, median of 31 seconds), the other story types, except for fires/accidents, were within three percentage points of each other. Political stories had a median duration of 34 seconds (fig. 5.8).

In Denver, soft news emerged as the most prominent story type, using over one-quarter (27 percent) of broadcast time, and they were also the longest stories with a median of 34 seconds. Crime (median of 27 seconds), political ads, and public issues (29 seconds) formed the second tier of story types within two percentage points of each other. Political stories (accounting for 14 percent of broadcast time with a median of 33 seconds) were only more prominent than fires and accidents (fig. 5.9).

The audience in the Phoenix television market saw a relatively more balanced distribution of the story types. Public issues (28 seconds median) and crime (27 seconds) were first and second in the proportion of time (22 percent and 20 percent, respectively). Political stories (14 percent, 30 seconds) were only more prominent than fires/accidents (10 percent, 25 seconds) (fig. 5.9).

In Cedar Rapids, soft news was king (26 percent, median of 34 seconds), but political ads were second (22 percent) closely followed by public issues (20 percent, median of 34 seconds). The time devoted to political stories (14 percent) was substantially below these story types, but they were slightly longer than all of the other stories with a median of 38 seconds. Interestingly, both crime and fires/accidents occupied less than one-tenth each (fig. 5.10).

In Milwaukee, soft news was the order of the day—accounting for almost one-third of broadcast time (31 percent, 36 seconds). It was also one of the markets in which political stories (13 percent) occupied more broadcast time than political ads (12 percent). Moreover, the political stories in Milwaukee, with a median duration of 68 seconds, were about twice as long as all of the other stories (fig. 5.10).

The stations in the Cleveland market were decidedly enamored with soft news stories—they accounted for 43 percent of broadcast time and they were the second longest stories at 42 seconds. That more than doubled public issues

(19 percent, 31 seconds) and more than tripled crime (13 percent, 30 seconds). It was over four times the time allotted to either political ads or political stories (11 percent each). That said, political stories were also the longest (46 seconds) in Cleveland, but not by much (fig. 5.11).

In San Francisco, the use of broadcast time was more evenly distributed. Soft news and public issues were neck and neck, each accounting for about one-fifth of the time. But soft news stories were significantly longer, 42 seconds and 36 seconds, respectively. Crime was a relatively close third (18 percent, 36 seconds). San Francisco was one of two markets (the other was Milwaukee) in which political stories accounted for more time than political ads (15 percent and 13 percent, respectively). And, political stories were significantly longer than all of the other stories with a median duration of 66 seconds (fig. 5.11).

In looking across the markets, it is clear that the news selection process that was employed in each of them yielded different mixes of story types. The different shapes within the graphs make that point. Regardless of the differences, though, there were some consistencies. Soft news accounted for more broadcast time than any other type in eight out the ten markets, in some cases overwhelmingly so. The comparison between political ads and political stories showed that, in six of the ten markets, political ad time exceeded political story time, sometimes by siginificant margins. For example, in Las Vegas, the market that saw the highest number of political ads, the time allotted to political ads almost doubled that used for political stories. That said, political stories were longer, sometimes substantially so, than all of the other stories in seven out of the ten markets. The important point for my examination is that the proportion of broadcast time allotted to political stories never came in higher than third behind the other story types on the broadcasts in any of the markets.

Political Stories and Ads by Races

My main concern here is the relationship between political ads and political stories across the presidential and down-ballot races. How did that play out across the markets? First, some clarifications. There were 3,845 political stories among the broadcasts; 3,494 were logically attributable to either the presidential or down-ballot races. The other 351 stories centered around announcements of early voting, absentee ballots, and similar stories and could not be categorized as one or the other. Those topics addressed both races and, as such, I excluded them from my analysis regarding the distrubution of political stories by race.

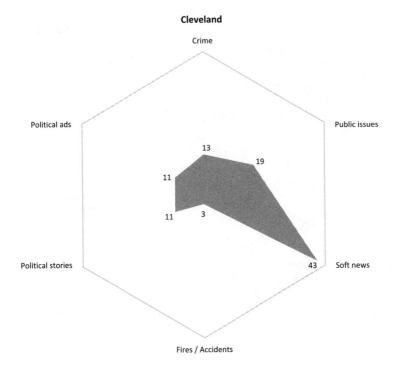

Cleveland

Crime

Political ads

Public issues

13

19

11

11 3

Political stories

Soft news

43

Fires / Accidents

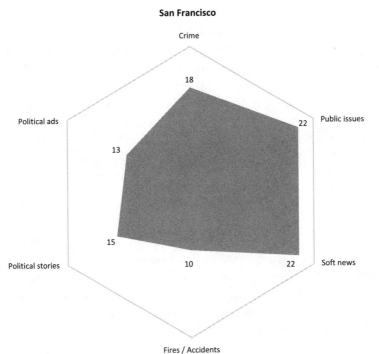

San Francisco

Crime

18

Political ads

Public issues

22

13

15

10 22

Political stories

Soft news

Fires / Accidents

Figure 5.11. Airtime by story type in Cleveland and San Francisco (in percent).

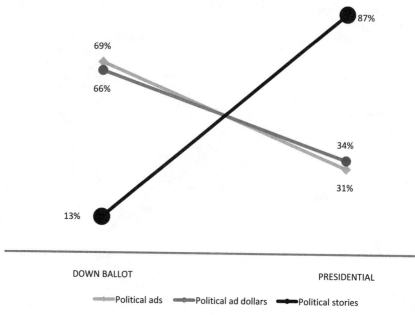

Figure 5.12. Distribution of political ads, revenue, and political stories by race.

The striking feature of the political stories across the races in all markets was that they were overwhelmingly directed toward the presidential race. Across all markets, almost nine out of ten (87 percent) of the stories talked about presidential politics (or 3,066 stories), leaving just 13 percent (428 stories) in the down-ballot column (fig. 5.12). That is in stark contrast to the distribution of political ads and political ad money in which the down-ballot races saw almost seven out of ten political ads and two-thirds of the political ad revenue (see fig. 4-1 in the previous chapter). There was clearly a difference between the emphases of the political ad buyers and the news selection calculus of the producers of the newscasts regarding which races to address.

How did this distribution of political stories play out in the individual markets? Some variation occurred, but the proportion of political stories directed at the presidential race did not dip below 80 percent in any of the markets. Cleveland lead the charge—97 percent of political stories there focused on the presidential race (fig. 5.13). But it was closely followed by Las Vegas, Denver, Philadelphia, and Tampa, all of which were above 90 percent. The other markets fell between 80 and 90 percent with San Francisco registering the lowest total—but that was still at the 80 percent level.

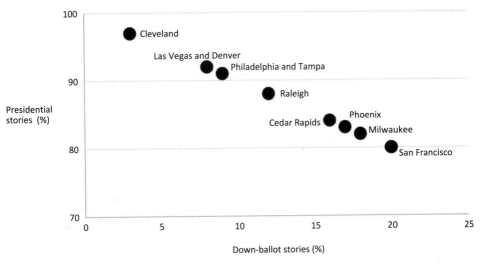

Figure 5.13. Comparison of stories for presidential versus down ballot races.

Political Stories and Political Ads by Market

The distribution of the political stories within the markets varied greatly, as news directors responded to the demands—economic, organizational, informational—that influenced them. In the following chart (fig. 5.14), the markets are presented in the rank order of the total number of political stories that was presented on the stations. The rank order of political stories did not correspond to the amount of time that the stations in the markets devoted to political ads. There was no linear order to the number of political stories. The round marker on the vertical line represents the first number that accompanies each market name. It is its rank among the ten markets regarding the number of political stories that appeared on the newscasts. The triangle marker on the line represents the second number and it indicates the market's rank regarding the number of political ads that were aired in the market. The distance between the two markers on the line shows the difference in the ranks.

San Francisco had the highest number of political stories (553), but the lowest number of political ads, and the numbers reflect that along the vertical line that links the market's ranking for political stories and political ads (fig. 5.14). At the other end of the spectrum, the market with the lowest number of political stories (164) had the third highest number of political ads—Raleigh. However, as I mentioned previously, I had a reduced number of broadcasts

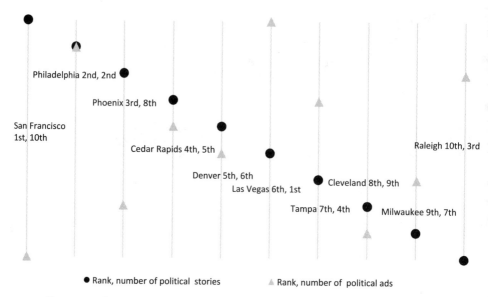

Philadelphia 2nd, 2nd

Phoenix 3rd, 8th

San Francisco
1st, 10th

Cedar Rapids 4th, 5th

Raleigh 10th, 3rd

Denver 5th, 6th

Las Vegas 6th, 1st

Cleveland 8th, 9th

Tampa 7th, 4th

Milwaukee 9th, 7th

● Rank, number of political stories   ▲ Rank, number of political ads

Figure 5.14. Comparison of the rank of markets by number political stories and political ads.

from the Raleigh market due to a technical error. The market with the highest number of political ads, Las Vegas, had only the sixth highest number of political stories. The most consistent market was Philadelphia, it came in second in both categories. The other markets in which the numbers of political stories and political ads were within one position in rank were Cedar Rapids (fourth and fifth), Denver (fifth and sixth) and Cleveland (eighth and ninth). The important point here is that the number of political ads that were presented by the stations in the market did not necessarily translate into the number of political stories that appeared on their air.

Political Stories by Types, Time, and Races

In order to better understand the nature of the political stories that the stations presented, I applied a specific coding scheme to them that yielded five types of political stories. In rank order by the number of stories they were:

Campaign event: These stories included coverage of the candidates' rallies, speeches, debates, and other public appearances in campaign mode. I included the debates in this group because they met the criterion of campaign stories and there were relatively few of

them. This coverage was generally characterized by an announcement of the event before it occurred or a short description of the
event after it was over. In many ways, these stories were almost ste-
nography rather than journalism and they were relatively inexpen-
sive to produce. That is, the information that the reporters gave the
audience was, in the first instance, derived from a press release from
the campaign—the when and where of the event. The reporting
after the event was most often focused on the fact that it did occur,
the size of the crowd, and some reiteration of what the candidate
said. These stories were not characterized by probing journalism.
However, they did represent a cost to the station to produce in the
use of reporters and, sometimes, photographers to convey the information. I counted 1,438 of these stories totaling 34 percent of political story time with a median duration of 35 seconds.

Local status report: These stories covered the present status of the
campaign, both at the presidential and down-ballot levels. They
included polling results (horse race), candidates' positions, and
comments on each other's positions. However, these stories were
produced and presented by reporters from the local station, therefore, the stations incurred the costs of production. There were 1,184
such stories accounting for 31 percent of political story time with a
median duration of 46 seconds.

National status report: Like the local status report, these stories covered the present status of the campaign, including the latest poll
results (horse race), candidate positions that were taken on the campaign trail. These stories were presented by national network reporters after a "toss" from the local anchor. That is, the story began with
a brief introduction by the local anchor who referred the audience
to the network reporter who delivered the substance of the story.
Essentially, the local station incurred no cost in the production of
this story. There were 504 stories that comprised 16 percent of political story time. However, they were, by far, the longest stories at a
median duration of 77 seconds.

Issue: These stories included overage of a campaign issue that was discussed by the candidates (such as immigration, jobs, healthcare), a
reference to or mention of a political ad of the candidate or an
examination of the accuracy or the effect of an ad. Relative to the
other political story types, these stories could be seen as the journalism that the stations would bring to the task. Issue stories numbered
only 486, accounting for about 14 percent of political story time.

However, they were also the second longest in duration—a median
of 50 seconds.

Other: These stories referred to the political campaigns but did not fit
in the above categories. For example, they included a story about
campaign posters that had been destroyed. These stories were the
fewest in number (233), about 5 percent of political story time, and
the shortest, a median duration of 37 seconds.

Local television news broadcasts wrestle with a precious commodity—
time. It is finite and the amount of broadcast time that is devoted to one story
versus another is an indication of its importance in the news selection process.
Therefore, I show here how the political stories were treated from that perspective—first, for all of the markets combined and then, for each individual
market.

As I mentioned earlier, the total amount of news time available to news
producers was 515 hours. But for purposes of the following discussion, I use
minutes. So, the 515 hours translate into 30,900 minutes, of which the broadcast news directors used 3,816 minutes (about 12 percent) for the coverage of
political stories, defined as directly addressing the presidential or down-ballot
campaigns. Out of that time for political stories, the overwhelming majority
addressed the presidential race (3,309 minutes, 87 percent); only 507 minutes
(13 percent) were dedicated to the down-ballot races.

The campaign event was, by far, the most prominent type of political story
that made the news, accounting for 1,307 minutes at the presidential level
versus just 88 at for down-ballot races, 34 percent of all political story time
(fig. 5.15). The median duration of these stories was 35 seconds.

Local status reports were second with 895 minutes and 183 minutes at the
presidential and down-ballot races, respectively (31 percent of political story
time). The median duration for these stories was 46 seconds. Both the local
and national status report stories were essentially recaps of information: the
horse race nature of the races, who said what, who responded, and the like.
National status reports accounted for just 16 percent of the political story time,
but they were the longest, by far, at a median duration of 76.5 seconds. And
remember, the national status reports were produced by the network affiliates
and the local stations incurred no cost for their presentation except the time
that it took to "toss" the story from the local anchor to the network reporter.

The important finding is that the political stories that: addressed issues
that were a topic in the ads, referenced or mentioned a political ad, or examined the claims of a political ad came in last among the political story types,

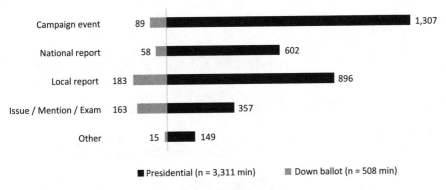

Figure 5.15. Time spent on political story type (in minutes).

notwithstanding the "other" category that was a collection of disparate topics (5 percent of political story time, median of 37 seconds). They accounted for only 357 minutes of airtime in the presidential race and 163 minutes for the down-ballot races (14 percent of political story time), and their duration had a median of 50 seconds. So, even among political stories, little time was devoted to references or queries of the ads that took up so much of the stations' commercial time.

Political Stories within the Markets

In all of the markets, the stations spent much more time covering the presidential race compared to the down-ballot contests. While it is instructive to know the general trends in the use of political story time, the real decisions about how the races were covered occurred in the individual markets. News directors decided what was covered, how it was covered, when it was covered and how much time was devoted to any story. And the use of that scarce resource, time, gives us a very important window into those decisions. The percentages in the following information refer to the proportion of time that was allocated to political story types. The median durations refer to the 3,494 stories that addressed either the presidential or down-ballot races.

In Las Vegas, campaign events and national reports took up much of the time for political stories (29 percent and 27 percent of the total time devoted to political stories, respectively). The local report followed with a total of 76 minutes (21 percent of the total time). The issue stories only accounted for 39 minutes on the presidential side and just 16 minutes for down-ballot races (15

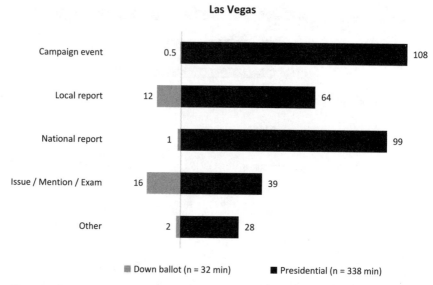

Figure 5.16. Minutes spent on political story type by race in the Las Vegas market.

percent of total time). That said, it is important to note that, as a proportion across the races, the issue stories had more time devoted to the down-ballot races than the other types, 16 minutes (fig. 5.16).

In addition to the proportion of time each type occupied, it is important to consider the median duration of the stories. The longest stories, by far, were issue stories at a median of 109 seconds. Local and national reports were relatively equal, 63 and 57.5 seconds, respectively. Interestingly, the *other* stories were significantly long at a median of 79 seconds. Campaign event stories, the most prominent type by proportion of political story time, were also the shortest—39 seconds.

In Philadelphia, the distribution was quite different from Las Vegas. Although campaign event stories were prominent (36 percent of the total time), local reports on the campaign carried the day at 169 minutes for the presidential race and another 22 minutes at the down-ballot level (40 percent of the total time). The stories that addressed issue, mentions, and ads totaled just over 29 minutes (6 percent of political story time).

There were significant differences in the duration of the story types. The issue stories led the way with a median of 130 seconds, followed by the national reports at 115 seconds. Campaign event stories came in at 59 seconds. But, the most prominent of stories by proportion of time, local reports, had a median

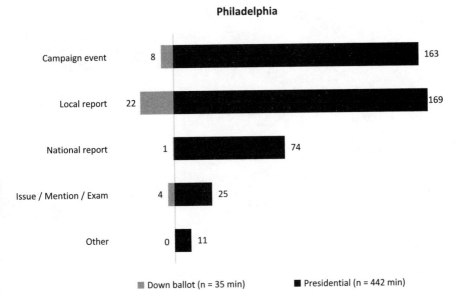

Figure 5.17. Minutes spent on political story type by race in the Philadelphia market.

of 97 seconds, and they devoted more time to the down-ballot races (22 minutes) than the other story types. The shortest stories were the *other* category at 44 seconds (fig. 5.17).

In Raleigh, campaign event stories ruled the day with 95 minutes for the presidential race and another 15 minutes for the down-ballot races. That accounted for almost two-thirds of the time devoted to political stories (63 percent), but they were the second shortest stories in the market with a median of 26 seconds. Local reports were a distant second with 16 percent of political story time and they were longer at 38.5 seconds. The two longest story types were issue stories and national reports at median times of 89 and 72 seconds, respectively. But they comprised very small percentages of the time allotted to political stories, 5 and 11 percent, respectively. Even though the percentages were small, Raleigh was only one of two markets (San Francisco was the other) in which there was more time spent on issue stories for the down-ballot races than the presidential contest—13 minutes to 5 minutes (fig. 5.18).

Tampa was decidedly different. Although campaign event stories occupied the most time (37 percent), they were also the shortest at a median of 26 seconds. Issue stories were second (29 percent, median of 39 seconds). Importantly, these stories also spent the most time on the down-ballot races, 24

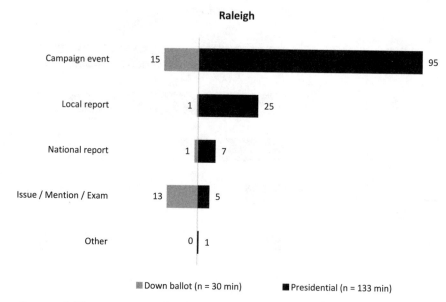

Figure 5.18. Minutes spent on political story type by race in the Raleigh market.

minutes. The local and national reports occupied about the same proportion of political story time (16 percent and 14 percent, respectively), but there was a difference in their median durations, 41 and 47 seconds, respectively (fig. 5.19).

In Denver, campaign event stories (39 percent) were first on both sides of the ledger (129 and 19 minutes, respectively for presidential and down-ballot races), but they had the second shortest duration at a median of 29 seconds. Local reports accounted for over one-third of political story time and were the second longest at a median of 38 seconds. National reports and issue stories, although comprising just 12 percent and 10 percent of story time, were the longest at a median of 43 seconds (fig. 5.20).

In Phoenix, campaign event stories accounted for most political story time (36 percent), but they were among the shortest (median of 26 seconds). Local reports accounted for over one-quarter of time (27 percent) and they were about one-third longer than campaign event stories at a median of 34 seconds. The longest stories in Phoenix were issue stories at a median of 39.5 seconds, but they only comprised 14 percent of the political story time. Most importantly, though, the Phoenix stations devoted the exact same amount of time for issue stories to the presidential and down-ballot races, 30 minutes (fig. 5.21). That was quite different from the general trend across the markets.

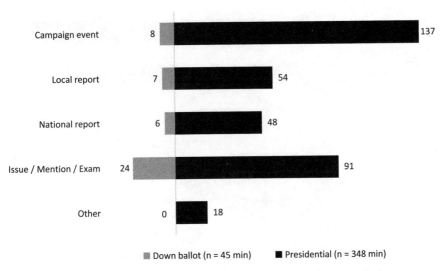

Figure 5.19. Tampa: Minutes spent on political story type by race in the Tampa market.

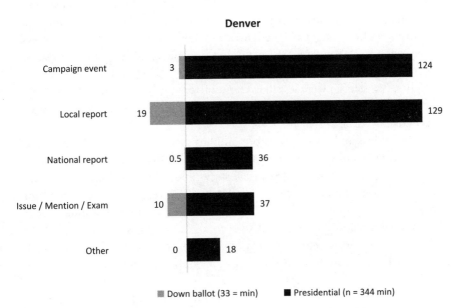

Figure 5.20. Minutes spent on political story type by race in the Denver market.

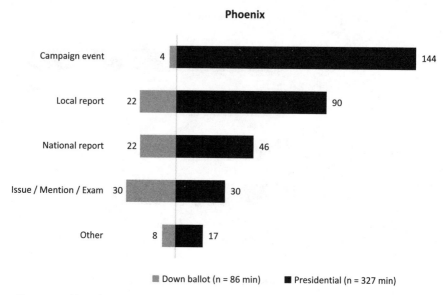

Figure 5.21. Minutes spent on political story type by race in the Phoenix market.

In Cedar Rapids, campaign event stories accounted for over one-third (36 percent) of political story time at the presidential level; local reports came in second (93 minutes) and first (34 minutes) on the down-ballot side. Campaign event stories were longer at a median of 37.5 seconds compared to local reports at 29 seconds. National reports accounted for about one-fifth of the stories and they were the longest at a median of 54 seconds. However, important for my inquiry, issue stories were less than one-tenth (7 percent) of political story time even though they were the second longest in the market at a median of 50 seconds (fig. 5.22).

Milwaukee audiences saw more emphasis on local reports, both in the presidential races (87 minutes) and at the down-ballot level (31 minutes), accounting for 38 percent of political story time. They were also the second longest at a median of 96.5 seconds. Campaign event stories accounted for over one-fourth of political story time and they were almost a minute shorter than local reports at a median of 39 seconds. The longest stories were those that addressed an issue, mentioned an ad, or examined the claims of an ad. They had a median of 98 seconds, but they only accounted for 11 percent of political story time (fig. 5.23).

In Cleveland, the stations spent virtually no time on the down-ballot races (only 14 minutes). At the presidential level the overwhelming story of choice

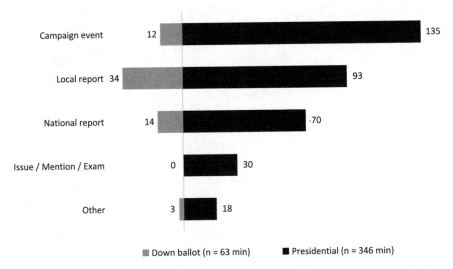

Figure 5.22. Minutes spent on political story type by race in the Cedar Rapids market.

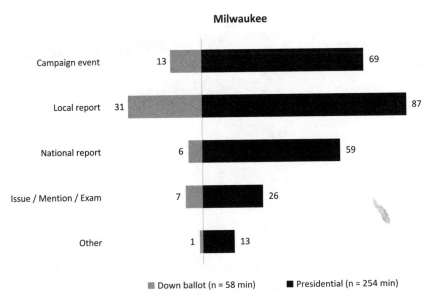

Figure 5.23. Minutes spent on political story type by race in the Milwaukee market.

was the campaign event (167 minutes). Those stories comprised almost half of political story time and had a median time of 38 seconds. Local reports occupied over one-quarter of political story time and they were substantially longer at a median of 49 seconds. National reports, with only 9 percent of political story time, were the longest at a median of 58 seconds and all of them were directed toward the presidential race. Issue stories, although accounting for 12 percent of political story time, were shorter at a median of 52 seconds (fig. 5.24).

In San Francisco, virtually all of the political story types were covered. The striking feature is that the time spent on down-ballot issue stories significantly exceeded the presidential side of that ledger, 56 to 36 minutes, respectively. Of course, the issue stories accounted for only 16 percent of political story time, but they were also the longest at a median of 102 seconds (fig. 5.25).

Campaign event stories were one-third of political story time—the most prominent—with a median duration of one minute. National reports occupied exactly one-fourth of political story time with a median duration of just over a minute (66 seconds). Local reports, at just under a quarter of political story time, were the second longest at a median of 81 seconds.

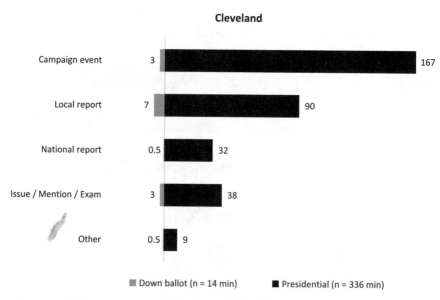

Figure 5.24. Minutes spent on political story type by race in the Cleveland market.

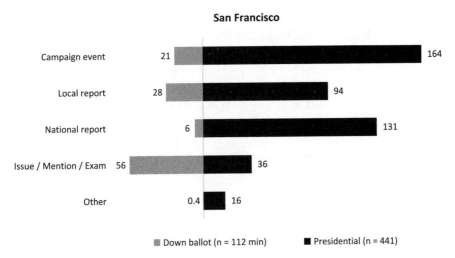

Figure 5.25. Minutes spent on political story type by race in San Francisco.

Summary

I found great variation among the markets in the time devoted to political stories. We might expect that, as news directors tend to claim that they are responding to their audiences, or, at least, to the economic conditions of the media market. However, in each of the markets, to one extent of another, they overwhelmingly directed their attention to the presidential race. And the news selection process is a zero-sum game. So, if attention and resources went to the presidential race, by definition that reduced the time and resources they dedicated to the down-ballot races. Further, the type of political stories that was the most prominent in seven out of the ten markets—the coverage of campaign events—was arguably the least expensive to produce. Much of the information that comprised the narrative of the story was information provided by the campaigns—who was going to be there, when, where, what they were going to say. Even in stories that covered the campaign event after it had occurred typically used videotape from the event as the basis for the story and reiterated the who, what, and where narrative. There was not much investigative time involved in the production process.

By contrast, the political story type that would have required the use of more resources—the issue, mention, and examine pieces—often accounted for the least amount of time in the markets. In fact, that was the case in seven out of the ten markets. To be sure, the stations were reluctant to tackle the claims of political ads. The reasons for that reluctance are understandable from an economic sense. Those stories cost money and they might expose the station to the dissatisfaction of some viewers and of political ad buyers. Further, there is an economic incentive to show as many ads as possible and let the audience try to sort out the accuracy and reasonableness of the various claims through their own devices. In fact, that is precisely what happened.

In the next chapter, I look at the campaigns in each of the markets and how the relationship between political ads and political stories played out on the local newscasts.

6

The Markets

*

The overall findings for all of the markets are instructive. However, the central question was really directed at the markets themselves—individually, not as a group. Media firms always make the argument that comparing their performance across markets is unfair because they are suppliers of a good (news) in a particular market that has its own demand structure. Therefore, the supply of news would be different across the markets owing to the demand, however, the stations determine that demand. That is a reasonable position, to a point. I will touch on that, but my main purpose in this chapter is to see how the political ads, political stories, and the money played out across the stations in the markets during the sixty-four-day campaign period between September 5 and November 7, 2016.

The profiles that follow treat the markets as separate entities and they are arranged in the same rank-order based on the number of ads that appeared in the market that I used in earlier chapters. The profiles contain several pieces of information, all based on the performance of the individual stations in the market. I did that because the stations were the primary actors in the market that deliver both the political ads and the news in the market. The decisions of the news directors, as well as other managers of the station, were crucial to what the public saw.

First, I looked at the races themselves. I tracked polls in September, October, and November, as well as the final election results for both the presidential and US Senate races. I defined races that had election results within five percentage points as those that were competitive. My findings confirm the conventional wisdom that competitive races draw the most money and political ads. Las Vegas and Philadelphia aired, by far, the most political ads and realized the largest revenue compared to the other markets.

Second, for each station, I show the total number of ads by presidential and down-ballot (DB) races, the total estimated revenue, the station average cost per ad, and the ratio of presidential to DB ads.

Third, the relationship between presidential and DB campaign ads is important. However, the central concern here is the relationship between political ads and political stories. I looked at that relationship through a set of ratios, both for the number of political ads and stories and, perhaps more importantly given the scarcity of time on newscasts, the amount of time that was devoted to each. I do so because the political ads were all 30 seconds in duration and the median duration of all political stories across all ten markets was 43 seconds. It was 49 seconds for all issue stories. Therefore, basing the ratios only on the numbers of political ads and political stories would be accurate, but they would not show a more nuanced relationship. I show ratios to compare the time that the stations devoted to political ads and to political stories. First, I show the ratios of presidential to DB stories; second, the ratios of political ads to all political stories; and third, the ratios of political ads to the political stories that address an issue in the ads, mention an ad, or examine the claims of an ad. These stories represent the enterprise reporting of the stations in which they exhibited some level of journalism.

Las Vegas, NV

In Nevada, Democrat Catherine Cortez Masto narrowly defeated Republican Joe Heck: 47.1 percent to 44.7 percent. The September and October polls showed a slight advantage for Heck. However, the early November poll gave Masto her first lead over Heck. The final result fell within the competitive 5 percent; Masto, however, was able to maintain her lead on Election Day (table 6.1). In the presidential race, a poll in September showed a two-point lead for Trump. However, the October, November, and Election Day results ended up in Clinton's favor (table 6.2).

Table 6.1. Senate Race

Candidate	Party	NBC/WSJ/Marist Sep 6–8	Monmouth Oct 14–17	Survey Monkey Nov 1–7	Official Result
Catherine Cortez Masto	D	45	42	50	47.1
Joe Heck	R	47	45	45	44.7

Table 6.2. Presidential Race

Candidate	Party	Monmouth Sep 11–13	CNN/ORC Oct 1–15	Emerson Nov 4–5	Official Result
Donald Trump	R	44	46	46	45.5
Hillary Clinton	D	42	50	47	47.9

Both Clinton and Masto outspent their Republican counterparts during the election which could explain the shift in poll results closer to the election. Clinton spent $5.5 million compared to Trump's $3.76 million, and Masto spent $4.4 million compared to Heck's $2.99 million.

In the races for the US House of Representatives, three of the four Nevada districts are part of the Las Vegas television market. Before the election, the Republicans controlled two of the three seats. After the election, they controlled none. In District 1, incumbent Dina Titus defeated her top opponent, Mary Perry, by a whopping 33 percent. The races in Districts 3 and 4 were much closer. In District 3, the incumbent Joe Heck resigned to run for Senate—a race he lost. In his place, Danny Tarkanian, the son of the University of Nevada, Las Vegas' legendary basketball coach, Jerry Tarkanian, became the Republican nominee. He lost the race to Democrat Jacky Rosen by a very slim margin of 1.3 percent. In District 4, Democrat Ruben Kihuen defeated Republican Crescent Hardy by 4 percent—another competitive race.

Political Ads and Revenue by Stations

Las Vegas is ranked number 40 among the 210 television markets in the United States, as measured by the number of television households, with just over 750,000 households (Nielsen 2016). The market encompasses three counties in Nevada. The four network affiliate stations are KLAS (CBS), KSNV (NBC), KTNV (ABC), and KVVU (Fox).

In total, over 46,000 ads were presented in the market during the sixty-four-day campaign period for a total estimated revenue for the four stations of about $55 million, and they had an estimated average cost per ad of just under $1,200 (table 6.3). There were over 36,000 ads directed toward the DB races compared to just over 10,000 for the presidential contest—a ratio of 3.51:1 of DB to presidential ads. But there were significant differences among the stations.

Table 6.3 is organized by the rank-order of the total number of ads that each station aired. The table shows the variation in the cost of doing business across the Las Vegas stations and that was due to the size of the audience that each station commanded. KVVU presented the highest number of ads and by a

Table 6.3. Political Ads Aired by Station, 2016

Station	Political Ads Total	Down-ballot Ads	Presidential Ads	Ratio	Estimated Ad Revenue	Average Cost per Ad	Revenue* ($)	Political Ad Revenue of Total Revenue (%)
KVVU	14,068	11,061	3,007	3.7	9,251,570	658	42,000,000	22
KSNV	10,929	8,295	2,634	3.1	16,489,990	1,509	59,000,000	28
KTNV	10,844	8,430	2,414	3.5	7,455,010	687	30,000,000	25
KLAS	10,749	8,482	2,267	3.7	21,779,640	2,026	62,000,000	35
Total	46,590	36,268	10,322	3.5	54,976,210	1,180	193,000,000	28

* Source: BIA/Kelsey, 2018

good margin over the others (about 22 percent). The station saw just over $9 million in estimated revenue as the average estimated cost of an ad was only $658. KTNV was in a similar situation regarding its average cost per ad ($687), but it did not present the number of ads that would increase its estimated revenue which was last among the stations at just under $7.5 million.

The revenue from political ads was immensely important to all of the stations. Remember, the political ad revenue only accounts for the last two months of the campaign. Yet, the political ads in that period contributed substantial money to the stations. KLAS brought in $62 million in all of 2016 (BIA/Kelsey 2018), yet political ad revenue was almost $22 million in the sixty-four-day campaign period that I covered—that's 35 percent of the total revenue. The other stations ranged from 28 percent (KSNV) to 22 percent (KVVU). The stations realized between one-fifth and one-third of their total revenue in just two months of the campaign. Such was the importance of the revenue of political ads to the stations' bottom lines.

The clear winner in the ad sweepstakes was KLAS. It aired the fewest number of ads (10,749) and realized the highest estimated revenue—almost $22 million, with an average cost per ad of over $2,000. That was about 24 percent more on both counts than its nearest competitor, KSNV.

That said, KLAS also had the highest ratio of DB to presidential ads, 3.74. That is, for every presidential ad, KLAS presented almost 4 DB ads.

Comparing Presidential and Down-Ballot Stories and Ads

While KLAS enjoyed the most revenue in the market, it also had the highest ratio of the number of presidential stories to those addressing the DB races

(19:1). That means that the station broadcasted nineteen stories that featured the presidential race to every story devoted to the DB races. That was much higher than its competitors at 12:1 for KVVU, 11:1 for KSNV, and 10:1 for KTNV (fig. 6.1). The most important relationships for my purposes were those between political ads and political stories, and, more specifically, between political ads and the issue, mention, and examine type of political stories which I call issue stories here. These are the stories in which the stations carried out some version of journalism. There were two relationships: between political ads and political stories in general, and between political ads and the issue stories.

As was the case with presidential and DB stories, KLAS was the clear leader in the ratios of ads to stories metric as well political ads to issue stories. Looking at the relationship of political ads to political stories, KLAS's ratio for the number of each was 7:1—for every seven political ads it aired, it showed one political story. Again, that ratio was higher than any other station in the market.

The imbalance between political advertising and political stories was starker when I looked at ads and a particular *type* of political story—those that discussed an issue raised by the ads, mentioned an ad or examined the claims of an ad. Once again, KLAS was out in front. With a ratio of 56:1, it showed 56 ads to every issue story that it broadcast. By contrast, KVVU was 40:1 and KSNV was the lowest at 16:1 (fig. 6.1). The ratios that are based on the *number* of stories and ads are instructive. However, as I explained earlier, comparing the stations' performance based on the time that they devoted to ads and stories gives us a more nuanced view of the stations' activities. It may be a fairer measure of the relationship between ads and stories.

Looking at the time devoted to presidential and DB stories, KLAS's ratio is quite different than the one based just on the number of stories. In fact, it increases dramatically to 39:1 (fig. 6.1). That is, the station broadcast 39 seconds of presidential stories to every one second of DB stories. That was about 350 percent higher than the second-place station, KTNV, with an 11:1 ratio.

When I looked at the time ratios of political ads to political stories, in general, the stations were closely bunched. Both KLAS and KTNV broadcast 2.2 seconds of ads to every 1 second of political stories. KVVU and KSNV had ratios of 1.6:1 and 1.4:1, respectively. Clearly, the longer duration of political stories (median of 59 seconds) compared to the 30-second political ads was at play here.

The political story type that could be seen as enterprise reporting were those that I called issue stories. Remember, among the political story types, issue stories accounted for only 16 percent of broadcast time with a median duration of almost double (median of 58 seconds) that of political ads. Still,

Las Vegas

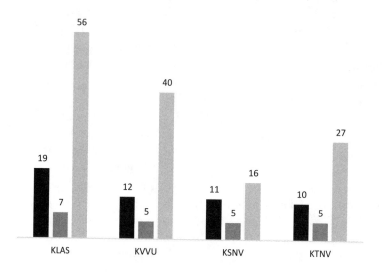

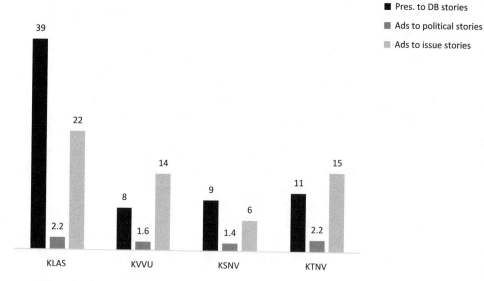

Figure 6.1. Ratio of number of ads (*top*) and time (*bottom*) for presidential to down-ballot stories, ads to political stories, and ads to issues stories in Las Vegas.

the time devoted to ads won out. KLAS led the way at 22:1—22 ad seconds to every 1 second of issue stories. We can see that both KVVU and KTNV still had significantly wide ratios at 14:1 and 15:1, respectively. KSNV, by contrast, had a ratio of 6:1—by far, the lowest among the stations.

Consider the point—KLAS realized an estimated revenue in the sixty-four-day period of almost $22 million compared to KSNV's $16.5 million. They were the two largest revenue totals in the market by a wide margin. However, as measured by the time they devoted to political ads and to issue stories, KSNV was more inclined to do some enterprise reporting. Yet a larger point should not be lost here: A 6:1 ratio only looks good when we compare it to a 22:1 ratio. It still means that the stations spent significantly more time on political ads than issue stories.

Philadelphia, PA

The polls and results in the Pennsylvania Senate and presidential races were very similar to those in North Carolina, another market with very competitive races. Republican incumbent Senator Pat Toomey held a narrow lead in September and October polls with a November poll showing challenger Katie McGinty with a four-point lead. However, Toomey ended up narrowly winning reelection by less than two percentage points (table 6.4). In the presidential race, Clinton maintained a five- to six-point lead throughout the campaign. But she did not hold that lead in the final election results as the state went for Trump by less than two percentage point (table 6.5).

These races gained attention because Toomey managed to keep his race close by running his campaign separately from Donald Trump and by

Table 6.4. Senate Race

Candidate	Party	Quinnipiac Aug 31–Sep 7	Quinnipiac Oct 1–16	Survey Monkey Nov 1–7	Official Result
Pat Toomey	R	46	49	45	48.8
Katie McGinty	D	45	45	49	47.3

Table 6.5. Presidential Race

Candidate	Party	Quinnipiac Aug 29–Sep 7	Quinnipiac Oct 1–16	Morning Call Oct 3–Nov 4	Official Result
Donald Trump	R	43	45	42	48.2
Hillary Clinton	D	48	51	48	47.5

withholding for whom he would vote on Election Day (Decker 2016). Donald Trump only spent $3.3 million in Philadelphia compared to Clinton's $6.76 million and benefitted from the link between McGinty and Clinton that the ads by Toomey were emphasizing. This link resulted in McGinty spending more money on ads ($3.26 million compared to Toomey's $2.6 million), which in conjunction with the negative Clinton link, could have led to voter fatigue at the end of the campaign.

The Philadelphia television market has all or portions of nine House districts in Pennsylvania and three in New Jersey. Going into the 2016 election, the Republicans held five seats in Pennsylvania and two seats in New Jersey. After the election, that stayed the same, and the races were not close.

In Pennsylvania District 1, Democratic incumbent Robert Brady overwhelmed Republican Deborah Williams with over 64 percent of the vote. In District 2, incumbent Chaka Fattah could not run due to his conviction on corruption charges. In his place, Democrat Dwight Evans became the nominee and he crushed Republican James Jones with 80 percent of the vote. They were the largest margins of victory for all of the House races in both states.

In District 6, incumbent Republican Ryan Costello defeated Democrat Mike Parrish by about 15 percentage points. In District 7, Republican incumbent Patrick Meehan registered a slightly larger victory (about 19 percentage points) over Democrat Mary Ellen Balchunis. Incumbent Republican Brian Fitzpatrick beat Democrat Steve Santarsiero, in a nasty race, by about 9 percentage points in District 8. The Democratic incumbent in District 13, Brendon Boyle, was unopposed. In Districts 15 and 16, Republicans won handily. Incumbent Charlie Dent won by 20 percentage points over Democrat Rick Daugherty in District 15; Lloyd Smucker overcame his Democratic opponent, Christina Hartman, by about 11 percentage points in District 16.

The House races in New Jersey were equally noncompetitive. All of the incumbents won handily by margins of victory that were around 20 percentage points. In District 1, Democrat Donald Norcross defeated Bob Patterson; in District 2 Republican Frank LoBiondo overcame David Cole; in District 3, Republican Tom McArthur won over Frederick Lavergne.

Political Ads and Revenue by Station

The Philadelphia television market was the fourth largest television market in the country in 2016 with just under three million television households (Nielsen 2016). The market stretches across three states covering eight counties in Pennsylvania, nine counties in New Jersey, and two counties in Delaware.

Table 6.6. Political Ads Aired by Station, 2016

Station	Political Ads Total	Down-ballot Ads	Presidential Ads	Ratio	Estimated Ad Revenue	Average Cost per Ad	Revenue* ($)	Political Ad Revenue of Total Revenue (%)
WCAU	9,316	7,005	2,311	3.0	12,701,470	1,363	85,000,000	15
KYW	9,054	6,737	2,317	2.9	14,394,910	1,590	105,000,000	14
WPVI	8,871	6,819	2,052	3.3	18,699,550	2,108	150,000,000	12
WXTF	7,631	5,433	2,198	2.5	10,992,660	1,441	80,000,000	14
Total	34,872	25,994	8,878	2.9	56,788,590	1,628	420,000,000	14

* Source: BIA/Kelsey, 2018

The network affiliate stations are KYW (CBS), WCAU (NBC), WPVI (ABC), and WXTF (Fox).

The four network affiliate stations broadcast almost 35,000 political ads and realized almost $57 million in estimated revenue in the sixty-four-day campaign period. On average, the cost of a political ad was $1,628 and the stations had an overall ratio of DB to presidential ads of 2.9:1 (table 6.6). However, there were significant differences among the stations. WCAU, the NBC affiliate, carried the most ads and realized estimated revenue from those ads of over $12.7 million. Its nearest competitor was KYW with about $14.4 million. Its ratio of DB to presidential ads was 3:1. Like the Las Vegas market, there was a clear winner in the political ad sweepstakes. WPVI, the ABC affiliate and perennial ratings leader, broadcast almost 8,900 ads, but it raked in the most money among the stations—$18.7 million. The average cost of ads on the station was the highest in the market at $2,108. Most significantly, it had the highest ratio of DB to presidential ads (3.3:1).

The financial importance of the political ads was clear in Philadelphia as it was in Las Vegas. The two-month revenue from the political ads accounted for 14 percent of the stations' total revenue in 2016. That is lower than Las Vegas, but it represents a large portion. WCAU was at the highest percentage in the market at 15 percent. WPVI came in at 12 percent. Certainly, political advertising meant serious money to the stations.

Comparing Presidential and Down-Ballot Stories and Ads

How did the stations perform when it came to stories and political ads? First, let's look at the presidential and DB stories across the stations. The stations'

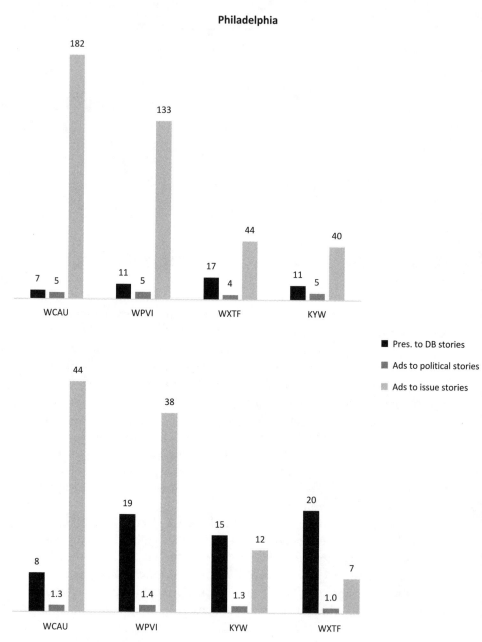

Figure 6.2. Ratio of number of ads (top) and time (bottom) for presidential to down-ballot stories, ads to political stories, and ads to issues stories in Philadelphia.

ratios ranged between 17:1 for WXTF to 7:1 for WCAU (fig. 6.2). WPVI and KYW were each at 11:1. So, at a minimum, depending on the station, Philadelphia audiences saw somewhere between 7 and 17 presidential stories for every story that addressed the DB races. The ratios were a bit tighter when I compared the number of political ads and political stories. The stations were remarkably consistent, either at 5:1 or 4:1 of political ads to stories.

The differences among the stations became glaringly obvious, when I looked at the relationship between political ads and issue stories. The stations fell into two camps—one with an *immense* imbalance between presidential and DB stories and the other with a *less immense* imbalance.

When it came to the number of political stories that the stations broadcast for each race, WCAU and WPVI were in their own class. With ratios of 182:1 and 133:1, respectively, they *immensely* overwhelmed their audiences with presidential stories (fig. 6.2). WXTF and KYW registered ratios of 44:1 and 40:1, respectively. And while these ratios show a serious imbalance in the coverage of the two races, they pale in comparison to the performance of their competitors. It was if there were no issues that warranted examination in the campaign.

The ratios based on the numbers are revealing, but, as I mentioned earlier, it is important to understand how the stations spent their most precious resource, time. It is interesting to note that the ratios rise when it comes to the amount of time the stations devoted to presidential and DB stories. WXTF's ratio of 20:1 means that it broadcast 20 seconds of presidential story time to every one second of DB story time. WPVI ran a close second at 19:1. In each instance that was wider than the ratios based on the number of stories and that meant that the presidential stories were longer than those devoted to DB races. The other two stations, WCAU and KYW, had time ratios that were close to the number ratios. The median duration of political stories across all of the stations was 99 seconds. Looking at the ratio of time spent on political ads to political stories, the stations were quite similar, just a little bit over one ad to one story with a range between 1.0 and 1.4.

The imbalance between political ads and issue stories, however, remains when I looked at time, even though the median duration of issue stories was 130 seconds across all stations. They were reduced, certainly, but they still revealed that WCAU and WPVI broadcast 44 and 38 seconds of political ads, respectively, to every one second of political stories. My characterization of the imbalance as immense still applies. And these performances are from the stations that made the most money from the ads (WPVI), and the station that presented the most ads and for which the ads accounted for the highest proportion of its 2016 revenue (WCAU).

Raleigh, NC

North Carolina was incredibly competitive as it was the only state that the Cook Political Report rated as a "toss-up" for presidential, Senate, and governor races. This was reflected in the polls for both races with all of the results falling within the 5 percent competitive range.

However, both November polls showed small leads for the Democratic candidates despite the fact that both Republican candidates ended up winning the state in the election. That could be due to the fact that outside Republican groups spent more money on attack ads in the state than they had initially planned in an effort to maintain control of the US Senate (Douglas 2016). This makes sense when you see that incumbent Richard Burr ($1.7 million) and challenger Deborah Ross ($1.1 million) spent similar amounts in the market (table 6.7). Donald Trump again spent very little money ($801,410) and earned fewer votes (by percentage) than Burr and only narrowly beat out Clinton ($2.67 million) in the election (table 6.8).

While the presidential and US Senate races were tightly contested, there was much going on with the House contests. It all had to do with the intense debate over the congressional district maps in the state. In February 2016, the Fourth Circuit Court of Appeals threw out the Congressional district map used by the state saying that: "There is strong evidence that race was the only nonnegotiable criterion and that traditional redistricting principles were subordinated to race" (Ballotpedia 2016).

The North Carolina legislature immediately drew a new map, but critics charged that it was as flawed as the map that was struck down by the federal court, saying that instead of packing African American voters into two districts,

Table 6.7. Senate Race

Candidate	Party	Elon Sep 12–16	NBC/WSJ/Marist Oct 1–12	Survey Monkey Nov 1–7	Official Result
Richard Burr	R	43	46	43	51.1
Deborah Ross	D	44	46	47	45.4

Table 6.8. Presidential Race

Candidate	Party	Elon Sep 12–16	NBC/WSJ/Marist Oct 1–12	Quinnipiac Nov 3–6	Official Result
Donald Trump	R	44	43	45	49.8
Hillary Clinton	D	43	48	48	46.2

"it instead scattered them to the winds" (*Harris and Bowser* 2016, 1). In the filing on February 29, 2016, the plaintiffs were clear regarding the unacceptable provisions of the newly drawn map and the process by which it was rendered:

> Indeed, the General Assembly's remedial redistricting process is all too familiar. The same architects who oversaw the original plan instructed the same map drawer who drew the unconstitutional racial gerrymander to draw a new plan. Once again, the plan was drawn outside the supervision of any other legislators. Once again, the plan is couched in claims that race was not considered, only partisan politics. It is hardly surprising that the resulting "remedy" is no remedy at all. (2)

The plaintiffs did not prevail, however. In June 2016 the US District Court for the Middle District of North Carolina rejected the complaints of a partisan gerrymander in the plan. And, in a ruling that added insult to injury, it said that its hands were tied by a previous Supreme Court ruling. The Supreme Court said that it could find "no judicially discernible and manageable standards" for determining partisan gerrymandering (McGann et al. 2015, 295). In doing so, the Supreme Court said that the plaintiffs did not provide a standard that the court might use. The partisan gerrymandered plan remained in place for the November election. The voting for the US House occurred in this environment.

The Raleigh-Durham television market comprised some or all of five House districts in which the Republicans held a 3:2 majority going into the 2016 election. That stayed the same after the election as all of the incumbents easily won. The margins were very wide—the widest in District 1 where Democrat G. K. Butterfield steamrolled Republican H. Powell Dew by forty percentage points. In the District 2, Republican George Holding won by thirteen percentage points over Democrat John McNeil. There was a twenty-nine-point margin in District 4 as the Democrat David Price overwhelmed Republican Sue George. The Republicans almost matched that margin in District 7 with a twenty-two-point win for David Rouzer over Democrat J. Wesley Casteen. In District 13, Republican Tedd Budd beat Democrat Bruce Davis by the relatively small margin of about 12 percentage points (Ballotpedia 2016). As in other markets, the House races were not competitive—not even close.

Political Ads and Revenue by Station

The Raleigh television market ranks twenty-fifth in the nation with just over 1.3 million television households. Officially, the market designation is

Raleigh-Durham-Fayetteville but, for my purposes, I will call it Raleigh. The market covers all or parts of twenty-two counties in north-central North Carolina and one county (Mecklenburg) in southern Virginia. The four stations from which I gathered data were: WNCN (CBS), WRAZ (Fox), WRAL (NBC), and WLFL (CW). As I mentioned earlier, because of a technical glitch in the system that captured the broadcasts, the content for the ABC affiliate WTVD was unavailable. However, WTVD produced the daily news program that was aired at 10 PM on WLFL, the CW affiliate.

The four stations in Raleigh presented over 22,500 political ads during the sixty-four-day campaign period with an overall ratio of 2.29 DB ads to one presidential ad (table 6.9). But that varied among the stations. WRAL presented the most ads and realized the most revenue, over 7,500 ads for over $6.7 million, and the station aired just over two DB ads to presidential ads. Further, the average cost of an ad on WRAL was the highest in the market ($897). Although WRAZ came in third for the number of ads it aired, it came in second in the revenue the ads provided, almost $4 million. The station that presented the fewest ads, WLFL, also realized the lowest estimated ad revenue. It also had the highest ratio of DB to presidential ads, 2.52:1.

As in other markets, the political ad revenue accounted for a substantial proportion of the stations' revenues in 2016—on average 12 percent for the entire market. Both WRAL and WRAZ, with the largest estimated political ads revenue, came in at 13 percent.

Comparing Presidential and Down Ballot Stories and Ads

Looking at the numbers, WNCN and WLFL broadcast substantially more presidential stories than those that addressed the DB races, 14:1 and 13:1, respectively (fig. 6.3). When it came to comparing the number of political ads

Table 6.9. Political Ads Aired by Station, 2016

Station	Political Ads Total	Down-ballot Ads	Presidential Ads	Ratio	Estimated Ad Revenue	Average Cost per Ad	Revenue* ($)	Political Ad Revenue of Total Revenue (%)
WRAL	7,529	5,140	2,389	2.15	6,751,590	897	52,000,000	13
WNCN	6,816	4,828	1,988	2.43	2,852,800	419	27,500,000	10
WRAZ	5,282	3,638	1,644	2.21	3,969,140	751	30,000,000	13
WLFL	2,927	2,096	831	2.52	1,012,200	346	12,700,000	8
Total	22,554	15,702	6,852	2.29	14,585,730	647	122,200,000	12

* Source: BIA/Kelsey, 2018

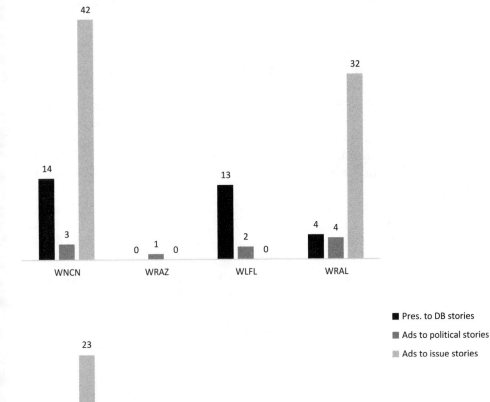

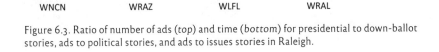

Figure 6.3. Ratio of number of ads (*top*) and time (*bottom*) for presidential to down-ballot stories, ads to political stories, and ads to issues stories in Raleigh.

and issue stories, the ratios for WNCN and WRAL were quite high, 42:1 and 32:1, respectively. The ratios that are expressed as zero need explanation. First, WRAZ; the ratios for the relationship between presidential and DB stories and the number of ads to issue stories are zero because the station did not broadcast any stories that dealt with the DB races or addressed any issue in the campaign. However, the station did present thirteen political stories, all directed to the presidential race. On the other hand, WLFL did present political stories (twenty-six of them), but none was an issue story. The zero ratio between the number of political ads and issue stories reflects these facts.

The median duration of political stories in Raleigh across all stations was 34 seconds, almost the same as the 30 seconds for political ads. However, that duration for issue stories was 89 seconds—virtually three times the duration of the ads. The ratios reflect the stations' activity.

WNCN still had the highest ratio of the time spent on presidential stories compared to the DB races, 8:1 (fig. 6.3). Again, reflecting the nonexistent DB stories on WRAZ, that ratio is zero. However, the station spent 470 seconds on those presidential stories. You could argue that was not a lot of time over the sixty-four-day period, but that is my point. On the broadcasts that I examined, WRAZ used only about 8 minutes to present political stories. Even then, it paid no attention to the DB races.

The imbalance was more pronounced when it came to the comparison of political ads to issue stories, which had a median duration of 130 seconds. For the stations that did present issue stories, the ratios were wide. For WNCN it was 23:1; WRAL came in at 12:1. WLFL, like WRAZ, did not present any issue stories.

Tampa, FL

In Florida, Republican incumbent Marco Rubio won reelection by more than the 5 percent competitive margin, despite the polls showing a shrinking lead with the final poll in November, giving a one-point edge to the Democratic challenger Patrick Murphy (table 6.10). The presidential race on the other hand stayed incredibly competitive with November polls showing the two

Table 6.10. Senate Race

Candidate	Party	CNN/ORC Sep 7–12	Quinnipiac Oct 1–16	Survey Monkey Nov 1–7	Official Result
Marco Rubio	R	54	49	48	52.0
Patrick Murphy	D	43	47	49	44.3

Table 6.11. Presidential Race

Candidate	Party	CNN/ORC Sep 7–12	Quinnipiac Oct 1–16	Quinnipiac Nov 3–6	Official Result
Donald Trump	R	50	45	46	49.0
Hillary Clinton	D	46	49	46	47.8

dead even at 46 percent. Donald Trump ended up winning Florida by less than two points in a historically significant swing state (table 6.11).

The close margin in the polls for the Senate race was reflected in the spending by both candidates with Murphy slightly outspending Rubio ($1.65 million compared to $1.25 million). Donald Trump ($3.28 million) again spent significantly less than Clinton ($5.6 million) which occurred in eight out of the ten markets I tracked.

Like North Carolina, Florida saw a redistricting battle that was referred to the courts. The challenge to the Florida congressional district map was brought by the League of Women Voters and a coalition of other groups. In July 2015 the Florida Supreme Court agreed with plaintiffs and ruled that the congressional district map was unconstitutional. The court imposed an August 25 deadline for the legislature to produce a new map. The house and senate both produced maps, but they could not agree on a version to present to the court. So, the issue was back in the Second Circuit Court in September 2015. Following the trial, the judge recommended the map that was offered by the coalition groups to the state supreme court. In December 2015, it upheld that map. It was a very different outcome than the one that prevailed in North Carolina.

The Tampa television market includes seven US House districts, some of which are completely within the market and others which only have a portion of the district within the market. Prior to the 2016 election, the Republicans held six of those seats. After the election, the totals were five Republicans and two Democrats. The margins of victory were quite wide except in District 13 where former Republican Governor Charlie Crist ran and won as a Democrat, ousting incumbent Republican David Jolly by about four percentage points. In District 11, Republican Daniel Webster replaced the retiring Richard Nugent and won by thirty-four percentage points over Democrat Dave Koller. In District 12, Republican incumbent Gus Bilirakis won by an even bigger margin (thirty-seven percentage points) over Democrat Robert Matthew Tiger. In Districts 14, 15, 16, and 17, incumbents retained their seats by significant margins—Democrat Kathy Castor in District 14 by twenty-five percentage points and Republicans Dennis Ross (District 15), Vern Buchanan

(District 16), and Thomas Rooney (District 17) by fifteen, twenty, and twenty-seven percentage points, respectively (Ballotpedia 2016).

Political Ads and Revenue by Station

The Tampa-St. Petersburg-Sarasota television market is the eleventh largest in the country with almost 1.9 million television households. It is comprised of all or a portion of eleven counties on the western side of the state. The network affiliated stations in the market are: WFTS (ABC), WTSP (CBS), WTVT (Fox) and WFLA (NBC). However, as I mentioned previously, due to a technical glitch, I could not acquire the content of WTSP. Therefore, the findings reflect the activity of the other three affiliate stations.

The three stations aired almost 19,000 political ads for a total estimated revenue of over $21.5 million (table 6.12). Although they showed slightly more DB to presidential ads, that margin was small enough to result in a ratio of 1:1. Indeed, there were virtually no differences among the stations when it came to that ratio. There was, however, a significant difference in the average cost of ads across the stations. WFLA showed the fewest number of ads, but they cost an average of $1,401, the highest in the market.

Across all of the stations, the political ad revenue accounted for 12 percent of their total 2016 revenue. That ranged from 10 percent for WFLA to 14 percent for WFTS, even though that station had the lowest average cost per ad ($965).

Comparing Presidential and Down-Ballot Stories and Ads

The relatively even distribution of political ads across both races in Tampa was not entirely matched by the ratios of ads to political stories. For example, the ratio for the number of presidential to DB political stories was the highest for WFLA, 13:1 (fig. 6.4). However, both WTVT and WFTS had significant ratios,

Table 6.12. Political Ads Aired by Station, 2016

Station	Political Ads Total	Down-ballot Ads	Presidential Ads	Ratio	Estimated Ad Revenue	Average Cost per Ad	Revenue* ($)	Political Ad Revenue of Total Revenue (%)
WTVT	7,082	7,005	3,528	1.0	8,146,690	1,150	65,000,000	13
WFTS	6,518	6,737	3,277	1.0	6,288,230	965	44,000,000	14
WFLA	5,082	6,819	2,369	1.1	7,121,800	1,401	68,800,000	10
Total	18,682	5,433	9,174	1.0	21,556,720	1,154	177,800,000	12

* Source: BIA/Kelsey, 2018

Tampa

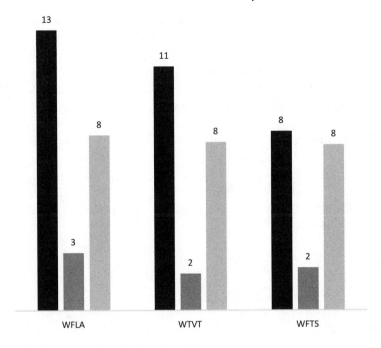

- Pres. to DB stories
- Ads to political stories
- Ads to issue stories

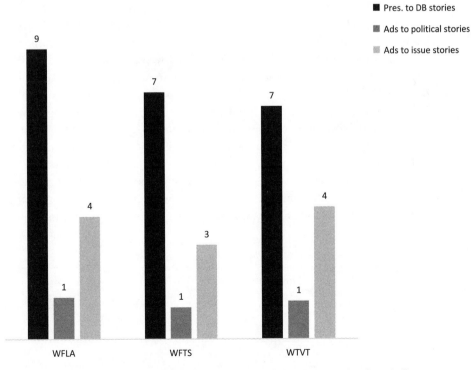

Figure 6.4. Ratio of number of ads (*top*) and time (*bottom*) for presidential to down-ballot stories, ads to political stories, and ads to issues stories in Tampa.

too—11:1 and 8:1, respectively. The ratios for the number of political ads to political stories were all relatively low, hovering around 3:1 or 2:1. As in the other markets, the ratios jumped when I looked at the number of political ads and issue stories—all were 8:1. When I looked at the time devoted to ads and stories, the ratios dropped. WFLA's ratio for the time devoted to presidential compared to DB stories was 9:1. The other two stations were not far behind at 7:1 both.

The median duration for a political story in Tampa was 34 seconds. That similarity was seen in the ratios of time for political ads and political stories, 1:1 for all of the stations. That changed when it came to issue stories. Even though issue stories were not much longer than other political stories (39 seconds), the stations used between three and four times more of the broadcast for ads than issue stories.

Denver, CO

In Colorado, Democratic incumbent Michael Bennet won reelection over Republican Darryl Glenn 49.1 percent to 45.4 percent. The polls from September, October, and November showed that despite the slightly wider October margin, the race was going to be close to the competitive 5 percent threshold (table 6.13). This is surprising considering that Michael Bennet's campaign spent over three times the amount on political ads then challenger Darryl Glenn ($2.1 million to Bennet's $680,240). However, the increasing number of political ads that were shown in later weeks could have led to ad fatigue and thus a narrower margin of victory than expected. In the presidential race, Hillary Clinton defeated Donald Trump 48.2 percent to 43.3 percent. A September poll showed both candidates tied at 47 percent, although the October and November polls showed Clinton putting enough distance between them to take the battleground state on Election Day (table 6.14).

Denver itself had a strong Democratic lean (73.7 percent for Clinton). Yet there was a significant amount of money spent on political ads during the campaign. Clinton's campaign spent $905,950 whereas Trump's campaign, perhaps recognizing the Democratic lean of Denver, spent $3.76 million.

Table 6.13. Senate Race

Candidate	Party	Quinnipiac Sep 9–13	Quinnipiac Oct 1–16	Survey Monkey Nov 1–7	Official Result
Michael Bennet	D	52	56	52	50.0
Darryl Glenn	R	43	38	45	44.3

Table 6.14. Presidential Race

Candidate	Party	Quinnipiac Sep 13–21	Quinnipiac Oct 1–16	Public Policy Polling Nov 3–4	Official Result
Donald Trump	R	47	40	43	43.3
Hillary Clinton	D	47	51	48	48.2

The Denver television market encompasses all or a portion of four House districts. Before the election, there were two Republicans and two Democrats. The election did not change that as all of the incumbents won, and by wide margins. The "closest" race was for District 3 in which Republican Scott Tipton had a fifteen-percentage-point victory over Democrat Gail Schwartz. The race in District 1 was the most lopsided as Democrat Diana DeGette won by forty points over Republican Casper Stockham. Jared Polis, Democrat, won by twenty percentage points over Republican Nicholas Morse in District 2. Republican Doug Lamborn beat out Democrat Misty Plowright by thirty points in District 5. Again, the House races in the Denver market, as in other television markets, were not competitive.

Political Ads and Revenue by Station

The Denver television market is ranked number 17 with almost 1.6 million television households. The market is comprised of all or a portion of fifty-eight counties, forty-four in Colorado, fourteen in Nebraska, and four in Wyoming. The network affiliate stations are: KMGH (ABC), KCNC (CBS), KDVR (Fox), and KUSA (NBC).

Table 6.15. Political Ads Aired by Station, 2016

Station	Political Ads Total	Down-ballot Ads	Presidential Ads	Ratio	Estimated Ad Revenue	Average Cost per Ad	Revenue* ($)	Political Ad Revenue of Total Revenue (%)
KUSA	5,315	3,806	1,509	2.5	10,548,340	1,985	94,000,000	11
KCNC	4,234	3,187	1,047	3.0	5,234,750	985	76,000,000	7
KMGH	4,138	2,857	1,281	2.2	3,973,150	748	50,000,000	8
KDVR	3,910	2,758	1,152	2.4	3,325,640	626	35,000,000	10
Total	17,597	12,608	4,989	2.5	23,081,880	1,311	255,000,000	9

* Source: BIA/Kelsey, 2018

During the campaign period I studied, the four affiliated stations in Denver aired over 17,500 political ads—the overwhelming majority of them at the DB level for a DB to presidential ad ratio of 2.5:1 (table 6.15). And, in the Denver market, there was a pattern that held a direct link between the number of ads a station showed, its revenue, and its rank order in the market along those two dimensions. The more ads, the more money. However, there was a clear leader in the political ad sweepstakes—KUSA. It not only broadcast the most ads in the market (5,315), it also had an estimated political ad revenue of twice its nearest competitor—over $10.5 million to KCNC's $5.2 million. Further, its average charge for a political ad of just under $2,000 equally outstripped the others, the closest of which was KCNC with $985.

KUSA also depended on the political ad money as a higher proportion of its total 2016 revenue than the other stations, 11 percent—that is 11 percent of $94 million, its total 2016 revenue. The closest competitor regarding that percentage was KDVR at 10 percent. But that station only had total revenue of $35 million in 2016.

Comparing Presidential and Down-Ballot Stories and Ads

The stations were decidedly focused on the presidential race when it came to the number of political stories at each level. KCNC and KDVR had about the same ratio of presidential to DB stories, 16:1 and 17:1, respectively (fig. 6.5). At the other end, KUSA, the market leader in number of ads and money, had the lowest ratio, 8:1. The ratio of the number of ads to political stories hovered between 3:1 and 2:1 for the stations. However, when it came to issue stories, the ratios jumped significantly. KCNC aired forty-two ads to every political story—the market leader. The others had ratios that were below 20:1.

As in the other markets, when we looked at the time that the stations devoted to ads and political stories, the ratios were smaller for all of the stations, except for KUSA, the money leader in the market, it rose from 8:1 to 9:1 (fig. 6.5). The median duration of a political story in Denver was 34 seconds and that was reflected in the ratios of the time devoted to political ads and political stories across the stations. They ranged between 1 and 1.4 ads to stories.

The real differences showed up, once again, in the time devoted to ads and issue stories, the median duration of which was 43 seconds in the market. That was relatively close to the 30-second duration of the ads. However, the stations did not spend time with these stories. KCNC had a ratio of 19:1 and the others were all around 10:1.

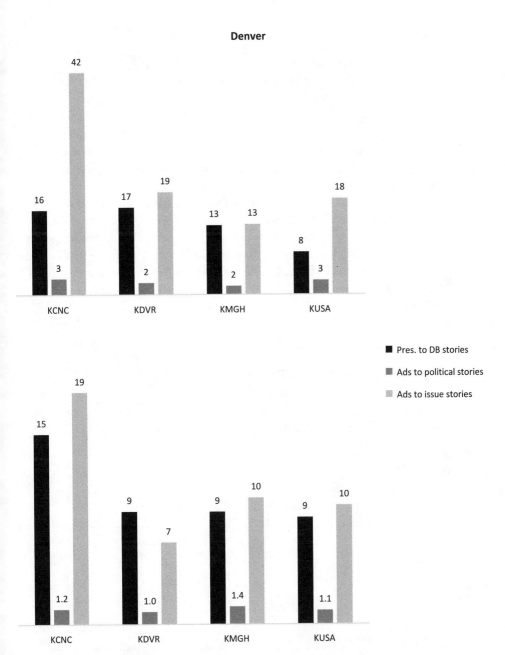

Figure 6.5. Ratio of number of ads (*top*) and time (*bottom*) for presidential to down-ballot stories, ads to political stories, and ads to issues stories in Denver.

Cedar Rapids, IA

In Iowa longtime Republican incumbent Chuck Grassley had a strong lead throughout the campaign and won reelection easily over Democratic challenger Patty Judge (table 6-16). The presidential polls on the other hand were extremely competitive early on with September and October polls showing a one-point lead for Trump. The November poll showed a seven-point lead in Trump's favor that coincided with the increased coverage of Clinton's FBI email scandal. The final result ended up being even more significantly in Trump's favor with a nearly ten-point win (table 6-17).

Only one House district was part of the Cedar Rapids market—District 1. The Republican incumbent Rod Blum retained his seat over Democrat Monica Vernon by 8 percentage points (Ballotpedia 2016). That seemed a rather close race in a state that reelected its senator by 25 points and went for Donald Trump by 10 points. In fact, Blum had more than doubled his margin of victory compared to the 2014 election. It seems as though Trump's strong showing in Iowa had DB effects.

Political Ads and Revenue by Station

The Cedar Rapids-Waterloo-Dubuque television market is ranked ninetieth in the country with just under 350,000 television households. It was the smallest market I examined. It encompasses all or a portion of twenty counties in eastern Iowa. The network affiliated stations are: KCRG (ABC), KGAN (CBS), KFXA (Fox) and KWWL (NBC).

Table 6.16. Senate Race

Candidate	Party	Quinnipiac Sep 13–21	Quinnipiac Oct 2–26	Survey Monkey Nov 1–7	Official Result
Chuck Grassley	R	55	56	57	60.1
Patty Judge	D	43	38	39	35.7

Table 6.17. Presidential Race

Candidate	Party	Quinnipiac Sep 13–21	Quinnipiac Oct 2–26	Des Moines Register Nov 1–4	Official Result
Donald Trump	R	44	47	46	51.1
Hillary Clinton	D	43	46	39	41.7

Table 6.18. Political Ads Aired by Station, 2016

Station	Political Ads Total	Down-ballot Ads	Presidential Ads	Ratio	Estimated Ad Revenue	Average Cost per Ad	Revenue* ($)	Political Ad Revenue of Total Revenue (%)
KWWL	5,625	4,067	1,558	2.6	3,101,440	551	19,000,000	16
KGAN	4,736	3,037	1,699	1.8	1,310,750	277	9,700,000	14
KCRG	4,247	2,908	1,339	2.2	2,490,150	586	26,100,000	10
KFXA	3,232	1,985	1,247	1.6	819,800	254	5,900,000	14
Total	17,840	11,997	5,843	2.1	7,722,140	433	60,700,000	13

* Source: BIA/Kelsey, 2018

The stations combined to air a total of almost 18,000 political ads, bringing in almost $8 million (table 6.18). The stations in this market showed about as many ads as the stations in Denver but garnered less than one-third of that revenue (see table 6.15). And, on average, they showed over twice as many DB than presidential ads, a 2.1:1 ratio. The station that aired the most ads, KWWL, also brought in the most money (over $3.1 million) and had the highest ratio of DB to presidential ads, 2.6:1. That is in contrast to the station that had the lowest ratio, 1.6:1. It aired the fewest total number of ads and saw an estimated revenue of just over one-quarter of that of KWWL.

On average, the political ads accounted for 13 percent of the stations' revenues in 2016. For the leader in ads and money, KWWL, that proportion was 16 percent of its revenue of $19 million for the year. For KCRG, the station that had the highest total revenue in 2016, over $26 million, the political ads accounted for just about 10 percent of the total. Clearly, KWWL relied more heavily on the political ad revenue than the other stations.

Comparing Presidential and Down-Ballot Stories and Ads

Looking at the ratios of the number of presidential to DB stories, KFXA, the station with the smallest revenue, had an imbalance in favor of presidential stories with a ratio of 11:1 (fig. 6.6). That was followed by KGAN at 8:1. The ratios of the number of ads to political stories was fairly consistent among the stations, ranging between 5:1 and 3:1. True to form with the other markets, when it came to the ratios of the number of ads versus issue stories, there was no contest. The money leader, KWWL, had the largest imbalance. It broadcasted seventy-nine political ads to every one political story. Further, the station did not air one issue story for the DB races. Its competitors also did not cover issue stories with ratios between 34:1 and 50:1.

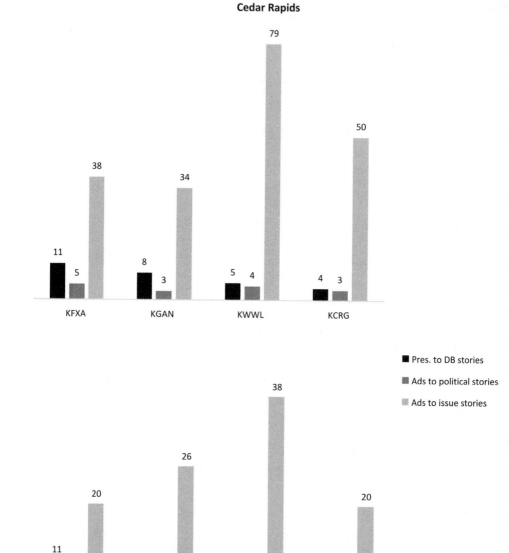

Figure 6.6. Ratio of number of ads (*top*) and time (*bottom*) for presidential to down-ballot stories, ads to political stories, and ads to issues stories in Cedar Rapids.

The median duration of political stories in Cedar Rapids was 37 seconds; for issue stories, it was 50 seconds When it comes to looking at the time the stations devoted to ads and stories, the ratios narrow somewhat. However, they are still substantial. The most important ratio for my purposes is that of the relationship between political ads and issue stories. Even looking at time, where the longer stories would somewhat lessen the effect of the shorter ads, the stations' preferences were clear. Even though the ratios drop, KWWL aired 38 seconds of political ads to every one second of issue stories (fig. 6.6). The other stations followed suit—not to the same extent, but they still did not cover issue stories.

Milwaukee, WI

In Wisconsin, incumbent Ron Johnson won reelection over Democratic challenger Russ Feingold (50.2 percent to 46.8 percent). Early polls in September and October showed Feingold with a surprisingly wide lead, although the poll in early November showed Johnson with a one-point lead, which was much closer to the final result (table 6.19). The competitiveness of the race mirrored that of the financial race between both candidates in Milwaukee. Feingold outspent Johnson ($2.03 million to $1.4 million) which could have skewed the poll results in his favor. This makes sense, as it was extremely important for Feingold to win by a large margin in Milwaukee, as it is one of only three counties to vote Democrat in an otherwise Republican state (table 6.20).

Donald Trump narrowly defeated Hillary Clinton (47.2 percent to 46.5 percent). The September, October, and early November polls all were in

Table 6.19. Senate Race

Candidate	Party	Marquette Sep 15–18	Monmouth Oct 15–18	Survey Monkey Nov 1–7	Official Result
Ron Johnson	R	41	44	49	50.2
Russ Feingold	D	47	52	48	46.8

Table 6.20. Presidential Race

Candidate	Party	Marquette Sep 15–18	Monmouth Oct 15–18	Remington Research Nov 1–2	Official Result
Donald Trump	R	42	40	41	47.2
Hillary Clinton	D	44	47	49	46.5

Clinton's favor, although surprisingly the margin increased closer to the election. It appears that Hillary Clinton's FBI email scandal that dominated local news in the final two weeks of the election may have had a drastic impact on voters between the final poll and Election Day.

Neither candidate spent much money on political ads in Milwaukee: $896,850 for Clinton compared to only $994,700 for Trump. This may have been due to Milwaukee's strong Democratic lean, which was reflected in their voting (28.6 percent Trump and 65.5 percent Clinton).

The Milwaukee television market had all or a portion of four House districts—three Republicans and one Democrat. All of the incumbents won, so the balance did not change in 2016. The largest margin of victory occurred in District 4, where Democrat Gwen Moore won by 65 points over Republican Robert Raymond. In District 1, Speaker of the House, Paul Ryan, beat Democrat Ryan Solen by 35 points. Jim Sensenbrenner, Republican, had a similar margin (37 points) in District 5 over Khary Penebaker, Democrat. Republican Glenn Grothman registered a two-point win over Democrat Sarah Lloyd in District 6 (Ballotpedia 2016).

Political Ads and Revenue by Station

The Milwaukee television market ranks thirty-fifth in the country with almost 890,000 television households. Bordered by Lake Michigan to its east, the market is comprised of eleven counties. The network affiliated stations are: WISN (ABC), WDJT (CBS), WITI (Fox) and WTMJ (NBC).

The stations presented almost 15,000 ads in the sixty-four-day campaign period for which they earned an estimated revenue of over $12.8 million (table 6.21). They presented 2.8 DB ads to every presidential ad, but that varied greatly

Table 6.21. Political Ads Aired by Station, 2016

Station	Political Ads Total	Down-ballot Ads	Presidential Ads	Ratio	Estimated Ad Revenue	Average Cost per Ad	Revenue* ($)	Political Ad Revenue of Total Revenue (%)
WITI	4,144	3,087	1,057	2.9	4,231,050	1021	32,000,000	13
WTMJ	3,993	2,921	1,072	2.7	3,423,440	857	34,000,000	10
WISN	3,719	2,531	1,188	2.1	2,882,250	775	39,000,000	7
WDJT	2,932	2,344	588	4.0	2,346,840	800	27,000,000	9
Total	14,788	10,883	3,905	2.8	12,883,580	871	132,000,000	10

* Source: BIA/Kelsey, 2018

among the stations. For example, WDJT presented the fewest number of ads in the market and brought in the least amount of political ad money (just over $2.3 million), but the station greatly favored DB ads with a ratio of 4:1. On the other hand, WITI presented the most ads (4,144) and, as a consequence, made the most money (over $4.2 million) and also had the highest average cost for ad ($1,021). Its ratio was at 2.9:1.

Across the stations, the political ads in the sixty-four-day period accounted for 10 percent of the 2016 revenues. For the ad and money leader, WITI, that figure was 13 percent. Interestingly, WISN, the station that had the highest revenue in 2016 ($39 million), realized only about 7 percent of its income from the ads during the period.

Comparing Presidential and Down-Ballot Stories and Ads

Looking at the stations' presentation of ads and stories revealed quite different performances. WDJT, the station that showed four DB ads to every presidential ad, had the largest imbalance when it came to the number of presidential and DB political stories, 31:1 (fig. 6.7). The other stations had much lower ratios—7:1, 5:1, and 2:1. The ratios of the number of political ads to political stories were between the 4:1 and 1:1 range. As in the other markets, the imbalance between political ads and issue stories was substantial. WDJT was the market leader at 35:1, while both WISN and WITI came in at 24:1.

The consideration of time changed the ratios, but the order of magnitude was still significant. The median duration of all political stories in Milwaukee was 69 seconds; for issue stories, it was 98 seconds. Both were considerably longer than the 30-second ad spots. Still, the time devoted to ads won out. For example, WDJT's emphasis on the presidential race remained clear with a ratio of 23:1 regarding presidential and DB stories. For WTMJ, the time ratio was larger (11:1) than the ratio based on the numbers (7:1), indicating that even when they presented DB stories, they were significantly shorter than the presidential stories it aired. Moreover, WITI, the ad number and ad revenue leader, had the largest imbalance between the ads and issue stories (14:1).

Phoenix, AZ

In Arizona, long-time incumbent John McCain won reelection easily over Democratic challenger Ann Kirkpatrick 53.7 percent to 40.7 percent (table 6.22). However, October and early November polls showed a narrower race than the overall result as McCain had to deal with Donald Trump at the top of the ballot. The competitiveness was seen more in the amount of money spent

Milwaukee

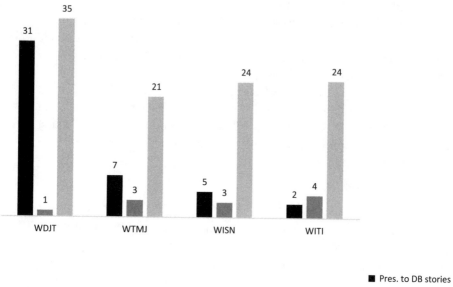

- Pres. to DB stories
- Ads to political stories
- Ads to issue stories

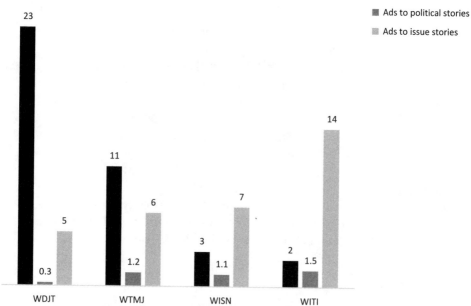

Figure 6.7. Ratio of number of ads (*top*) and time (*bottom*) for presidential to down-ballot stories, ads to political stories, and ads to issues stories in Milwaukee.

Table 6.22. Senate Race

Candidate	Party	NBC/WSJ/Marist Sep 6–8	Ipsos/Reuters Oct 6–18	Survey Monkey Nov 1–7	Official Result
John McCain	R	57	48	50	53.7
Ann Kirkpatrick	D	38	38	45	40.7

on political ads in Phoenix with McCain's campaign spending $2.2 million to Kirkpatrick's $1.3 million. This was due to the fact that Phoenix resides in Maricopa County, which, despite voting favorably for McCain (55 percent to 39.5 percent), was much more narrowly split between Trump (47.7 percent) and Clinton (44.8 percent) (Ballotpedia 2016). The presidential race in Arizona, however, was nearly too close to call as Donald Trump edged out Hillary Clinton 48.7 percent to 45.1 percent. The polls I tracked from September, October, and early November expressed the conflicted feelings of a traditionally Republican state toward a nontraditional Republican candidate in the narrow lead that Trump held throughout the campaign and in the final result (table 6.23).

Despite the tight race, neither candidate spent much money on political ads (Clinton: $2.4 million; Trump: $16,680). This is likely due to the fact that both Phoenix (Maricopa County) and Arizona had been Republican strongholds in previous elections.

In the Phoenix market, the public had to watch the races of four House districts. Before the election there were two Republicans and two Democrats. All of the incumbents won—nothing changed in 2016. The margins of victory were significant—the largest was in District 7 where Democrat Ruben Gallego won by 50 points over Republican Eva Nunez. Republicans David Schweikert and Trent Franks won by 24 and 37 points, respectively over their Democratic opponents in Districts 6 and 8. In District 9, Democrat Kyrsten Sinema beat Republican Dave Giles by 22 points (Ballotpedia 2016).

Table 6.23. Presidential Race

Candidate	Party	NBC/WSJ/Marist Sep 6–8	Arizona Republic Oct 1–15	NBC/WSJ/Marist Oct 3–Nov 1	Official Result
Donald Trump	R	42	38	46	48.7
Hillary Clinton	D	41	43	41	45.1

Political Ads and Revenue by Station

The Phoenix television market is ranked twelfth in the country with just over 1.8 million television households. It encompasses all or part of ten counties. The network affiliated stations are: KNXV (ABC), KPHO (CBS), KSAZ (Fox), and KUSA (NBC).

The stations in Phoenix presented 12,639 political ads that brought in over $11.2 million. That was 5 percent of the $219 million the stations received in 2016 revenue (table 6.24). They showed 3.1 DB ads to every presidential ad. The number of ads was relatively evenly distributed among the stations.

One station stood out regarding its content. KPNX made the most money from political ads, just over $4 million. It also had the highest average charge for an ad ($1,329)—almost twice its nearest competitor. Most important, the ads accounted for the highest percentage of its annual revenue (8 percent).

Comparing Presidential and Down-Ballot Stories and Ads

Looking at the numbers of ads and stories, we see that KPNX's preference for DB ads (see table 6.24) is turned on its head when it comes to presidential and DB stories. The station presented eleven presidential stories to each one that addressed DB races (fig. 6.8). The other stations all had similar turnabouts with ratios of 5:1 and 4:1. The ratios of the number of political ads to political stories were quite consistent across the stations, ranging between 3:1 for KPHO and 1:1 for KNXV. Yet the treatment of issue stories relative to political ads saw the same imbalance as occurred in other markets. KSAZ broadcast twenty-three ads to every issue story. The other stations also registered large ratios.

Examining the ratios of time, the stations devoted to presidential and DB stories, they did look much different than the number ratios. The ratio for KPNX came down to 8:1 (fig. 6.8). However, those same ratios for the other

Table 6.24. Political Ads Aired by Station, 2016

Station	Political Ads Total	Down-ballot Ads	Presidential Ads	Ratio	Estimated Ad Revenue	Average Cost per Ad	Revenue* ($)	Political Ad Revenue of Total Revenue (%)
KSAZ	3,304	2,438	866	2.8	2,584,970	782	56,000,000	5
KNXV	3,187	2,427	760	3.2	2,196,570	689	44,000,000	5
KPNX	3,081	2,425	656	3.7	4,094,510	1,329	54,000,000	8
KPHO	3,067	2,295	772	3.0	2,422,110	790	65,000,000	4
Total	12,639	9,585	3,054	3.1	11,298,160	894	219,000,000	5

* Source: BIA/Kelsey, 2018

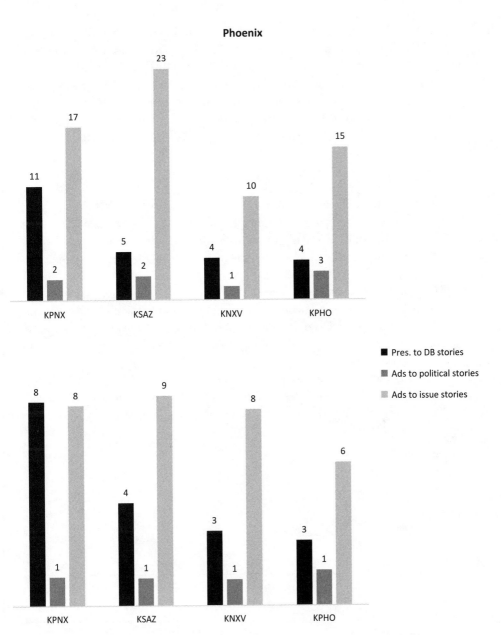

Figure 6.8. Ratio of number of ads (*top*) and time (*bottom*) for presidential to down-ballot stories, ads to political stories, and ads to issues stories in Phoenix.

stations were close to each other. The median duration of a political story in Phoenix was 30 seconds; issue stories were 25 seconds. It was the only market in which political stories matched, or were shorter than, political ads. That manifested in political ad to political story ratios that were 1:1 across all of the stations. Even with issue stories having a shorter median duration than political ads, the ratios still showed the stations' penchant for ads over issues, with similar ratios across the stations with KSAZ with a slight lead at 9:1.

Cleveland, OH

In Ohio, Republican incumbent Rob Portman easily led all Senate polls throughout the campaign, including the final election results (table 6.25). The presidential polls had a slightly closer margin but were also consistently Republican with the final result showing a larger margin of victory then any of the previous polls (table 6.26).

The large margin was also seen in the spending by both Senate candidates with Republican Rob Portman spending over double the amount ($2.5 million) that Democrat Ted Strickland spent ($1.08 million) which makes sense considering how many seats the Republicans needed to preserve in order to retain control of the Senate.

This was not the case for the presidential candidates as Hillary Clinton outspent Donald Trump ($3.98 million to $2.2 million), who was able to take advantage of the free media coverage he was generating throughout the campaign.

Table 6.25. Senate Race

Candidate	Party	Bloomberg Sep 9–12	CNN/ORC Oct 1–15	Survey Monkey Nov 1–7	Official Result
.0Rob Portman	R	53	56	57	58.0
Ted Strickland	D	36	40	39	37.2

Table 6.26. Presidential Race

Candidate	Party	Bloomberg Sep 9–12	CNN/ORC Oct 1–15	Emerson Nov 4–5	Official Result
Donald Trump	R	48	50	46	51.7
Hillary Clinton	D	43	47	39	43.6

This race was extremely important for Donald Trump as Ohio has backed the presidential winners in the past thirteen elections. No Republican in modern history has won the White House without capturing Ohio (Epstein 2016).

The Cleveland television market contained some or all of four House districts—two Democrats and two Republicans. Again, all of the incumbents won—nothing changed. Democrats Marcia Fudge (District 11) and Marcy Kaptur (District 9) won by large margins (65 and 37 points, respectively) over the Republican contenders. Republicans David Joyce (District 14) and Jim Renacci (District 16) won by 25 and 31 points, respectively, over the Democratic candidates (Ballotpedia 2016).

Political Ads and Revenue by Station

The Cleveland-Akron-Canton television market is ranked nineteenth in the country with just under 1.5 million television households. Bordered on the north by Lake Erie, it encompasses all or part of sixteen counties. The network affiliated stations are: WEWS (ABC), WOIO (CBS), WJW (Fox) and WKYC (NBC).

The Cleveland stations delivered 12,611 political ads for a total estimated revenue of over $15.1 million. It was the only market in the ten markets that I studied that showed more presidential ads than DB ads and that was reflected in the DB to presidential ad ratio of 0.6:1 (table 6.27). That is, the stations in the market—all of them—presented almost twice as many presidential to DB ads.

On average, the political ads revenue accounted for 8 percent of the total yearly revenue of the stations. However, there was one station that stood out. WOIO came in third regarding the number of ads it presented, yet it raked in

Table 6.27. Political Ads Aired by Station, 2016

Station	Political Ads Total	Down-ballot Ads	Presidential Ads	Ratio	Estimated Ad Revenue	Average Cost per Ad	Revenue* ($)	Political Ad Revenue of Total Revenue (%)
WJW	3,934	1,221	2,713	0.5	4,518,470	1,149	55,000,000	8
WEWS	3,691	1,525	2,166	0.7	2,789,920	756	54,000,000	5
WOIO	2,600	945	1,655	0.6	5,509,300	2,119	34,900,000	16
WKYC	2,386	839	1,547	0.5	2,334,890	979	55,000,000	4
Total	12,611	4,530	8,081	0.6	15,152,580	1,202	198,900,000	8

* Source: BIA/Kelsey, 2018

the most political ads revenue, over $5.5 million. And that accounted for a whopping 16 percent of its total 2016 revenues. That was possible because the station charged on average almost twice as much per ad ($2,119) than its competitors. Such is the power of ratings.

Comparing Presidential and Down-Ballot Stories and Ads

As the stations in Cleveland aired more presidential than DB ads, that pattern continued when it came to political stories. WOIO lead the way with a 47:1 ratio of presidential to DB stories (fig. 6.9). WJW and WEWS had ratios that were lower than that, but significant. WKYC came in at 18:1. The relationships between the number of political ads and political stories were fairly close across the stations—ratios of 3:1 and under. Things changed when it came to issue stories. WOIO aired thirty-nine political ads to every one political story. At the other end of the spectrum, WEWS had a ratio that was one-third of that, 13:1.

When I looked at the time ratios, the imbalances were more pronounced. WOIO—the money and percentage of ad revenue leader—had a presidential to DB story ratio of 139:1 (fig. 6.9). Both with the political ads and the political stories, the station went "all in" toward the presidential race. The ratios for the other stations had a wide range—44:1, 18:1 and 8:1—but they were not close to WOIO. The median duration of all political stories in Cleveland was 46 seconds. Issue stories came in at 52 seconds. Only WKYC spent more time on political stories than political ads with a ratio of ads to stories of 0.6:1. As in the other markets, the treatment of issue stories relative to political ads was decidedly in favor of the ads. The largest ratio was WJW at 20:1. The others were substantially below that yet significant nonetheless.

San Francisco, CA

San Francisco and the state of California are consistent Democrat strongholds, and this was reflected in all polls and the final election results. The Senate race had two Democrats and no Republican candidate which reflects the liberal nature of the state (table 6.28). Neither race was ever competitive as incumbent Kamala Harris and Hillary Clinton won by extremely large margins (table 6.29).

The audience in the San Francisco television market saw the fewest number of political ads than any of the other markets in the study. The market had a portion or all of nine House districts, all of which had Democratic incumbents. Eight of the nine incumbents won reelection and so nothing changed.

Cleveland

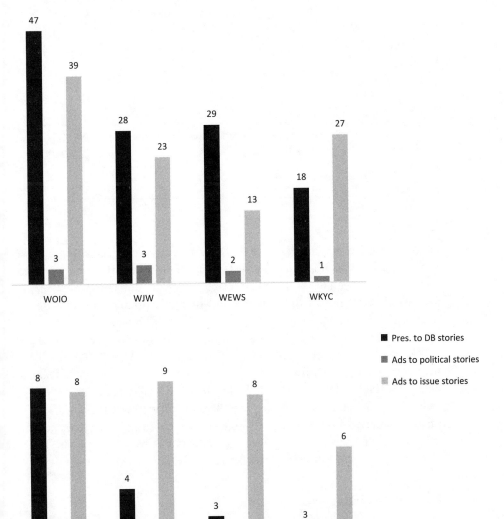

Figure 6.9. Ratio of number of ads (*top*) and time (*bottom*) for presidential to down-ballot stories, ads to political stories, and ads to issues stories in Cleveland.

Table 6.28. Senate Race

Candidate	Party	KABC/SurveyUSA Sep 8–11	KABC/SurveyUSA Oct 13–15	Survey Monkey Nov 1–7	Official Result
Kamala D. Harris	D	44	45	52	61.6
Loretta Sanchez	D	27	24	31	38.4

Table 6.29. Presidential Race

Candidate	Party	KABC/SurveyUSA Sept 8–11	KABC/SurveyUSA Oct 13–15	KABC/SurveyUSA Oct 28–31	Official Result
Donald Trump	R	32	30	35	31.6
Hillary Clinton	D	57	56	56	61.7

However, there were some twists to the story. In most states, the party primaries are held in which registered voters choose their own party's nominee to
stand for the general election. In California, things are different. California's
primary election uses a two-top system in which the two highest vote-getters
move on to the general election, regardless of party affiliation. All voters can
vote, and all candidates can run. That means that, in the general election, the
contest could be between candidates of the same party. That is exactly what
happened in 2016. In District 17, Democrat Ro Khanna beat incumbent Democrat Mike Honda by 22 points. He had challenged him in 2014.

The average margin of victory across the other districts was 53 points. That
included House Minority Leader Nancy Pelosi's and Jackie Speier's 62-point
wins in Districts 12 and 14. In District 13, Barbara Lee won by 82 points. The
closest race was in District 9 in which Jerry McNerney won by 15 points.

Political Ads and Revenue by Station

The San Francisco-Oakland-San Jose television market is ranked sixth in
the country with just under 2.5 million television households. The network
affiliate stations are: KGO (ABC), KPIX (CBS), KTVU (Fox), and KPIX
(CBS). With the Pacific Ocean to its west, it covers all or some of twelve
counties.

The San Francisco market was the only market among the ten that I examined that was not in a battleground state in the 2016 election. Clinton handily
defeated Trump by about 30 percentage points. The DB races were also not

Table 6.30. Political Ads Aired by Station, 2016

Station	Political Ads Total	Down-ballot Ads	Presidential Ads	Ratio	Estimated Ad Revenue	Average Cost per Ad	Revenue* ($)	Political Ad Revenue of Total Revenue (%)
KGO	861	629	232	2.7	698,360	811	100,000,000	0.7
KPIX	636	434	202	2.1	663,180	1,043	99,000,000	0.7
KTVU	579	382	197	1.9	803,250	1,387	100,000,000	0.8
KNTV	262	142	120	1.2	291,270	1,112	72,000,000	0.4
Total	2,338	1,587	751	2.1	2,456,060	1,050	371,000,000	0.7

* Source: BIA/Kelsey, 2018

competitive. That was reflected most clearly in two ways. Firstly, the stations in the market showed only 2,338 ads during the entire sixty-four-day period I studied for about $2.5 million (table 6.30). That's almost 10,000 fewer ads than the ninth-place market, Cleveland. And that's over $5 million less political ad revenue than in Cedar Rapids, the ninetieth market in the country (see table 6.18). Secondly, the San Francisco stations had $317 million in revenue in 2016, but less than 1 percent of that money came from political ads during the campaign period that I examined. It was the only market that was below that level. The next lowest market percentage was Phoenix at 5 percent (see table 6.24). Having said that, the overall ratio of DB to presidential ads was 2.1:1, much like most of the other markets. So, it seems that neither the competitiveness of the races (the number of ads) nor the proportion of total revenue that was derived from the ads made a difference in where the emphasis was. The ads for DB races prevailed.

Comparing Presidential and Down-Ballot Stories and Ads

How did that work out for the ratios? When it came to the number of presidential and DB stories, like the other markets, the San Francisco stations preferred the presidential race. KNTV had the largest ratio of presidential to DB stories at 6:1 (fig. 6.10). The ratios of political ads to political stories was very consistent across the markets at 4:1 and 3:1. And, like the other markets, the San Francisco stations showed significantly more political ads than issue stores with KGO having the highest ratio of 18:1.

The median duration of a political story in San Francisco was 67 seconds; the issue stories were 102 seconds. Again, even given the market's differences

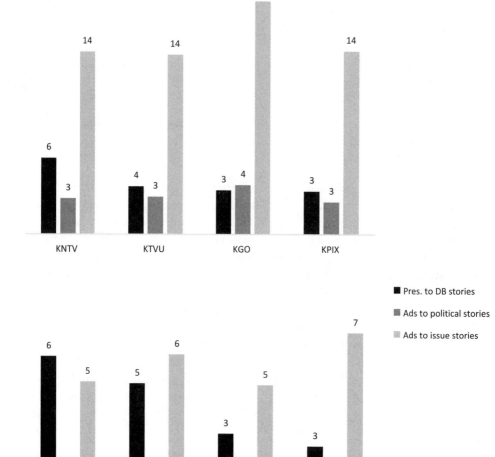

Figure 6.10. Ratio of number of ads (*top*) and time (*bottom*) for presidential to down-ballot stories, ads to political stories, and ads to issues stories in San Francisco.

from the others regarding the prominence of political ad money, the ratios are not that different from the other markets. KTVU had a ratio of 6:1 for the time it spent on presidential versus DB stories. KTNV was just a bit tighter at 5:1 and the other two stations were at 3:1 (fig. 6.10). When it came to comparing the time devoted to political ads and political stories, the ratios were relatively equal. In fact, KTVU spent more time on political stories than ads with a ratio of 0.8:1.

You might have thought that the one place in which the San Francisco stations may have outperformed the other markets was with regard to issue stories. Those stories were relatively longer than they were in the other markets and, given the noncompetitive nature of the races, the stations might have had more of an inclination to look at issues rather than just the races. However, that was not the case. They still devoted a significant amount of time to ads over issue stories, the highest ratio was KGO's 7:1.

Summary

This look at the markets individually was important because it gave us a view of the major actors in the relationship among political ad, political stories, and money—the television stations themselves. That is where the fundamental decisions are made regarding the treatment of the political campaign and how the money and political ads themselves might affect that coverage. Let's take the points one at a time.

First, the money—particularly the proportion of revenue that the political ads provided for the stations. Las Vegas aired the most ads and was second, behind Philadelphia, in total ad revenue. More importantly, that revenue accounted for 28 percent of the total revenue in 2016. For one station (KLAS), it was 35 percent. And the ad revenue that I included here only refers to the last two months of the campaign. The stations aired political ads throughout the primary season as early as February 2016. The revenue that they received for those ads is not part of the 28 percent. By definition, then, the proportion of 2016 total revenue that the ads represented was certainly higher and perhaps substantially so. Whatever that figure would be, political ads were a major revenue stream.

And, that is especially important for smaller markets. Remember, Las Vegas is number 40 in the country and realizing at least 28 percent of your revenue from one source gets attention. Philadelphia, on the other hand, is number 4 and it brought in over $56 million in political ad revenue during those last two months. That only accounted for about 14 percent of total 2016 revenue in the market. That is still a hefty percentage, but the stations

collectively had revenues of $420 million. There is much room in that amount
of revenue to affect content.

Consider that the political ad revenue in Raleigh accounted for, at least, 12
percent of 2016 revenues, but those stations collectively brought in almost $300
million less than the stations in Philadelphia (about $122 million). That is a lot
of money, but the Raleigh stations had nowhere near the financial wiggle
room to apply to content that the stations in Philadelphia did. In terms of the
effect on the stations' capacities, 12 percent of $122 million is a whole lot more
than 14 percent of $420 million.

Second, the ads. As I mentioned previously, the stations really had no
choice in the number of ads that they aired. In fact, they worked very hard to
get that business. They aired the ads for whichever races the ads were purchased. And, so, the ratios of DB to presidential ads that appeared on the air
was a response to market demand—the demand of political advertisers for
commercial time on their stations. However, the ratios were not consistent
across stations or across markets.

Third, the content, particularly political stories. The stations had complete
control over stories they would produce—their type, the races that they would
cover, where they would place them in the newscast, and so on. All of those
decisions had economic implications. A news director had to decide how to
use the news team resources (most often a reporter and a video person), what
production mode to choose, and how much of the scarce time of a newscast
to devote to the story. All of them meant money.

In looking at the presidential and DB races, it is clear that the stations
decided that the presidential race was the way to go for stories. In Cleveland,
for example, the station that made the most money from political ads had the
highest ratio of the number of presidential to DB stories—47:1. Not to be out-
done, a Las Vegas station came in at 39:1. For each station, the ads accounted
for, at least, 16 and 35 percent of total 2016 revenue.

My real concern is the stories that would provide the public with political
information that might inform political choices. They were the stories that
either covered an issue that the ads raised, mentioned the ad, or examined the
claims of an ad. I called them issue stories. Among the types of political stories
that the stations presented, these came closest to what we might call journalism. How did that fair in the scheme of things? Not well.

For the purposes of this summary, I will limit myself to highlighting the
amount of time the stations devoted to these stories compared to the political
ads. There was wide variation across the markets as well as across the stations
within the same market. For example, in Philadelphia, one station's time ratio
of political ads to issue stories was 44:1; that is, it aired 44 seconds of political

ads to every 1 second of issue stories. Within that same market, another station's ratio for the same relationship was 7:1. Clearly, the stations are reading the demand for content very differently within the same market. That said, though, there was no station with a ratio below 4:1. There were even two stations in the same market that presented no issue stories at all.

In short, political ads carried the day over political stories of any sort and especially over issue stories, which were the rarest of political stories. Even when any political story was presented, it was overwhelmingly directed at the presidential race. If we consider that in light of the fact that the significant majority of political ads addressed the DB races, the information imbalance was obvious. This is not to say that citizens did not learn something from the ads. Some research suggests that they do (Ridout and Franz 2011; Ridout, Franz, and Fowler 2013; Valentino, Hutchings, and Williams 2004). But that is not the learning that concerns me here. The political ads, quite correctly, are geared toward persuasion, not simply information. Local television news stories about issues in the campaign are different, and they carry with them an obligation to provide citizens with political information that they can use as a basis for thought and action. In a nutshell, that type of story was mostly absent from the content that I studied.

7

The Business of News

Before we consider how the media are organized in the United States, it is useful to summarize the research and the findings that it revealed. At the heart of this book is the relationship among political ads, money, and news content, particularly the comparison between the presidential and down-ballot races. The findings revealed the work of the "media-and-money election complex," as Nichols and McChesney (2013) characterize the system. Here are some of the important points to consider.

I focused on ten television markets across the country—nine of which were in battleground states. They ranged in size from Philadelphia (number 4) to Cedar Rapids (number 90).

The campaign period was the sixty-four days between September 5 and November 7, 2016. In that time, the viewers in the ten markets saw 200,511 political ads on the thirty-nine network-affiliated stations—an average of over 3,100 ads per day combined. In return for airing those ads, the stations earned over $220 million. But, of course, neither the ads nor the money was evenly distributed across the campaigns, the markets, or the stations.

As I mentioned at the outset of the book, there were stark imbalances: Two were the result of decisions made by the candidates and their sponsors; the third one was the result of decisions made by the local stations. The second and third imbalances were what drew my attention.

The first imbalance was how the political ads were distributed between the presidential candidates. Hillary Clinton sponsored 75 percent of them. But even with that three-to-one advantage, she could not overcome the $5 billion in free coverage that the media lavished on Donald Trump. Tweets won. Les Moonves got his wish.

The second imbalance was how the ads fell across the campaigns—presidential and down-ballot. There were over twice as many ads directed at the down-ballot race than at the presidential race—69 percent to 31 percent. And, of course, the money followed the ads—66 percent (down-ballot race) to 34 percent presidential race). Further, the ads and the money were not distributed evenly across the markets. Las Vegas and Philadelphia, markets in which there were competitive local races, aired the most ads and made the most money. Las Vegas aired the most ads, over 46,500, and got about $55 million; in Philadelphia, there were just under 35,000 ads for which the stations received about $57 million. Remember, Las Vegas is number 40 among the markets whereas Philadelphia is number 4. As a result, it costs more money to advertise in Philadelphia. That's why the stations in the market saw more revenue than those in Las Vegas, even though they aired over 11,000 fewer ads.

The most glaring imbalance was the result of how the stations decided to cover the campaigns. There were three parts to that calculus: how many resources would be devoted to campaign coverage; how to cover the campaigns; and how to distribute that coverage between the presidential and down-ballot races.

Let's take the first part of that. I examined the content of 1,552 local newscasts during the campaign period. In that representative sample of broadcasts, the stations aired a combined total of 10,229 political ads and a combined total of about 29,000 stories, but they only dedicated 3,845 of them to the political campaigns—about 13 percent. The news directors opted for other topics—human interest/soft news were the most prominent. So, even in the middle of a white-hot campaign, in general, news directors did not direct much of the stations' resources to campaign coverage.

Even when they did, the stations offered five types of political stories: campaign event, local status report, national status report, issue stories, and other. Of the five types, the issue stories were those that covered an issue that was discussed by the candidates, made reference to a political ad, or examined the claims of an ad. These were the stories that I identified as a form of enterprise journalism in which the reporters had the opportunity to delve into the campaign to provide viewers with political information on which they might act.

However, before I discuss the political story types, it is useful to compare the number of political ads and political stories and the amount of time the stations dedicated to them in general. I calculated a ratio to make that comparison. For the number of political ads and political stories, it was relatively close, 2.9:1. That is, the stations presented about three ads to every political story. Those ratios applied to all political stories.

As I mentioned previously, a more nuanced examination of that relation-ship required considering the time that was used for each. There are two rea-sons for that approach. First, time is the scarcest resource for a television broadcast. It is finite. Second, the political ads were all 30 seconds long, while the duration of political stories was variable; the median was 43 seconds. Just to add a more detailed view, the mean was just over 65 seconds with a standard deviation of almost 58 seconds indicating that the duration of those stories varied widely. Therefore, when I looked at the ratio for time devoted to politi-cal ads and political stories, it was almost even at 1.3:1.

The campaign event, local status report, and national status report stories combined accounted for 81 percent of the broadcast time of political stories, with the campaign event being the most prominent. What is important about that is these stories, by their construction, did not delve into any of the issues of the campaign. The campaign event stories (34 percent of political story broadcast time) simply announced when and where campaign events were going to happen or, after they happened, they reported that the event had taken place. Some would reiterate what the candidate said on the stump and often give an estimate of the size of the crowd in attendance.

Both the local and national status reports confined themselves to just the status of the campaign. They focused on the latest polls and the horse race nature of the campaign. In addition, they would also reiterate the statements of the candidates regarding a particular topic of the day. It was the proverbial "he said, she said" coverage. The distinction between the local and national status reports referred not to the topic of the story but rather to the resources that were used to convey the narrative, either local station or national network resources. For the most part, however, national status reports were directed at the presidential race. Rarely did a national reporter offer a status report of a down-ballot race. When it did occur, it referred to a very tightly contested race and what national implications it might have. That was a concern for me because my interest was how the stations used the $220 million that they received for airing the political ads.

Local status reports (31 percent of political story broadcast time) had the same attributes of the national status stories, but they were delivered by anchors and reporters from the local station. Therefore, the station had to expend resources to construct the story and then to present it. The news direc-tors made decisions about the newsworthiness of the story and whether it would capture an audience.

National status reports (16 percent of political story broadcast time) were stories that were conveyed by national reporters of the affiliated network. They were introduced by a local anchor and then the story was "tossed" to the national correspondent. The local station incurred no real cost in the presentation of the story. In almost every instance, these stories focused on the presidential campaign.

Issue stories (14 percent of political story broadcast time) reported on an issue that was raised in the campaign, mentioned a political ad, or examined the claims of a political ad. There were 486 of these stories that we coded. The overwhelming topic of these stories was the controversy surrounding Hillary Clinton's emails; they accounted for 101 of the stories (just over 20 percent). No other topic—including propositions in California, political ad issues, or the sexual misconduct accusations against Trump among others—had proportions out of the single digits. Therefore, even when it came to issue stories, the preferred topic choice of news directors was clear. The news selection decision is reflected in the ratios that I calculated for issue stories. The ratio for the number of political ads to issue story was 21:1; for the time devoted to each, the ratio was 9:1. Both ratios indicated a significant imbalance. Further, unlike other researchers, I did not find that many of the issue stories referred to political ads—either their mention or their evaluation of ad claims (Fowler and Ridout 2009).

The third imbalance was the distribution of the political stories between the presidential and down-ballot races. When it came to the types of political stories that would be covered, news directors opted overwhelmingly to just tell us some basic information about the campaign without delving into any of its substance. But that was only the first decision. The second decision they had to make was the race to which to direct their attention. Out of the 3,845 political stories, only 3,494 could be logically attributed to the ether race. The others were general stories about early voting and absentee ballots among others, that applied to both races. In addition to the decision about what aspect of the campaign the stations would cover, news directors made a decision about which race would receive their attention. There was no contest—the score was 87 percent for the presidential race to 13 percent for the down-ballot races. The local news directors, just like the broadcast and cable networks, decided that covering the "circus" as Moonves called it, was the best way to use their reporting resources.

That was borne out in the distribution of time between the races the stations used for the political stories, to wit: the proportion of story time directed toward the presidential race—94 percent of campaign event stories, 91 percent of national stories, 83 percent of local status reports and 69 percent of issue stories.

While sobering, these facts need to be understood in the context of how the political ads and the money that supported them were distributed. Remember, unlike the political stories, the political ads (69 percent) and the money (66 percent) overwhelmingly went to the down-ballot races. The political stories that might have assisted voters with information about those races were simply not there.

However, before I level too harsh a judgment regarding the performance of the stations' coverage of the campaign, I must consider Doris Graber's (2001) cautions about what television does. She contends that journalists often choose poorly when it comes to framing and the tone of political content. However, she observes that, in an environment with diverse audience tastes, "the wisdom of nearly every story choice becomes contestable. Television does present a caricature of the political world, as charged, but that is the nature of the broadcast beast. When selection is necessary, distortions are inevitable" (121). Graber concludes that, "television, despite its many serious shortcomings, makes major contributions to political action and to the public's understanding of political issues" (128).

Graber's caution is instructive as I consider how the television stations covered the 2016 campaign. Political stories were conveyed as campaign events, local status report stories, national status report stories, and issue stories (not considering the "other" stories here). It is true that each of those stories gave the audience information about the Presidential and down-ballot races. It was important to know that campaign events were taking place—where, when, which candidate. Citizens could and did use that information to guide action. No doubt, those who attended the rallies learned something about the candidate while there. The local and national status reports that included the results of polls, statements by the candidates or assessments about who was trending up or down gave citizens a sense of how things were going. I do not want to diminish the contribution of those stories to the political knowledge of voters.

While these stories offered information to citizens, none involved enterprise reporting. The stations' reporters did not break new journalistic ground about the campaign. I looked at the issue stories for that kind of coverage. Specifically, these stories included a mention of a political ad, the coverage of an issue that was referenced in a political ad, or the examination of the claims of a political ad. There were few of them—fewer than any of the other types of political story. Yet citizens want that information as I stated previously and, by my analysis, it was seriously lacking among the stations' coverage.

There is the argument that voters had other avenues to learn about politics. That is true. But, as I demonstrated previously, they came to local television news programs to learn about local politics. The advertisers invested $220 million to persuade that audience. However, judging by the metrics that I cite here, the local stations essentially abrogated their public interest obligations to inform that audience and that gave the advantage to the advertisers. When it came to local television and local races, political communication and political reality were bought.

The News System in the United States

My conclusion about bought reality and the dismal performance of local television stations in the coverage of the 2016 election cycle should not surprise us. In fact, we should have expected it. We designed the system that way.

Whatever the critiques of the media and their place in society, a fundamental issue is the economic model on which it rests. News production in the United States is burdened by an inherent dilemma, because the news system is based on the delivery of a public good (news) by private means. Newspapers, television stations (except for public stations), and radio stations (except for public stations) are private enterprises whose main goal is to maximize profit. That is the way we set it up from the beginning. Today, that model of the media in the United States has an air of inevitability which we do not question. But there were very real and conscious decisions about how to organize the electronic media in the United States in the 1930s (McChesney 1999; 2004; Bagdikian 2004). Even when there were serious challenges to that model in the 1940s to consider the media's public service obligations in light of its monopolistic use of the public airwaves, the structure of a privately owned media system prevailed (Commission on Freedom of the Press 1947; Pickard 2015). If we compare the United States to the developed world, its model of private ownership is the exception. Comparing eighteen developed countries, the average spent on public broadcasting was $86 per capita in 2014 with Norway topping the list at $180. The United States came in last at $3 per capita (Coren 2018).

The dilemma is foundational because it requires media firms to treat the news either as a public good or as a private good—a commodity. The tension is how do news producers present information that is both in the public interest and profitable. Media reform advocates claim that as news becomes commodified, profit trumps public interest. Media executives assert precisely the opposite reality. Reformers contend that when citizens are overwhelmed with spin, infotainment, and news framing, they opt out of the news system. It becomes too difficult for citizens to uncover the facts of a particular story and the easiest response is not to engage the body politic. News producers challenge that this disengagement arises when news does not capture consumers' attention. Media executives maintain that news produced in an entertainment framework provides citizens with the media system that they want and, by definition, that means that news is serving the public interest. This logic conflates the public interest with what the public is interested in. If it seems as though they are talking past each other, they are.

The public trustee doctrine has been repeatedly upheld by the courts against First Amendment challenges on the grounds that the broadcast spectrum is a scarce resource and the licensees who use that spectrum have a public interest obligation. However, there is a critical assessment that the public trustee doctrine has been a failure because, since its inception, "broadcasters have successfully opposed nearly all efforts by the Congress and the FCC to define, quantify and enforce the public interest standard" (Varona 2004, 5).

The profit-maximizing versus public interest calculus is played out every day at local television news stations in spades. News directors and reporters are constantly pushed by ownership to maximize the bottom line. And it takes its toll on the journalism that they produce and their own tolerance for the disconnect between what they want to do and what the insistence on the bottom line will let them do (Christin 2014).

Joseph White (2018), a local news journalist, recalls the day he "flamed out of television news" when he argued with his news director about covering a story in which a local health nurse was accused by the police of stealing $90,000 from a ninety-year-old patient. White pitched the story as a "jumping off point for a larger story on how those crimes are committed, and how you can protect the elderly and otherwise vulnerable members of your family" (1). White lost the argument. His news director wanted him to cover the cleanup of a downed tree that dropped across a driveway. By any measure, the driveway story was going to be much cheaper to cover. The video was going to be easy—chains sawing away the branches delivered the implicit message that the weather danger had been reconciled. On the other hand, doing an investigative report on elder abuse was simply too expensive to consider. That was the final straw for White as he identified four types of stories that made the news at his station; weather, breaking news, cry-on-camera and disagreements, "which are controversies that aren't actually controversial, but things about which we can let the viewer decide" (4).

White characterizes the news business as "impossibly hard to navigate because it's a contradiction. The news can't be beholden to corporations and profit margins, but that's what the business demands" (5). As he labored in his reporter's role, he felt that the scale was tipping away from the news and toward the business. Although I have no way of knowing, I think his news director may have been struck by the same contradiction, but he or she had the bottom line to satisfy.

The story about Joseph White is, to be sure, anecdotal. But I believe that his observations and warnings are accurate. That is borne out by other observers regarding the nature of television news. John McManus (1994) calls local television news content "infotainment." Mort Rosenblum (1993, 163) observed that television does not usually report the news that it covers; rather, it "creates little sociodramas, known as packages, to represent the situation at hand."

Lance Bennett (2005, 176) characterizes political content as being presented in "news reality frames," in part explained by market-driven journalism but, to be clear, also prompted by large numbers of the audience who are receptive to such emotional representations of politics. Dell Champlin and Janet Knoedler (2002, 459) argue that "news divisions have become just another profit center for their conglomerate parents that must yield the same rates of profit as the more lucrative entertainment divisions of the media empires." Alex Jones (2009) concluded that when local ownership of television stations was replaced by corporate ownership, the priorities changed, and content became tabloid because the stations put profit first.

The economic calculus of news content selection has changed dramatically over the last three decades. The news is now treated as a commodity (Adilov, Alexander, and Brown 2007) and the five Ws (who, what, when, where, and why) have been replaced by a decision process that fits that reality. James Hamilton (2004) identified a whole new set of questions that drive reporting: Who cares about a particular piece of information? What are they willing to pay to find out? What are others willing to pay to reach them? Where can media outlets or advertisers reach these people? When is it profitable to provide the information? Why is it profitable? The public interest doctrine I mentioned earlier is nowhere to be found in this model of news selection.

Scripps Broadcasting executive Sean McLaughlin expressed a clear-eyed view of the advantages and limitations of local television: "Our expertise in local communities is really significant, but we haven't been as strong in context and perspective. I get text alerts all the time telling me the news, but we're too one-dimensional. We need to be telling people things of real value. [TV news says that] everything is the most important, but it's not, and people see through that" (quoted in Wenger and Papper 2018, 9).

Perhaps, one of the harshest criticisms of local television news comes from Harry Jessell, cofounder of NewsCheck Media and a long-time observer, when he accuses it of having "journalistic shallowness, an obsession with crime, accidents, fires and other mayhem—the low-hanging fruit of journalism and a tendency to regulate public affairs to a Sunday morning talk show," among other things (quoted in Wenger and Papper 2018, 12). This critique is offered within an argument that local television news is also irreplaceable when it distinguishes itself in its reporting in the wake of disasters. Its local nature, its presence in the community over time, its immediacy and its preeminence as a news source in the aftermath of hurricanes, floods, fires, or other disasters make it a critical asset in the local media ecosystem.

Somewhat along the line of Jessell's criticism is Van Zuylen-Wood's (2017, 3) observation that the problem with local television is not that it is under-resourced or partisan—"the problem is that it is just lame." He notes that it is "weirdly" successful, judging by the profit it makes. But that success, he maintains, is the biggest hindrance to innovation. There is no impetus to change and even when local television news dallies with "digital" or "mobile"; many times, it is not trying to deliver news but to funnel viewers to television.

Local Television News Profitability and Consolidation

Whatever the criticisms and shortcomings, local newscasts are the profit and revenue centers of local television stations. In the 2016 edition of his annual RTNDA/Hofstra survey of newsrooms, media scholar Bob Papper (2017, 1) stated that 2016 "marked an extraordinary year for the local TV news business." He found that about two-thirds of newsrooms reported being profitable—the highest level, tied with 2013, since 1996, when it reached 72 percent. Only 4 percent of stations said that they lost money and they were very small news operations (Wenger and Papper 2018). Further, across all stations, local news accounts for a median proportion of 55 percent of the station's total revenues (Papper 2017). Think about that—the average station broadcasts 5.6 hours of news per day (Matsa and Fedeli 2018). That means that 45 percent of revenue comes from the other 18 or so hours that the station is on the air. Such is the importance of newscasts to the stations' bottom line.

This profitability should be understood in the larger context of the consolidation that is occurring among local television stations in the country. For the most part, the consolidation has happened out of the gaze of the public. The exception to that attention occurred in the case of Sinclair Broadcasting's ill-fated attempt to purchase Tribune Media. The deal was going to be worth $3.9 billion, and it was going to make Sinclair (already the largest station group) even larger—Sinclair was going to reach 72 percent of US television households, far above the 39 percent legal restriction. It made a lot of people nervous, including media public interest groups and other station group owners. It even prompted comedian John Oliver to devote an entire episode of his show, *Last Week Tonight*, to the implications of the pending merger. Oliver introduced Sinclair as, "the most influential media company that you never heard of." He gave a blistering critique of Sinclair's blatant ideological biases as it pushes a conservative agenda in segments that it requires all of its stations to run almost every day. One such segment is the Terrorism Alert Desk which is "designed to gin up xenophobia via local news" (Vogel 2018, 1). Another is the thrice-weekly commentaries of chief political analyst Boris Epshteyn, a former Trump advisor, whose sentiments were clear when he concluded in November 2018 that migrants at the southern border constituted an invasion threat to the United States. That "invasion" justified the use of tear gas to stop the attack. That position was even too far for the Sinclair corporate executives, and they distanced themselves from that commentary. In December 2019, Sinclair discontinued Epshteyn's commentaries with the final airing on December 13.

To Oliver and to many others, perhaps the most disturbing Sinclair must-run was a message in March 2018 that it forced its broadcast anchors (not reporters) to read. The statement denounced "the troubling trend of irresponsible, one-sided news plaguing our country . . . and that some members of the media use their platforms to push their own personal bias and agenda to control exactly what people think" (Domonoske 2018, 1). The message was seen to reinforce the same media criticism that Trump espouses every day.

The $3.9 billion Sinclair/Tribune deal blew up in spectacular fashion in July 2018 when FCC Chairman Ajit Pai announced that he would not support the merger. That was a complete about face for Pai. The Sinclair/Tribune deal had drawn withering criticism for over a year from many quarters across the political ideological spectrum, media reform groups as well as media firms who would have to compete with the new Sinclair (Kolhatkar 2018). But, all of Pai's public comments during the process were seen to be supportive of the deal.

For the deal to go through, Sinclair would have been required to relinquish control of certain stations to comply with FCC limits on the number and type of stations that one entity could control. Sinclair's actions to do that were grossly perverse. The station transfers that it proposed, through a series of shell companies and service agreements, were not transfers of control at all. Sinclair had a history of successfully pulling off that same scam (Kolhatkar 2018). And they did not try to hide the most recent perversion as the opponents to the deal continuously pointed out. Pai seemed unmoved and still supported the merger.

The Department of Justice indicated that it would not support the merger and that may have given the FCC chairman some political cover to oppose the deal. In the end, I think, Sinclair's hubris was simply a bridge too far for Pai. The five FCC commissioners voted unanimously to refer the matter to an administrative law judge (ALJ) within the FCC, a process that usually means the demise of the proposal. They cited Sinclair's potential misrepresentation and lack of candor for their decision (Eggerton 2018a). A month later, Tribune added insult to injury as it sued Sinclair for $1 billion seeking compensation "for all losses incurred as a result of Sinclair's material breaches of the merger agreement" (Miller 2018, 1).

When the FCC referred the deal to the ALJ, Sinclair withdrew its proposal. In doing so, Sinclair also asked the FCC to cancel the planned ALJ hearing and thereby avoided having to explain its actions. But that decision to cancel the hearing had to come from the newly appointed ALJ, Jane Hinckley Halperin. Curiously, only one month after the FCC's unanimous vote to refer the matter to the ALJ, the agency's enforcement bureau signaled that it was supportive of Sinclair's request for the termination of the hearing: "because the merger agreement between Sinclair and Tribune has been terminated; Sinclair wishes to dismiss the designated applications with prejudice; and neither applicant will seek to re-file those applications, the Bureau does not oppose a dismissal of the designated applications with prejudice and concurrent termination of the hearing proceeding" (quoted in Eggerton 2018b, 1). This is just one month after the FCC blew up a multi-billion-dollar deal because it found that Sinclair grossly misrepresented its intentions. Sinclair's misrepresentations would have been fully displayed in the hearing. Apparently, the FCC decided that simply losing the Tribune deal was enough pain for Sinclair to endure.

The FCC's recommendation was important, because the ALJ process would require a formal hearing on Sinclair's deception in the Tribune deal. And if that happened, then Sinclair's fitness as an owner of television stations in general would be questioned. That is precisely why some of its competitors and media reform critics of Sinclair wanted the ALJ process to proceed. Otherwise, the nature and extent of Sinclair's deception would not be visible to the public. In fact, the American Cable Association is trying to "force the FCC's hand on its assertion that there were material issues with Sinclair's presentation of the Tribune deal that needed resolving" (Eggerton 2018a, 1). It filed a petition with the FCC asking the agency to require Sinclair to file early renewal applications for several of its stations which would be a way for the FCC to "resolve the serious charges it leveled against Sinclair as soon as possible—charges that, if true, would speak to Sinclair's eligibility to retain any of its FCC licenses or acquire news licenses" (quoted in Eggerton 2018a, 1). The petition is exactly what it looks like. The American Cable Association was challenging Sinclair's fitness to hold any television license.

The issue was resolved on March 5, 2019, when the ALJ Halperin granted Sinclair's request to terminate the hearing. She did so saying that it would not be a prudent use of the FCC's resources because the application had been withdrawn. That rendered moot any consideration of three issues in the hearing designation order—"whether the deal violated FCC rules, whether it was in the public interest, and whether it should be granted" (Eggerton 2019c, 2).

Judge Halperin could have left it there. But, she didn't. One issue in the hearing designation order from the commissioners focused on Sinclair's "lack of candor." Judge Halperin found that to be a serious charge and Sinclair's alleged misconduct in that regard is neither "nullified or excused by the cancellation of its proposed deal with Tribune" (Federal Communications Commission 2019, 4). She pointedly noted that lying to the FCC can be grounds for the cancellation of a license. And even more to the point, Judge Halperin stated that Sinclair's misconduct should be considered within the context of a broader inquiry in a future proceeding in which Sinclair is seeking FCC approval for "a license assignment, transfer, or renewal" (4). There was no nuance in that warning. So, if Sinclair thought it dodged a bullet with the ALJ hearing termination, it may have stepped directly into the path of another one.

Yes, Sinclair had its ideological bias, but while that concerned media critics and public interest groups, that was not the worry of its station group competitors. They were about the business. They correctly saw the prospect of the largest station group among them getting much bigger and threatening their places in the market. In fact, Perry Sook, president and chairman of Nexstar Media Group, was concerned as far back as 2013 about what the local broadcast landscape would be in 2020: "10–12 major station groups, comprised of the four network-owned outfits, and a half-dozen other players reaching 20 percent or more of the U.S." (Malone 2013, 1). Then he amended his vision: "I would think that within 2–5 years, you'll see the emergence of what I call three or four super-groups, and I think you'll see a couple emerge sooner rather than later" (1).

Two Forms of Consolidation

Local television consolidation occurs in two forms. First, there is the outright purchase of stations by another station group. That activity has increased significantly over the past seven years. For example, in 2012, 95 stations were sold for a total of $1.9 billion (Mitchell and Page 2014). That increased by 300 percent in 2013 when 290 stations were sold for $8.8 billion. In 2016, 97 stations were sold for $5.28 billion and in 2017, 107 stations changed hands for a total sale of $4.68 billion (Lafayette 2018a). These totals in the billions of dollars represent significant investments and the tax bill passed by the Congress that reduced the corporate tax rate from 35 percent to 21 percent should increase the value of local television broadcast properties (Lafayette 2018a).

The second path to consolidation is through service agreements. These agreements are arrangements among stations in the same television market in which they share newsgathering resources, video, or marketing and management activities. They take several forms. There are broker (the controlling entity) and brokered (the noncontrolling entity) stations. Local news sharing agreements involve multiple stations that pool and share journalists, editors, equipment, and content. In a joint sales agreement, a licensed station sells some or all of its advertising time to another station in return for a fee or a percentage of the revenues. The FCC imposed a minimum of 15 percent— that is, if a station controlled more than 15 percent of another stations' advertising time, it was considered a controlling entity. Local marketing agreements occur when one station takes over the operation of another station, including programming and advertising. The fourth form of the service agreements is a shared services agreement in which the stations combine newsroom assets and personnel and share facilities and administrative functions (Yanich 2016). In 2017, 31 percent of stations reported being involved in a service agreement arrangement (Papper 2017). In 2014, these service agreements were present in 94 of the 210 television markets in the country (Mitchell and Page 2014). That number will increase as the consolidation trend continues.

The service agreements represent a departure for how local television stations have tried to reduce costs. Outsourcing station management is not new, "Broadcasters have been managing stations that belong to others for twenty years, but up until recently, such arrangements usually involved duopolies" (Coleman 2010, 2). Further, "a key difference with this new breed of managing companies is that they are seeking to manage stations, sometimes whole groups, regardless of whether they already have stations in the market" (2).

Media companies that provided outsourced station management, like Nexstar and Gray, were focused on a manage-to-own approach. Speaking of the managed station, investment banker Larry Patrick of Patrick Communications, characterized the arrangement as, "once you turn over management, whether or not there's an option to buy with the new manager, if the new manager can achieve economies of scale, he becomes the de facto buyer of the station" (quoted in Coleman 2010, 4).

Bert Ellis, a cofounder of Titan Broadcast Management, had no such intention: "We're not trying to buy stations. The owners want a totally neutral party to manage so they get the highest price for the stations when they sell" (quoted in Coleman 2010, 4).

The service agreements have been, and continue to be, a particularly intense flash point in the consolidation debate. They provide the perfect vehicle for the fundamental arguments around how the broadcast media should be organized in the United States—the role of the market versus regulation. The media industry contends that consolidation is needed to compete successfully against cable and the Internet. Media reformers counter that consolidation deprives the public of independent voices in the community and that it negatively affects the breadth of information that citizens receive. Some reformers have called them "covert consolidation." That is an accurate characterization. When I first became aware of service agreements and I realized how they were constructed and implemented, I thought that they may be a mechanism to skirt the FCC's regulatory principles of diversity, competition, and localism. My first step was to ask the FCC for information about service agreements—how many, where were they, which stations were involved, which owners were involved, among other things. Remarkably, the agency did not have that data. Station owners were entering into agreements which fundamentally altered the control of stations in television markets which it regulates, and the FCC did not know the extent or the nature of those agreements. Therefore, in order to examine them, I had to find them. I did that in collaboration with researchers at Free Press. In 2011, we were able to identify 55 television markets (service agreements are now operating in 94 markets).

In my examination of nine of those markets, I found that service agreements had an effect on the content of stations who were parties to the arrangement. Service agreements stations, on average, devoted less time to local stories than nonservice agreement stations (Yanich 2013b). They used their various stations to run duplicate stories, use the same scripts, and use the same video and graphics to report the same story (Yanich 2011). We should not be surprised. The parties to the service agreements said that they entered into the arrangements to achieve economies of scale, to become more efficient. They were true to their word. Yes, there were some references to more and better reporting. But that was an outcome that was offered as a result of the economies of scale.

Using these service agreements, media firms are trying to create new business models. In late 2010 Rich Boehne, former president and CEO of the E. W. Scripps Company, was clear about the direction he wanted to take: "I'm fully convinced that what we see today, both in local broadcast and in newspapers offering so much content for free, is not a sustainable model . . . we're going to experiment much more aggressively to try to create those models and take high-value premium content and derive much more revenue from it than we do today" (quoted in Malone 2010, 1). He continued saying that, as they moved away from syndicated shows such as *Wheel of Fortune* and *Oprah* (as her show ended), they would be replaced by local programming that "will improve margins; we'll make a lot more money" (1).

Beyond his own stations, Boehne wanted to extend the approach to other markets and he is forceful in his vision: "We very much believe that local broadcast markets over time will consolidate. It's time to build brands and take market share, mind share, audience share under a local brand when we have the opportunity" (quoted in Malone 2010, 2). Boehne was willing to work with anyone to build the brands he envisioned which, by definition, would consolidate local stations. He would like to take over the operations of rival stations in markets in which Scripps operated (as it was doing in West Palm Beach). He was confident enough in his assessment of local television station ownership that he extended the invitation: "We would like to do that in other markets, so if you know folks in those markets who you think should not be in the news business and you'd like us to take over their stations for them, just give us a call" (2). This was not a modest proposal. The service agreements that the station groups entered into are the perfect means to create the brands, market share, and mind share that Boehne envisioned.

The Honolulu Consolidation Case

The Honolulu case is most instructive. In August 2009, Raycom Media (owner of two of the five stations in the market) and MGB Capital Corporation (owner of one station) announced the establishment of a shared services agreement under which the companies would combine the three stations to "creatively and successfully address the impact of the negative economy and to secure the future of all three television stations in Hawaii" (quoted in Yanich 2013a, 245). The president of Raycom articulated the economic reasons for the merger:

> The purpose of the shared services agreement is to not only secure the future of KHNL, KFIVE and KGMB, but to operate them more efficiently and effectively without diminishing the quality of news and other programming provided to our customers in Hawaii. We realize there may be other financial and business options available, and while we are certainly open to discussing these with any interested party, the economic reality is that this market cannot support five traditionally separated television stations, all with duplicated costs. Rather than experiencing the loss of one, or possibly two stations in Hawaii, we intend to preserve three stations that provide important and valuable local, national and international programming in Hawaii. (245)

Under the agreement, the non-news programming was not affected. But the news programs underwent substantial changes. First, the news operations of all three stations were placed in one building. Second, the economies of scale were such that the merger resulted in the loss of 68 of the 190+ jobs that comprised the staff of all three stations. Third, and this was the most obvious to the viewers, two of the stations produced a simulcast of their news programs during time slots that accounted for three hours of news every day. Simulcasts were the airing of the exact same newscast—the exact same content—simultaneously on all three stations. The new "brand" of the shared services agreement was called Hawaii News Now. Talk about economies of scale.

But the Raycom deal was not without opposition. Honolulu was the only television market in the United States in which a local, nonprofit organization officially challenged the agreement. Media Council Hawaii (MCH), represented by the Institute of Public Representation at the Georgetown University Law Center, filed a complaint with the FCC to request relief in October 2009. It argued that the agreement would constitute "an unauthorized transfer of control in contravention of the Communications Act and FCC rules" (Campbell 2009, 1). MCH was specifically making the argument that the agreement violated the FCC's regulatory ownership principles and that the actions of Raycom "would harm the members of Media Council Hawaii and the general public by reducing the number of independent voices providing local news from four to three, and by substantially reducing competition in the provision of local news and the sale of advertising time" (6). My analysis proved MCH to be right. I was able to compare the stations' performance before and after the service agreement was implemented, and I found that the distribution of duplicate stories, the duration of stories, and the proportion of enterprise reporting stories were all affected by the agreement.

The Media Bureau of the FCC ruled against MCH in December 2011. However, it made its ruling on the narrow technical question regarding whether Raycom acquired control of a new license. The deal did not include a transfer of license. But the Media Bureau added a caveat that seemed to recognize that the technical point on which it ruled should be examined more carefully saying that, "further action on our part is warranted with respect to this and analogous cases . . . whether the action taken by the licensees in this case, or analogous actions by other licensees, are consistent with the public interest" (quoted in Yanich 2013a, 247).

It took three years, but the FCC finally ruled on these service agreements. Then-FCC Chairman Tom Wheeler characterized the agreements as "legal fictions." On March 31, 2014, the FCC issued a ruling saying that broadcasters generally could not form joint service agreements in which one station sells 15 percent or more of the advertising of another separately owned station in the same market. The ruling went further, stating that joint services agreements that were already extant were not "grandfathered" into the system. Rather, the stations who were party to the agreements had two years in which to make the case for a waiver on the basis that the joint services agreements served the public interest. The FCC (2014, 4542) made its position clear: "We reject arguments that we should automatically grandfather all television JSAs permanently or indefinitely. In these circumstances, we find that such grand-fathering would allow arbitrary and inconsistent changes to the level of per-missible common ownership on a market-by-market basis based not necessarily on where the public interest lies . . . Moreover . . . [current] licens-ees may seek a waiver of our rules if they believe strict application of the rules would not serve the public interest." It was no surprise that the opposition to the rule was fierce and immediate. The National Association of Broadcasters (NAB) filed two lawsuits challenging the grandfather ruling. They also brought intense pressure on the Congress. And, in the end, the broadcasters and the NAB won. In December 2015, the Congress, by wide bi-partisan mar-gins, passed a massive spending bill that contained a very short rider. It extended the time in which extant joint services agreements had to make their case from two to ten years, thereby effectively "grandfathering" them into the system. So, the legal fictions that Wheeler derided were still the order of the day.

The Numbers of Consolidation

Pew researcher Katerina Matsa examined the ownership of stations among the five largest station groups from 2004 through 2016. The groups included, in rank order by the number of full-power commercial stations that they con-trolled, Sinclair, Gray, Nexstar, Tegna, and Tribune. In 2004, there were 1,193 full-power commercial stations in the United States. The five station groups controlled 179 of them, 15 percent. By 2014, that number and percentage had more than doubled and the station groups controlled 378 (32 percent) of the 1,181 full-power commercial stations in the United States. Only two years later, in 2016, the station groups controlled 443 (37 percent) of 1,197 full-power tele-vision stations in the country (Matsa 2017).

This consolidation has an effect on the number of stations that *originate* local television news versus the number of stations that *carry* local news. In 2013, there were 1,026 that carried local TV news. However, only 719 origi-nated the news they carried. They produced their news and the news content for the other 307 stations. So, about 30 percent of stations that carried news did not produce the news it carried. The proportion rose steadily from 2014 to 2016. By 2017 the number of stations that carried news had risen to 1,072. But the number of stations that carried, but did not produce its news, rose from 307 in 2013 to 369, about 34 percent of stations (Papper 2018). The trend is clear—as stations consolidated, the production of news content was increas-ingly produced by fewer stations. This should come as no surprise; the express purpose of the consolidation is to achieve economies of scale. It's all about the money.

There is a very important milestone in the consolidation that occurred between 2004 and 2014. It was the *Citizens United* ruling in 2010. The ruling created a huge boon to the advertising fortunes of local television stations because that is where the vast majority of the money that was released by the ruling would be directed (see chapter 4). Political ads are the major mechanism through which candidates convey their message, and those ads are shown on local television stations. There is much money to be made in that arrangement. For example, the total combined political ads revenue in election years of six station groups rose from $573 million in 2012 to almost $700 million in 2014 to almost $843 million in 2016 (Matsa and Fedeli 2018).

Retransmission Fees

Beyond the tremendous amount of revenue that stations realized from political ad buys, there is another revenue source that is proving to be as important, if not more so, because it does not rely on the political cycle—retransmission (retrans) fees. These are the payments that cable and satellite systems pay to local channels to carry their content.

The notion of retransmission of content is based on the requirement of "must-carry" under the Communications Act of 1934, as amended. It stipulated that full-power television stations are entitled to mandatory carriage of their signal on any multichannel video programming distributor (MVPD), a service provider that delivers a wide variety of TV channels to users (cable TV, satellite TV, Verizon Fios, for example) located within their local market. But there is some nuance to that requirement. The stations have two choices regarding how they want to assert that mandatory carriage. One, if the broadcasters assert their "must-carry" rights, the cable operator must carry the signal and it cannot interrupt that carriage. However, in that scheme, the broadcasters cannot accept any compensation from the MVPD operator. In the second choice, broadcasters may elect "retransmission consent." In this scenario, retransmission consent is dependent on, among other things, the negotiated terms of compensation to the broadcasters by the MVPD systems. If they cannot reach agreement, the MVPD is prohibited from carrying the local station's signal. Therefore, broadcasters have the choice: assert the must-carry rule to guarantee carriage, but without compensation, or chose retransmission consent with compensation, but the possibility of the interruption of the carriage.

Interruptions in carriage have become much more frequent as broadcasters and cable operators haggle over fees. In July 2019, the stations of Meredith Corporation went dark to DISH satellite subscribers in twelve markets (Farrell 2019a). In June 2019, local stations on DirectTV went dark for seventeen stations in fourteen markets across the country (Farrell 2019c). In July 2019, 120 Nexstar Media Group stations in ninety-seven markets also went dark on DirectTV (Farrell 2019a).

The retransmission fees have risen rapidly and dramatically over time. In 2006, they totaled $215 million. By 2014, they had risen to over $4.8 billion—a 2,160 percent increase in less than a decade. In 2016, they totaled almost $9.4 billion and they are projected to be over $12.8 billion in 2023 (Matsa 2018). Within the span of seventeen years, the revenue that television stations would receive from retransmission fees will undergo a projected increase of over 5,800 percent. That is a whole lot of money, and it is precisely what has caught the attention of station group owners and those entities, especially private equity firms, that want to *become* station group owners. It is important to note that, for the first time in television history, a major station group reported advertising as the second-most important revenue source, behind retransmission fees. It happened in the first quarter of 2019. As Hank Price (2019, 1) states, "it was the first quarter in a non-political, non-Olympic year, and yes, the rest of the year will put advertising back on top, but the fact remains that Nexstar reported more total revenue from retransmission fees . . . than from spot sales." In that quarter, retransmission fees accounted for over 50 percent of Nexstar's revenue (Jessell 2019d).

The capacity to command those increasing retransmission fees is directly related to how large the station group is because controlling a large number of stations confers leverage in the negotiations with cable and satellite systems. The mantra of "go big or go home" plays out here as in no other endeavor. The negotiations are the ultimate "hard ball" game and they have real consequences. In 2017, three million Dish customers lost access to twenty-eight CBS-owned local stations in twenty-eight markets because Dish and CBS could not come to an agreement about the retransmission fees (Bode 2017).

The playing field is not level as the station groups have the upper hand by blocking content. And the more content they control by owning many stations, the more pressure they can exert on cable and satellite systems (Farrell 2019b). As you might have guessed by now, the real victims in these retransmission feuds are the consumers. One way or another, we pay for the counterproductive actions of the executives who play with the system.

Locast: A Threat to Retransmission Fees

Retransmission fees are completely dependent on the arrangement that the content of local stations is provided to consumers through the wires of the cable companies—ergo, the *retransmission*. Previously, in the days of television antennas, the local television station signals, were freely available over the air. Actually, they still are, and there is a growing number of television households that have opted for antennas as a reaction to the increasing high cost of cable or satellite service. In January 2019, 16 million homes had television antenna viewers, a 48 percent increase since 2011 (Kuchinskas 2019).

What if that local content could be provided to viewers without using MVPDs or antennas? What if you could get access to that content over the web? Enter Locast.

Locast is a non-profit organization that calls itself a "digital translator," boosting local broadcasters' reach by streaming the content over the web (Locast 2019). To stream the broadcast signals without payment or permission, the service relies on title 17, chapter 1, section 111a of the Copyright Act. The act grants an exemption from exclusive broadcast transmissions if "the secondary transmission is not made by a cable system, but is made by a governmental body, or other nonprofit organization, without any purpose of direct or indirect commercial advantage, and without charge to the recipients of the secondary transmission other than assessments necessary to defray the actual and reasonable costs of maintaining and operating the secondary transmission service" (Eggerton 2019g, 3).

As of February 2020, Locast was available in sixteen cities accounting for 35 percent of the US television market and reaching over forty-one million people. The cities include the eleven largest markets in the country by designated market area (DMA) size, based on the Nielsen 2020 television market estimates: New York (number 1), Los Angeles (number 2), Chicago (number 3), Philadelphia (number 4), Dallas (number 5), San Francisco (number 6), Washington, DC (number 7), Houston (number 8), Boston (number 9), Atlanta (number 10), Phoenix (number 11), Seattle (number 13), Denver (number 17), Baltimore, (number 26), Sioux Falls, SD (number 113), and Rapid City, SD (number 169) (Locast 2020).

Use of the service is straightforward. Any user must register and, from that information, Locast derives a geolocation that places the user within one television market. That is important because Locast can provide access to the local stations for any user only in the market in which the consumer lives. It is a free service. However, Locast asks for a donation, saying that there is a cost of maintaining the service. It offers several donation plans on the website from $5 per month to $100 per year. In order to test the service, I registered as a user (without making a donation) and indeed, I was able to view local television station programming on the web. Moreover, Locast is available on Apple iOS, Android, Roku, and Hooper. It added iPad, Apple TV, and Android TV in May 2019 (Eggerton 2019g).

Locast seemed to operate under the radar for about eighteen months. However, that was simply not going to last. The revenue from retransmission fees is much too important for the broadcasters. At the end of July 2019, the four major US television networks sued the service saying that Locast, which is backed by a large donation ($500,000) from AT&T Inc., "is not the Robin Hood of television; instead, Locast's founding, funding, and operations reveal its decidedly commercial purposes" (Coster 2019, 1). The National Association of Broadcasters supported the suit.

Locast has fought back. In September 2019, the service responded by filing its own suit against the broadcasters. Locast owner, lawyer David Goodfriend and a former staffer at the FCC, claimed that the service is not a violation of copyright and that the company "fits squarely" into the "Congressionally-designated exception to infringement" (Gardner 2019, 1). But Goodfriend did not stop there. He goes on a counterattack. He turns the notion of copyright abuse for which he had been sued into an indictment *against* the broadcasters. The broadcasters, he charged, "have colluded to limit the reasonable public access to the over-the-air signals that they are statutorily required to make available for free, and have opted instead to use their copyrights improperly to construct and protect a pay-TV model that forces consumers to forgo over-the-air programming or to pay cable, satellite, and online providers for access to programming that was intended to be free" (2). And he goes further: "By limiting access to the over-the-air signals that Plaintiffs have committed to make freely available, and simultaneously using the copyrights in their programming to drive revenue for the local programming that consumers cannot now effectively receive over the air through their pay-TV model, Plaintiffs have colluded and misused copyrights to expand their market power beyond what those copyrights were intended to protect. The pay-TV providers get rich. Plaintiffs get rich. The public gets fleeced" (1).

The cases will not be settled until after this book has been published. However, given the money that is at stake, the outcome of the cases will necessarily affect the retransmission arrangements between broadcasters and MVPDs. It seems to me that anything is possible.

The New FCC Ownership Rules

The local television space will become more consolidated. A lot has happened since 2016, particularly since Donald Trump appointed Ajit Pai to become the FCC chairman and there is a three-to-two Republican advantage among the five FCC commissioners. The majority pushed through significant rule changes in a series of three-to-two votes. Almost immediately, the new FCC rescinded some decades-old broadcast ownership rules, along with others. To wit: the FCC eliminated the newspaper-broadcast and radio-television cross-ownership rules; it now allowed dual-station ownership in markets with fewer than eight independent voices after the duopoly, creating an opportunity for one entity to own two of the top four stations in the market; and, very importantly, it eliminated attribution of joint sales agreements as ownership. That means that the very legal fictions that Wheeler warned about would continue unabated (Eggerton 2017).

But this FCC did not stop there. In April 2017, it reinstituted the UHF discount which allows the stations to count half of the audience of its UHF channels against the 39 percent cap of television households that any one broadcaster can reach. The discount was put in place in the 1980s when UHF signals were not as powerful and poorer in quality than VHF signals. The transition to digital television eliminated those differences. The FCC recognized that reality and abolished the rule in 2016. By reinstating it, the new FCC effectively allows the station groups to exceed the audience cap. The reinstatement withstood a legal challenge when, in July 2018, the federal appeals court in Washington, DC, ruled that the reinstatement of the rule by the FCC would remain in place. The court did not rule on the merits of the case. Rather, it rejected the plaintiffs' petition (which included Free Press, Common Cause, Media Alliance, Media Mobilizing Project, the National Hispanic Media Coalition, Prometheus Radio Project, and the United Church of Christ Office of Communication) because it said that they did not have standing. In its unpublished order, the court acknowledged the petitioners' argument regarding the connection between the reinstatement of the discount and consolidation, but that was not the basis for the ruling. "The administrative record here identified a proposed merger (between Sinclair Broadcast Group and Tribune Media Company) that petitioners contend would result in a degree of broadcaster consolidation permissible only with the reinstatement of the challenged discount. But the record did not contain—and petitioners' initial submission failed to provide—evidence that any member of any petitioner organization is a viewer in an affected market or otherwise stands to be injured by the identified consolidation" (Johnson 2018, 2). The response to the ruling by Jessica Gonzalez of Free Press was blunt; they were "disappointed that this panel of judges refused to rule on the FCC's phony math and poor excuses for the harmful and obsolete UHF discount" (2).

That said, there is an argument that the FCC should raise the national cap (the proportion of television households that any one broadcaster can reach) from 39 to 50 percent. Mark Fratrik (2018, 3 senior vice-president and chief economist for BIA Advisory Services, argues that a 50 percent national cap "would maintain a diversity of competitive voices while allowing local television station groups to compete more effectively in today's local video marketplace." Fundamentally, he makes the same economic argument that the media industry has made for over two decades—the competitive television market does not consist of just television stations, but rather the entire media ecosystem, including cable and the Internet. As a result, he concludes that the 50 percent cap will specifically encourage consolidation and that is a preferred outcome so stations can more effectively compete in this definition of the relevant media ecosystem.

The broadcasters go even further. In March 2019, twelve broadcast groups, including Nexstar and Tribune, introduced a filing with the FCC, saying that the national cap should be 78 percent—twice the present limit. They said that the increase should be the least the FCC could do (Eggerton 2019h).

The broader definition of the relevant competitive media market that Fratrik espouses was the subject of a two-day workshop convened by Makan Delrahim, the antitrust chief of the Department of Justice, in May 2019. Its purpose was to examine the impact of online advertising on the local broadcast television market. His remarks seemed to split the difference between a broad and more narrow definition of the relevant competitive media market. "He extolled the virtues of ad-supported content while he also acknowledged the rise of digital competitors. However, he said that it was not clear how much of a substitute online ads were for broadcast ad buys" (Eggerton 2019b, 1). The conclusion that I draw from Delrahim's comments is that the Department of Justice is still trying to understand how different media channels (defined broadly as broadcast and digital) compete.

FCC Commissioner Michael O'Rielly makes the same argument about what the FCC should consider as the relevant competitive market in its quadrennial review of broadcast ownership. In addressing the National Association of Broadcasters State Leadership Conference in Washington, DC, in late February 2019, the commissioner urged the broadcasters to engage policymakers to advance their views of the ownership issue. By so doing, "it will allow the Commission to jettison its myopic vision that broadcasters experience little competition in favor of one that recognizes the fulsome competitive forces in the current marketplace" (quoted in Eggerton 2019f, 1). O'Rielly urged broadcasters to address the quadrennial review process even if they had no intention to merge with anyone because it is in their interest to have the FCC view the marketplace broadly and that will have an impact on regulatory—"and hopefully deregulatory"—actions (1).

While O'Rielly's vision represents a fundamental change in the FCC's conception of the competitive marketplace, it has taken steps within the current rubric to assist broadcasters. One of those steps in October 2017 was the elimination of the main studio rule, which mandated that a television broadcast station had to maintain a studio located in or near its community of license. It had been a requirement for decades. Specifically, the agency eliminated "the requirement that the main studio have full-time management and staff present during normal business hours and that it have program origination capability" (Federal Communications Commission 2017, 1). The FCC made an economic argument. The main studio costs money and broadcasters could use the savings in other ways including equipment upgrades and news-gathering. It even suggested that repealing the rule "will encourage the launch of new broadcast stations in small towns and rural areas and help prevent existing stations in those areas from going dark" (1). Further, the FCC asserted that, as communications technologies have advanced, the public would be unlikely to visit the station as there are more efficient means—telephone, email, social media—to contact the station.

The FCC has it backwards. The real purpose of being in the community of license is not so the community can reach the studio, it is so the studio can reach the community. A fundamental ownership regulating principle of the FCC is localism. How can that possibly happen without the broadcaster actually being local? How can the broadcaster understand the needs of the community if it is not there? How can the broadcaster respond to the citizen information needs that the FCC's very own research identifies as critical? The FCC has an answer for that. The same technology that allows for community-to-station communication will be used for station-to-community purposes. Problem solved.

The FCC's actions under Ajit Pai during the first two years of the Trump presidency should be seen in an historical context. In very real ways, Pai's FCC has returned the agency to its stance on media regulation that was affirmed in the Telecommunications Act of 1996, a stance that favored market rather than regulatory instruments to determine the nature of telecommunications in the United States. Media scholar Ben Scott (2004) points out, though, that approach changed after the FCC's disastrous attempt in 2003 to relax broadcast ownership limits. The new rules were not routine because they amounted to a "striking change in the structure of the media system" (645). They permitted "a substantially increased media concentration in local and national television markets, tilting market conditions to favor larger firms and conglomerates" (645–646). Public response to the new rules was overwhelmingly negative as, "remarkably, the policies and regulations which shape the media system became political issues for the American people . . . something that had not happened for seventy years since the FCC was formed" (646). As you might imagine, Congress got the message, and in a bipartisan effort moved to oppose the changes. The rule changes were a "flashpoint where the political objectives of media policy most recently reaffirmed by the architects of the Telecommunications Act of 1996 collided with the sensibilities (political and otherwise) of the American public" (647). As a result, FCC broadcast ownership policy and the public viewed media concentration in the hands of a few large corporations as not a good idea. There is the argument that, even with political sensibilities about media consolidation, the FCC failed to enforce its own rules and "covert consolidation" continued throughout the period when the FCC was, nominally, concerned about the phenomenon (Turner 2014). But that changed when Donald Trump became president. That *nominal* concern about consolidation went out the window.

Consolidation Continues

Consolidation has been a fact in the television broadcast industry for a long time. It did not just increase since the new FCC came into power. In fact, the year that had the highest total value for television station mergers and acquisitions was 2006 at over $18 billion (Matsa and Fedeli 2018). That activity was due to the major broadcast television realignment that occurred in which the two second-tier broadcast networks, UPN and WB, ceased to exist and their operations were transferred to the CW Network (which stands next to ABC, CBS, Fox, and NBC). In that sense, the activities of that year represented an outlier in the mergers and acquisitions history.

That history notwithstanding, the actions by the new FCC since 2017 have created an environment that virtually guarantees consolidation. In fact, that seems to be the FCC's underlying purpose. What better way to allow market forces to work than to remove all the barriers to their actions? That is a long-standing and sincere belief of Chairman Pai, which he has articulated forcefully over time. From that position, the FCC has created the conditions that media firms, hedge funds, and other potential station group owners will use to their advantage.

Looking at the activity over the past couple of years: Sinclair is out, but everybody else is in. Perry Sook, of super-group prediction fame, is now the president of Nexstar Media Group. After the Sinclair/Tribune fiasco, Sook recalculated what was possible in the market. Now, instead of being a possible target of hedge fund buyers, Nexstar would be a prominent buyer itself. And there was no better target than Tribune. In 2019 Nexstar agreed to buy Tribune in a $6.4 billion deal. The FCC approved the merger in September 2019 after Nexstar divested itself of some stations in order to comply with FFC ownership rules. In the end, the deal was worth $7.1 billion, and it makes Nexstar the largest broadcast company in history with the control of 197 full-power stations in 115 television markets. Given its size, Nexstar now reaches over 60 percent of US television households (Eggerton 2019d). Nexstar calculated that the deal would result in $160 million in reduced costs and added revenue. Another advantage of the deal would allow Nexstar to impose its retransmission fee rates to the Tribune stations bringing a gain of $75 million (Lafayette and Eggerton 2018). With the deal, Sook characterizes Nexstar as the "industry's leading consolidator" (6).

The logic of consolidation is such that, as large station groups become even larger, what were once medium-sized station groups must follow suit or risk being overwhelmed. The leverage that these firms have in negotiating retransmission fees with cable and satellite systems and the cost of political ads with sponsors is greatly enhanced by the size of the group. And, as I mentioned, these two sources of revenue have become absolutely fundamental to the bottom line of the stations.

In keeping with that logic, "another regional television station owner will become a national powerplayer" (Tompkins 2018, 1). In June 2018 Gray Television announced the $3.6 billion purchase of Raycom, making it the third-largest station group (behind Nexstar and Sinclair) with 142 stations in 92 television markets. In addition, in February 2019, Gray purchased three television stations from United Communications, bringing its total to 145 stations, for $45 million as that company left the broadcast ownership market (Miller 2019c).

Let's take stock of those numbers. The FCC states that as of March 31, 2018, there were 1,375 full power commercial stations in the United States. The mergers have been approved and Nexstar, Sinclair, and Gray now control a combined total of 552 of those stations. That means that these three station groups will control over 40 percent of the television stations in the country. In 2016 five station groups controlled 37 percent of the stations. In less than three years, things will have changed drastically as the consolidation takes the course that the FCC has opened for it.

In addition to these transactions, in October 2018, E. W. Scripps Company purchased the fifteen television stations in ten markets from Cordillera Communications for $521 million. That will give Scripps fifty-one stations in thirty-six markets. The deal will leave Cordillera with one remaining station in Tucson, Arizona. Scripps did not buy that station because it already owns a duopoly in the market (Micheli 2018). Scripps's consolidation plans were clear as President and CEO Adam Symson stated that the acquisition will benefit the company's portfolio to "pursue incremental and transformative deals for television stations" (2). Translation: Scripps understands the "go big or go home" nature of the local television station market.

Apollo Global Management, LLC is a private equity firm and it is "lining up to become a force in U.S. broadcasting" (Baker and Roumeliotas 2019, 1). Previously, in separate attempts, it had tried to acquire both Nexstar and Sinclair—a private equity firm that wanted to go "all in" in its bid to enter the television station marketplace, setting its sights on the largest station groups. In fact, before the Sinclair/Tribune deal exploded, there was speculation that Nexstar would be a prime target because it had lost out on its own earlier bid to acquire Tribune. Once the Sinclair deal crashed and burned, Nexstar transformed from a possible target of a private equity buyer to a buyer itself. Apollo's failure to get Nexstar or Tribune did not stop its interest in local television stations. In February 2019, it announced a deal worth about $3 billion to own Cox Enterprises' fourteen regional television stations, as Cox is another station group that is leaving the market. It is Apollo's biggest move to date to enter the television station marketplace.

Interestingly, Apollo could still benefit from the Nexstar/Tribune deal. Ownership deals have a domino effect as the FCC's regulations that govern television ownership limit the number of stations that can be controlled by one entity in a market. Apollo is a bidder for a portfolio of stations worth about $1 billion that Nexstar plans to shed in order to comply with those limits (Baker and Roumeliotas 2019; Ahmed and Porter 2019).

Consolidation Comes to a Screeching Pause

The deregulatory scheme that Pai's FCC had put in place since January 2017 was dealt a very serious blow on September 23, 2019. The US Third Circuit Court of Appeals in Philadelphia ruled, in a 2:1 decision, against the FCC in a challenge to Pai's decision "to eliminate the broadcast-newspaper ownership rule, allow dual station ownership in markets with fewer than eight independent voices after that duopoly created an opportunity for ownership of two of the top four stations in a market on a case-by-case basis (the FCC was not calling it a waiver); and eliminate the attribution of joint sales agreements as ownership; and created a diversity incubator program" (Eggerton 2019a, 1).

This was the fourth time in sixteen years that the Third Circuit Court had heard cases on the FCC's ownership rules, all brought by the same set of petitioners led by Prometheus Radio Project. The FCC lost in each case.

The court issued the ruling saying that the FCC "did not adequately consider the effect of its sweeping rule changes will have on ownership of broadcast media by women and racial minorities" (quoted in Eggerton 2019a, 1). The court, as it had done previously, remanded the issues back to the FCC to find a remedy.

Although the decision decisively vacated Pai's deregulatory scheme, a partial dissent by one of the three judges hearing the case, Anthony Scirica, echoed the same argument that Pai had been making for years. Indeed, the judge said that he would have the FCC ownership rules go into effect: "The realities of operating a viable broadcasting enterprise today looks little like they did when the FCC enacted the current ownership rules. Despite all this, the FCC's broadcast ownership rules remained largely static for fifteen years" (quoted in Eggerton, 2019a, 3). Indeed, the court offered a road map to a successful remand:

> We vacate the Reconsideration Order and the Incubator Order in their entirety, as well as the "eligible entity" definition from the 2016 Report & Order. On remand the Commission must ascertain on record evidence the likely effect of any rule changes it proposes and whatever "eligible entity" definition it adopts on ownership by women and minorities, whether through new empirical research or an in- depth theoretical analysis. If it finds that a proposed rule change would likely have an adverse effect on ownership diversity but nonetheless believes that rule in the public interest all things considered, it must say so and explain its reasoning. If it finds that its proposed definition for eligible entities will not meaningfully advance ownership diversity, it must explain why it could not adopt an alternate definition that would do so. Once again, we do not prejudge the outcome of any of this, but the Commission must provide a substantial basis and justification for its actions whatever it ultimately decides. (3)

The FCC is seeking to reinstate Pai's deregulatory scheme. It filed a petition for review on November 7, 2019, in which it argued that the issue should be decided by the full court rather than the three-judge panel who issued the ruling (Eggerton 2019e). That was denied on November 20, 2019. There is too much money at stake, not to mention Pai's genuinely held faith in market mechanisms. In fact, the day after the court issued its ruling in September 2019, the FCC approved a deal that would be prohibited by the court's actions. The FCC approved Gray Television's purchase of a broadcast station in Sioux Falls, South Dakota, owned by Red River Broadcast. The purchase created the ownership of two top-rated stations by the same entity in a small market. In granting its approval, the FCC stated that the court's mandate had not gone into effect, and "Furthermore, the commission intends to seek review of that decision" (Jessell 2019a).

The spokesperson for the Commission was exactly right. While the two Democratic FCC Commissioners (Jessica Rosenworcel and Geoffrey Starks) praised the ruling, the three Republicans (Chairman Pai, Michael O'Rielly, and Brendan Carr) were outraged. They had strong language for the court. Commissioner O'Rielly called the ruling "a classic case of judicial activism and legislating from the bench" (O'Rielly 2019, 1). And he implored the chairman to take the case to the US Supreme Court. He expanded his criticism beyond the case at hand to the entire judicial branch of government. The ruling, he said, "further justifies the ongoing fight for reforming the judiciary" (1). That seems to be a remarkable step to take.

Chairman Pai (2019, 1) was also blunt, specifically expressing his frustration with the court:

> For more than twenty years, Congress has instructed the Federal Communications Commission to review its media ownership regulations and revise or repeal those rules that are no longer necessary. But for the last fifteen years, a majority of the same Third Circuit panel has taken that authority for themselves, blocking any attempt to modernize these regulations to match the obvious realities of the modern media marketplace. It's become quite clear that there is no evidence or reasoning—newspapers going out of business, broadcast radio struggling, broadcast TV facing stiffer competition than ever— that will persuade them to change their minds. We intend to seek further review of today's decision and are optimistic that the views set forth today in Judge Scirica's well-reasoned opinion ultimately will carry the day.

On December 23, 2019, it reinstated the ownership rules that the Third Circuit required only because it had to do it. The FCC made it clear by its actions and its official response to the ruling by the Republican majority about its intentions. This is not a halt to the FCC's deregulatory path, it is just a pause.

Why Buy Local Television Stations?

Why would private equity firms find local television stations appealing? Why would local television station groups want to get bigger? Why would they assume the billions of dollars of debt to consolidate? Because there is money to be made. Local TV stations "are prime targets of private equity firm buyouts because they are reliable cash generators that require little capital expenditure" (Sherman 2018, 2). The control of many stations gives station groups and private equity firms significant leverage in negotiating the twin and growing revenue streams of political ads (Nichols and McChesney 2013) and the cash-rich retransmission fees (Baker and Roumeliotas 2019). The retransmission fees, as mentioned earlier, are projected to be almost $13 billion by 2023.

The cash-producing capacity of retransmission fees may be the real jewel in the deals that private equity firm Apollo Global Management is considering as it is works to construct a large, new station group by combining all of the stations of Cox Media Group and Northwest Broadcasting. That is because Apollo will take advantage of the "after-acquired" clauses in retransmission contracts that station groups have with cable and satellite systems. They are applied when station groups are consolidated. This provision allows for the imposition of the higher retransmission fees of one station group to be implemented for all of the newly acquired stations. That results in a huge jump in cash flow for the new buyers. That is precisely what media commentator Harry Jessell (2019b) suggests might be happening in the Apollo/Cox/Northwest deal. He points out that the owner of Northwest Broadcasting, Brian Brady, may have negotiated some of the most lucrative retransmission deals in the nation and, upon completion of the merger, those fees would automatically be used by all of the Cox stations. Jessell surmises that, "what Apollo is buying from Northwest is not TV stations or Brady's genius at running TV stations; it's buying Brady's retrans contracts" (2).

An increasing number of US television consumers are cutting the cable cord. In 2018, cord cutters numbered 33 million people (about 13 percent of people eighteen and older). Yet in that same year, about 187 million people were still watching cable, satellite, or telco-provided pay TV (Perez 2018). Projections are that by 2022, there will be over 55 million cord cutters, but that would still only be about 21 percent of the adult population (Perez 2018). That is important because it means that the risk that station groups and private equity firms are taking in gobbling up television stations is a good one, because as long as there are cords, there will be retransmission fees. Further, as long as those cords represent viewers on the other end, political ads will be there, too.

Of course, there is the argument that as streaming technology and social media become the locus of consumption for content and political ads, the bonanza that retransmission fees from cable and political ads presently deliver will shrivel. But the near- and mid-term prospects are very good, and, frankly, I do not know if any private equity firm that wants to own television stations right now is looking beyond that timeline. For example, in April 2019, seven publicly traded station groups registered double digit stock price gains year to date, three of which were over 50 percent—Nexstar, Gray, and Scripps. Five others had gains of over 20 percent (Seyler 2019).

In addition to the political ads and retransmission factors, station owners are "feeling pressure from networks and syndicators to pay more for programming" (Tompkins 2018, 2). Just like the retransmission and political ad negotiations, larger station groups are in a much better position to hammer out better deals for themselves. Further, technology provides stations with opportunities to create hubs for some station operations such as master control, graphics production, business offices, and recruiting. From an organizational standpoint, larger station groups can provide upward mobility for staff to move from smaller to larger markets (Tompkins 2018).

Political ad and retransmission revenue, programming costs, and organizational economies of scale are here-and-now reasons for consolidation. What about the long term? Poynter's Al Tompkins (2018) asks, why would anybody buy television stations when younger audiences are increasingly turning away from the medium, especially local TV news? He makes the crucial point that the real opportunity for big media owners may not be in the present but in the future as over-the-top (OTT) viewership will grow. OTT is that content that comes to the viewer over the top of the cable box. Think Netflix, Hulu, and the like. Younger audiences definitely know that method of consuming content. OTT will deliver a whole new advertising model for local broadcasters and they can take advantage of it because they already produce the content that can easily be delivered through OTT. That delivery model "puts them on the same footing as social media and search engines in being able to deliver micro-targeted advertising" (5). Of course, the success in achieving and maintaining any audience, of whatever age, comes down to the content—What is required to make local television news desirable to young people? I will talk about that in the next chapter.

The Effects of Consolidation

The FCC bases its regulation of broadcast media on three principles: diversity, competition, and localism. As the principles are applied, they only have meaning in the 210 television markets across the United States—that is, their effect is local. The question is whether or not a television market is sufficiently diverse, sufficiently competitive, and arranged to sufficiently cover local issues to serve the audience in that market. Therefore, any arrangement that consolidates stations in television markets must be evaluated against those principles.

However, the FCC has never been very clear on what the adherence to those principles means in practical terms. For example, what does diversity mean? Diversity of owners? Diversity of points of view? If we look at the competition, the television markets in the United States are oligopolies rather than fully competitive markets with a few major firms dominating the playing field. Localism has been the least studied of the principles and, arguably, it has suffered the most from a lack of clarity (Napoli 2004). But even with this ambiguity, there are attributes of consolidated markets whose effect on the principles are apparent. I mentioned some of my own work previously, and I make the point that the nature of the consolidation that has been implemented by television station groups is perfectly consistent with the profit-maximizing calculus that the station groups, as private firms, apply to the transactions. There have been other critiques.

Stucke and Grunes (2009), writing at the beginning of the Obama presidency, argued that the FCC must look beyond what mergers might do to advertising rates and it must examine how the merger might affect the marketplace of ideas. Their critique is clear: "One cannot rely on flawed laissez-faire beliefs that unregulated market forces will provide the efficient level of information. Nor can one assume that the current haphazard patchwork of media policies will remedy the current ailments in the media industry today or promote the unrestrained flow of information" (52).

A media consultant who asked that his identity remain confidential told media scholar Bob Papper, "From the viewer's perspective, there's no upside to consolidation" (quoted in Van Zuylen-Wood 2017, 11). But, "for the stations, it has been a windfall" (11). That said, 54 percent of the marketing directors of stations say that ownership consolidation is not good for business; about 30 percent are unsure, and only about 15 percent say that it is good for business (Greeley 2014).

David Scott, Robert Gobetz, and Mike Chanslor (2008) found that there was a difference in the performance of television stations that were owned by large chains and independent owners. The independent stations—what the authors called small station groups—produced more local news, more local video, used more on-air reporters and had fewer news promotions than chain-based broadcast groups.

Those findings were also consistent with a five-year study carried out by the Project for Excellence in Journalism (PEJ) in which it found that smaller station groups "overall tended to produce higher quality newscasts than stations owned by larger companies—by a significant margin . . . stations with cross-ownership—in which the parent company also owns a newspaper in the market—tended to produce higher quality newscasts" (Pew Research Center 2003, 2). As PEJ found a higher quality of news with cross-ownership, Yan found that cross-ownership had no significant effect on the presence or quantity of local public affairs programming on commercial television (Yan 2006).

According to Michael Yan and Yong Park (2005), duopoly stations significantly increased their local news programming between 1997 and 2003, but so did nonduopoly stations located in duopoly and nonduopoly markets. They found that, contrary to the argument that relaxing ownership rules to allow joint ownership would increase local news, no such increase occurred in the minor stations to the deal.

PEJ also found that "local ownership did not protect against newscasts being very poor and did not produce superior quality" (Pew Research Center 2003, 2). That is, the argument that local control also means better quality was not borne out by the research.

PEJ asks the question regarding an ideal ownership type. Its findings suggest that different ownership structures have virtues as well as weaknesses. For example, they found that stations that were owned and operated by the networks to which they were affiliated had a variety of viewpoints on the newscasts, but the quality of their newscasts was mediocre. Likewise, small station group companies were the best in overall newscast quality, but mid-sized station groups had more enterprise reporting as well more local coverage (Pew Research Center 2003). Pew contended that ownership does matter. But, even with these caveats, it expressed concern with the concentration of "vast numbers of TV stations into the hands of a very few very large corporations . . . and though it may prove the most profitable model, [it] is likely to lead to further erosion in the content and public interest value of the local TV news Americans receive" (8). Pew's warnings came in 2003—much before the consolidation among full-power commercial stations that I previously presented.

To this point, I have talked about ownership and content. Yet there was a demonstration of what was possible among large media corporations when it came to advertising. In 2018, the US Department of Justice filed an antitrust suit against seven media companies, including the two largest, Nexstar and Sinclair, for anticompetitive exchanges of sensitive advertising information. The purpose of the exchanges was to manipulate the advertising rates in the markets in which they operated, thereby negating the competition that would naturally occur in a competitive market. It was a neat trick. Eliminate competition and then charge advertisers whatever rate they wanted. The Department of Justice antitrust division chief, Makan Delrahim, commented, "robust competition among broadcast stations allows American businesses to obtain competitive advertising rates. The unlawful sharing of information reduced that competition and harmed businesses and the consumers they serve" (quoted in Eggerton 2018c, 1).

All of the companies settled with the Department of Justice in December 2018. But none of the settlements included a fine. As the saying goes, no harm, no foul.

Think about the sheer hubris of those arrangements. They included seven major station groups—along with Nexstar and Sinclair there were Raycom, Tribune, Meredith, Griffin and Dreamcatcher—all colluding to eliminate the fundamental feature of a competitive market. And all, at one point or another in presenting themselves to the public, espouse the fundamental virtue of the market as the best means to deliver quality programming to the public.

Beyond content and advertising, there is one aspect of consolidation where economies of scale are the most visible and effective—jobs. The shared services agreement in Honolulu resulted in the loss of about one-third of the jobs at the combined stations. The shared services agreement between Fisher Communications and New Press Gazette in Idaho Falls, Idaho, came with the loss of twenty-seven jobs (Ariens 2011). In 2011, almost immediately after Citadel Communications in Bronxville, New York, bought WLNE, Channel 6 in Providence, Rhode Island, positions such as chief engineer, news photographer and audio engineer, and other technical positions were eliminated (Derderian 2011).

It is difficult to determine the overall extent of job losses due to consolidation because, as we might expect, the stations understandably do not make that information available. However, it is safe to say that the economies of scale that they seek in the consolidation arrangements are most immediately realized as they reduce staff.

I would be remiss if I did not acknowledge that station owners as well as the National Association of Broadcasters (NAB) make the claim that there are advantages to local television markets that consolidation can bring. The most important among them is the claim that smaller stations in small markets could not survive "and would have no news at all without the financial support of a stronger broadcast partner" (Eggerton 2011, 1). That may be the case, and, although I have not seen it, I would be very happy to find it.

Profits of the Big Three

We can see how well the station groups are doing within the context of the media space that they dominate, especially the three largest who control 40 percent of the full-power commercial stations in the country.

Nexstar, the largest station group, saw its revenue grow by 22 percent in the fourth quarter of 2018—to $798 million—over the same period in 2017. The real story is where that revenue came from. For the first time, revenue from retransmission fees (up 12.3 percent) exceeded television ad revenue. So, retransmission was more important to the bottom line than the historical revenue leader. Further, political ad revenue reached $140 million—an increase of 1,020 percent (Miller 2019e). For sure, that reflects the activity of political ad sponsors during the 2018 midterm election, while 2017 was a nonelection year. That is my point—retransmission fee and political ads are critical factors in the profitability of station groups. By its own assessment, Nexstar foresees continued record performance as it announced a 20 percent increase in the quarterly cash dividend to its shareholders (Miller 2019e). And these are Nexstar's numbers *before* it will have taken over Tribune.

Then, there is Sinclair, the second largest station group. Even though it suffered the loss of the Tribune deal, it also did well in 2018. Its fourth quarter revenue of $893.3 million represented an increase of 25.4 percent over that same period in 2017 (Miller 2019h). In the fourth quarter of 2018, Sinclair posted almost $150 million in political ads revenue compared to $15.5 million in the same period in 2017 (Lafayette 2019). In fact, CEO Chris Ripley is already looking forward to political ad spending in 2020: "Building on the base of $255 million in political ads spending for 2018 and a number of candidates already declaring their candidacy for the presidency, we expect 2020's political advertising to be yet another record year for us" (quoted in Miller 2019h, 2). In the third quarter of 2018, its retransmission revenue was up 12 percent from 2017 to $116.6 million (Lafayette 2018b).

Gray Television is the third station group among the big three, with its acquisition of Raycom. Its 2018 fourth quarter revenue grew by 40 percent to $328.2 million, over the same period in 2017, mostly due to political ads and increased retransmission fees. Political ad revenue increased over 1,000 percent to $83.2 million; retransmission fees brought in $93 million, a 34 percent increase. However, Gray also stated that after it subtracted reverse compensation payments, its net retransmission revenue came to $50.3 (Miller 2019d).

The "go big or go home" mantra was not lost on other station groups. Scripps (Miller 2019g) and Tegna (Miller 2019f) reported similar increases in revenue in the fourth quarter of 2018 over the same quarter in 2017. As expected, increased revenue for political ads between an election and non-election year did drive some of that increase. But, as for the largest station groups, the increase in retransmission fees was a major contributor to fourth quarter performance.

Summary

You might ask why I included the discussion of ownership and consolidation when only two of the ten markets that I studied had a measure of consolidation. In Raleigh, Capital Broadcasting owned and operated both WRAL and WRAZ. Likewise, in Cedar Rapids, Sinclair owned KGAN, but it also controlled the programing of KFXA through a local marketing agreement with its owner, Second Generation of Iowa, Ltd. The performance of the stations in covering the presidential and down-ballot campaigns was dismal. And that was under conditions that were relatively not consolidated. For sure, there were economic imperatives that the stations faced, and they certainly affected their coverage.

The fundamental tension between seeing the media as a profit-making enterprise or a trustee of the public interest continues to be the subject of intense debate, as it has been for decades. The present majority of the FCC decidedly favors the market model for delivering news and information to the public. Although it has been thwarted in the short run of pursuing that vision of the media by a court ruling, it is intent on implementing polices that will make the market model dominant. With Ajit Pai's appointment as FCC Chair by Donald Trump and the Republican majority that created among the five FCC commissioners, it has moved forcefully to make that happen.

The broadcasting policy decisions of the FCC have their most significant impact in the 210 television markets in the United States. That is, their effect is local—the local media system, the local information that citizens must have to pursue their daily lives. The local television space will become even more consolidated than it is now for all of the reasons I mentioned earlier—the new FCC rules (even with the pause in their implementation), the economies of scale, the virtual certainty of profits. As that happens, it will have a dramatic effect on the coverage of political campaigns and what information citizens receive.

Conclusion

Where Do We Go from Here?

The state of affairs in which we find ourselves regarding political ads, news content and money is the result of: (1) our politics which are based on what Francis Lee (2016) described as "insecure majorities"; (2) a political campaign finance system that almost guarantees that version of politics; and (3) a media system that benefits greatly from both our politics and campaign finance system. They seem like the attributes of a perfect storm.

Politics as Insecure Majorities

Former Speaker of the House John Boehner's letter in 2006 to his House Republican colleagues regarding minority status states: "What is the job of [a] Republican leader in the minority? It's to hold the job for as short a time as possible" (quoted in Lee 2016, 42).

Francis Lee (2016) gives Boehner's comment historical perspective. Over time, particularly since 1932, Democrats controlled the House and Senate for nearly fifty years. They were "by all appearances, the nation's party" (1). However, that has changed drastically since 1980. Between 1980 and 2016, the Democrats and Republicans have held the presidency about half of the time; the Senate majority has changed hands seven times, and in the House, the majority shifted three times during which time the Democrats and Republicans held the majority for nine Congresses. Therefore, every election has the potential of changing party control over major national political institutions. These competitive circumstances, according to Lee, have left their mark on political incentives in Washington: "Intense party competition for institutional control focuses members of Congress on the quest for partisan political advantage. When party control seemingly hangs in the balance, members and leaders of both parties invest in more enterprises to promote their party's image and undercut that of the opposition . . . the primary way that parties make an electoral case for themselves vis-à-vis their opposition is by magnifying their differences" (2).

When the majority is insecure and the possibility of control over the institution is in play, politics is played as a zero-sum game in which bipartisan efforts are the victim. In this version of politics, it is simply not in the minority party's interest to engage in bipartisan efforts to pass legislation or any other positive action because the credit for such an outcome will necessarily redound to the majority party. That legislative or policy success only serves to legitimate the control of the majority party. If that happens, it is much harder to claim to the voters that the majority must be thrown out and replaced by the minority party. Not only has this approach to politics taken root at the national level, it has also occurred in states in which two parties are competitive and where the legislatures are polarized by party (Lee 2016).

There is a corollary to this competitive environment that, at first, seems counterintuitive. That is, there was more bipartisan cooperation when the majorities were secure. Members and leaders had little reason to invest in partisan efforts when there was little chance that control would change. "A secure party behaves differently from a party that fears losing power. A minority party, optimistic about winning a majority, behaves differently from a hopeless minority" (Lee 2016, 4). It is in both of their interests to make the institution work.

But that is not the case now. Not by a long shot.

The rise of this competitive atmosphere has amplified the critical importance of getting the party's message out and that has sparked the creation and institutionalization of sophisticated public relations operations. The parties are highly proactive in making their case to the voters about why they should stay in power (if they are) or why they should be in power (if they are not). That message cannot be left to the whims of media coverage. That message requires the singularly proactive efforts of skilled public relations professionals.

Firstly, there is advertising—creating a favorable image but having nothing to do with issue content. It is also useful in tarnishing the opposition party's image. Secondly, there is credit claiming and blaming where parties claim credit for good policies and blame the other party for bad policies. Thirdly, the messages can stake out and communicate a position the party takes on an issue. The fundamental purpose of the messages is to make the case for the party to stay in power or to wrest power from the majority. It is not a process given to compromise. In fact, just the opposite (Lee 2016).

One of the consequences—or, should I say, tactics—of that effort is the rise of the partisan message vote—"votes staged for the purpose of highlighting the differences between the parties with no expectation of influencing outcomes" (Lee 2016, 6). And, "members and leaders who want to amplify the differences the voters perceive between the parties need to provoke partisan fights, not tamp them down" (49).

Former California Republican Congressman Elton Gallegy wrote an op-ed as he retired from the Congress in 2013. He was direct: "Today, Congress is constantly campaigning. Governing has fallen by the wayside" (quoted in Lee 2016, 49). It is a sobering conclusion from someone on the inside of the institution.

The competitive environment that Lee characterizes is seen as toxic by long-time congressional scholars Thomas Mann and Norman Ornstein (2013). In *It's Even Worse Than It Looks*, they conclude that the Congress has moved way beyond just competition. It has moved to the "new politics of hostage taking" (14). To illustrate their point, they recount the debt limit crisis of 2011. By way of context, the debt limit is a device to allow the Congress to issue longer-term debt instruments. The vote to extend the limit should be perfunctory because it refers to debts that *have already been incurred*. Politicians have often railed against it, but that opposition was substantively meaningless because the United States had to pay its debts. Otherwise, the full faith and credit of the United States would be damaged. Therefore, votes to extend the limit, although partisan and often with thin majorities, were taken under Democratic and Republican administrations. The looming possibility that the country would default on its debt virtually guaranteed that no one would want to go over that fiscal cliff.

But that is not how it played out in 2011. There was a new group of Republican lawmakers who called themselves the "Young Guns" who wanted to distinguish themselves from their older predecessors and their compromising politics. They were embracing confrontational politics. The Congress was obliged to have its vote regarding the raising of the debt limit. The "Young Guns" saw that vote as the perfect opportunity to implement their confrontational politics. They were going to use the vote as a way to enact more fundamental policy changes and they were so committed to that confrontation that they were perfectly willing to let the country default. A deal was reached two days before the deadline, but that did not stop a Standard and Poor's downgrade of the United States four days later. It cited the dysfunctional political process. It was the first time the United States suffered that fate.

What is striking about the episode is the willingness of members of Congress (particularly the Republicans) to place the permanent campaign above policy and that it was a perfectly acceptable course. Talking about the default issue, Senator Mitch McConnell (R, KY) said, "what we did learn is this—it's a hostage worth ransoming" (quoted in Mann and Ornstein 2013, 31). One of the so-called Young Guns, House Majority Whip Kevin McCarthy, went ominously further, "We weren't kidding around, either. We would have taken it down" (32).

Taken what down? The credit rating of the United States? Or was McCarthy referring to something more than the debt limit, as serious as that issue was? Was he referring to the policy-making apparatus of the Congress that, in the end, must rest on some basic level on compromise? He and his "Young Guns" colleagues were clear about their "win-at-all-costs" strategy. They told us in no uncertain terms—yes, they were willing to take it down and they were almost able to do it.

That approach prompted concerns for the Congress as an institution. Former Democratic Senator Paul Sarbanes of Maryland retired in 2006, but shortly before doing so he concluded: "There are fewer and fewer people in the Senate who think of it as an institution. They put first and foremost party allegiance" (quoted in Lee 2016, 204). From the other side of the aisle, Maine Republican Senator Susan Collins offered this indictment, "If I could compress all that has gone wrong in one phrase, it would be the perpetual campaign" (204).

Paying for Insecure Majorities

Now we have politics played as a toxic competitive game in which losing and winning have little to do with governing. To play that version of politics, you need money—which is where the campaign finance system in the United States comes in. That system, I maintain, perpetuates that version of politics.

Money has always been an integral part of political campaigns. But the new system that has come into being after the landmark decision of *Citizens United* in 2010 has changed the calculus (see chapter 3). That ruling and several others after it have introduced us to a campaign finance system that includes PACs, super PACS, nondisclosure of donors, dark money, joint fundraising committees and no real limits on contributions. Given the possibility that opponents can muster significant resources to challenge them, insecure incumbents spend a good deal of their time not legislating but raising money.

John Nichols and Robert McChesney (2013) provide one of the most insightful looks at the relationship between campaign financing and politics. They argue that we are late to the game in recognizing that our politics are corrupted by a system they identify as the "money and media election complex" that is "every bit as dismissive of the popular will as the military-industrial complex is" (18). This complex is comprised of a "set of commercial and institutional relationships involving wealthy donors, giant corporations, lobbyists, consultants, spinmeisters, corporate media, coin-operated think-tanks, inside-the-beltway pundits, and now super-PACs" (26). Their assessment of the effect on our democracy is harsh and unblinking. However, the comments from Senators Sarbanes and Collins fundamentally make the same point.

The Media and the Politics of Insecure Majorities

The politics of insecure majorities puts everything in play all of the time. There is the very real possibility in every election that the control of political institutions will change from one party to another. In fact, that has been the case for the last thirty-six years. And the money spent on campaign advertising has made that possible. Just consider the mid-term election of 2018. There were highly energized partisans on both sides of the Democrat/Republican fault line. Referring to the Congress, Donald Trump said that the race was about him. Incumbent Republicans whose positions were considered to be secure faced serious and well-financed challenges. Democrats who were on the bubble also felt the heat.

No race was more emblematic of that competitive reality than the contest for the Senate seat in Texas that was held by Ted Cruz. His Democratic challenger, Beto O'Rourke, raised almost $79 million to defeat him. Cruz spent $45 million to retain his seat. O'Rourke lost the election by just 2.6 percentage points, after an election night roller coaster ride that raised the possibility of a historic upset. O'Rourke swore off support from PACs, but almost 55 percent of his donations were large individual contributions whereas about 47 percent were small individual contributions (less than $200). For Cruz, those percentages were 43 percent and 31 percent, respectively. Whoever contributed to the campaigns, the local media benefitted handsomely. O'Rourke spent over $47 million (63 percent of the total expenditure) on the media; Cruz came in at $19.5 million (43 percent of his total) (OpenSecrets.org 2019).

Although O'Rourke did not accept contributions from PACs and super PACs, he was a clear beneficiary of their activity. For much of the race, an anti-Cruz organization, *Fire Ted Cruz PAC*, generated media attention in a series of online ads. Another anti-Cruz organization, a super PAC called *Texas Forever*, spent over $2 million in political ad buys (Svitek 2018). O'Rourke continued to say that he was not interested in this support. It came anyway, and it was mainly manifested in broadcasted political ads.

The fundraising of the O'Rourke campaign spooked Cruz and the Republican Party. Super PAC *Texans Are* spent about $5 million trying to level the playing field. In addition, the *Club for Growth*, a national anti-tax group, made a seven-figure investment to support Cruz (Svitek 2018).

In addition to the Texas Senate race, there were eight Republican House seats that were targeted by the Democrats and the outside spending for those races topped $13 million. When all was said and done, it was estimated that PACs and super PACs poured over $40 million into the state's election system (Svitek 2018).

And where did that money go? Overwhelmingly, it went to political ads on broadcast television.

In this view of things, I draw a straight line among the salient points of our present condition—the perpetual campaign pits insecure incumbents against political challengers because everything is in play for every election; incumbents and challengers and their surrogate supporters conduct politics with the sole purpose of winning, not governing, and they use a political campaign finance system to accomplish those ends; and they leverage a media system that is only too happy to accommodate the political advertising and the political coverage that are critical to the game because it makes them a lot of money.

Nichols and McChesney (2013) argue that, in the process of playing the political game, our media institutions do a terrible job in engaging the American public in political life. They are the immediate financial beneficiaries of an "absurd" election system that is based on their broadcasting of political campaign advertising. They embrace that election system because it makes them money—a lot of it.

Remember Les Moonves's comments in the introduction. Even he understood that the media system's approach to the campaign was "not good for America." But that did not matter. It was good for CBS, and by "good" he meant that the "money was rolling in." To be sure, money has always been a large part of campaigns and elections. But the present system relies so much on money that it endangers our capacities as citizens (Nichols and McChesney 2013).

Legendary CBS newsman Fred Friendly was asked in 1967 if there was anything seriously wrong with television. His answer was blunt and direct: "The heart of it is that television makes so much money doing its worst that it can't afford to do its best" (Friendly 1967, 58).

The Future of Local News

From the beginning, the question that prompted this book was about the political information system in local places, specifically about local television news. How do citizens learn about the candidates who would represent them? What information do citizens get that would help them hold their elected officials accountable? To help them make informed choices when casting their vote? That is particularly important now as almost seven in ten Americans say they suffer from news fatigue (Gottfried and Barthel 2018). Local journalism is at risk, more now than ever before. Journalism's losses, while significant at all levels, have been most deeply felt in local places.

My focus is on local television news because it is still the dominant source of local political information as I discuss in chapter 2. But there are serious indictments of its performance. Hanna Brooks Olsen (2017, 2) implores us to "stop watching your local news" because:

> Between the repetitive B-roll, the one-dimensional vox-pops and the cherry-picked experts, the underlying tone of many of the pieces was consistent: The world is both highly predictable but also in a state of flux. It is not what you think it is, and it's not how you remember it from when things were good, whenever that was. Crime is getting worse. Modern trends are necessarily worse than older ones. And that at the end of the day, the best way to solve your problems is not to vote, write your lawmakers, or get involved, but instead, to buy something.

But that presents the challenge. Local journalism is diminished to such an extent that we call it a crisis. Local news, "is both the type of journalism that's most endangered and the type most likely to build an informed and connected citizenry" (Green 2018, 1). Remember, the FCC said that local TV news is more important now that it ever has been. The necessity for its revitalization is much more than just a reference to building trust. Now, the clarion call is to rebuild the news itself. Finally, we come to addressing the elephant in the room.

Local television news sits in a strategic place in the struggle to revitalize local journalism. There are two aspects to that revitalization. The first is what local television news needs to look like in order to remain relevant for citizens—its production factors. The second is the structure that we would build in order to make local journalism sustainable and where local television fits into that picture. Let's consider them separately.

Innovating Local Television News

There is much to be done in local television news. It has important advantages. The first is that it is unscalable (Waldman 2015). Local is local. You could argue that the fact that it does not scale is a disadvantage, particularly when it comes to labor-intensive investigative reporting (Waldman 2011). That is certainly the case if we just look at the money. However, the very essence of local television news is that it is connected to the place in which it does its reporting. That is why the consolidation activities of station groups and the policies of the FCC that I discuss in chapter 7 are so devastating to the enterprise.

The Radio Act of 1927 and the Communications Act of 1934 both stipulated the standard that broadcasters, in exchange for their monopolies over parts of the airwaves, should operate in the public interest, convenience, and necessity. That obligation and the FCC's regulating principles of competition, diversity, and localism are manifest in local television markets. That is where the decisions of the FCC as well as the station groups have their most significant and meaningful effect. Local television can be a central actor in the effort to save local journalism. But it needs to change.

There is much activity to develop innovation in the local television news industry. The John S. and James L. Knight Foundation has been a major force in that effort. In 2018 it provided $2.6 million to five organizations to foster innovation. The bulk of that money, $1.9 million, went to the Walter Cronkite School of Journalism and Mass Communication at Arizona State University to promote innovation in three areas: experiments in television news broadcast formats and digital storytelling, a leadership program to promote digital transformation, and a digital hub that shares research and best practices.

Nieman Lab journalist Christine Schmidt (2019b) advances the idea that, as core resources of newsrooms are stretched, collaboration will be a core feature of newsroom work. That would certainly be an innovation as it would change the relationship among competitors in the television market. Local television stations are slow to adopt that strategy with cross-medium collaborators because there are inherent frictions—how news is defined, which story should be prominent. C. J. LeMaster, the chief investigative reporter for WLBT in Jackson, Missouri, points out that broadcasters are "stubborn . . . we like to stay in our silos but are still fiercely competitive among other stations. I think that hurts us in ways we could use opportunities for partnership with members of the print media and nonprofits" (quoted in Schmidt 2019b, 4). Extending that collaboration to other broadcast stations "when you're fighting for ratings is anathema to broadcasters," explains a spokesperson for the National Association of Broadcasters (4).

But even without collaboration, what should a "new" newscast look like to draw an audience that it presently does not have? Mike Beaudet and John Wihbey (2019), two researchers at Northeastern University conducted an experiment to learn how local television might engage younger viewers—and I might add other audiences, too. They worked with six television stations around the country and tested the effect on audiences of traditional news stories that were remixed, as they said, to look more like online content providers such as NowThis, Snapchat, Vice, and Vox than the traditional production of a local television news story. In the remixed versions of the stories they borrowed tactics from digital-native publications—incorporating animation, historical video, and animation. They showed the traditional and remixed stories to audiences in all six of the markets. The remixes for the soft and hard news stories had different resonances. The remix of the soft-news stories did not necessarily result in improved audience evaluations. But, and this is a big but, the remix certainly had an effect on the evaluations of the hard news stories—they improved. The remix not only added features to the storytelling but also increased the duration of the stories. As the authors pointed out, the findings, "were striking both in terms of the clear results and the implications for the type of news most vital to an informed democracy" (Beaudet and Wihbey 2019, 8).

To be sure, the experiment was limited. However, the authors made several suggestions for innovation to everyone in the newsroom: (1) take real risks, try something that is really new; (2) break the production mold, consider using graphics, animation, sound elements; (3) hire an animator; (4) infuse historical video to convey the whole story; (5) hire millennial and Gen Z journalists and involve them in all aspects of the newsroom; (6) tell relevant, innovative stories; (7) present your story in an authentic way; (8) achieve newsroom buy-in at all levels (Beaudet and Wihbey 2019).

Media scholars Debora Wenger and Bob Popper (2018) chronicle the awareness that some in local TV news understand about the future. In posing the question of change or die, they cite media executive Ellen Crooke's flint-eyed assessment: "We need to stop doing what we're doing. We say in our company that it's the 80/20 rule. Now maybe 20 percent (of what we're putting on air) is really interesting, and 80 percent is the commodity part of news—the standard crime and car crashes. We need to switch that around so that 80 percent is the really interesting part" (19). Wenger and Popper state that the change includes expanding investigative and enterprise reporting; hiring and training people with strong journalistic backgrounds; focusing on quality and accuracy; rewarding critical thinking in the newsroom; and diversifying the newsroom.

There is a particular attribute of local television news that gives it a path to create the innovation that it needs—it has pictures. Newspapers did not have that advantage. Television has always been about the pictures—often times to its detriment as it has substituted the picture over the narrative to tell citizens about important issues in their communities. We have all seen the dramatic video of the crime scene, the accident, and the fire as the anchor adds her voice to it. But that way to tell the story does not inform us. It just makes the story easier to sell to us so the station can sell us to their advertisers.

But television's pictures may be another important way to innovate. Over-the-top (OTT) media consumption has exploded in the last decade. That space is occupied by Netflix, Hulu, and Amazon among others. Tapping into OTT media consumption seems like a natural path for local television stations to distribute their content, particularly to younger viewers who have no experience with local television news. They are very much the audience that reflects the new relationship between news producers and news consumers. And, it is to that audience that local television news stations could directly stream their content. Bill Kovach and Tom Rosenstiel (2010) explain the change as moving from the "trust me" relationship of the old appointment news viewing behavior to the "show me" version in which news sources vie for our attention. This audience gets its news on demand using mobile devices. So, why not stream local news using that technology? The pictures are already there.

Some stations have experimented with the idea, but the results have been less than stellar (Jessell 2018). But there is a resurgence in local OTT services as stations begin to understand the potential it offers. In December 2018, CBS launched CBSN New York, a streaming news service, which provides content from its two New York stations. It is the first of the network's planned direct-to-consumer services that will offer anchored coverage of major news events in the markets in which the network has stations (Farrell 2018). It expanded to Los Angeles in June 2019 and Boston in September 2019. By early 2020 CBSN will be in all thirteen television markets in which CBS has a local television station. The remaining markets are Chicago, Philadelphia, Dallas-Fort Worth, San Francisco, Denver, Minneapolis-Saint Paul, Miami, Sacramento, Pittsburgh, and Baltimore (Miller 2019d). The network cites its commitment to local television news and the potential of digital systems. Mark Lund, president and general manager of WBZ and WSBK in Boston makes the point: "Our award-winning news department looks forward to providing comprehensive coverage of local stories to an even bigger audience thanks to this tremendous new distribution platform" (quoted in Miller 2019d, 2).

Sinclair too has expanded into streaming services. In January 2019 it launched STIRR, a free ad-supported streaming service that "combines content from a variety of national linear services, on-demand programming and local channel with material from the company's stations" (Lafayette 2019a, 1). Cox, Graham, and Gray are also considering streaming their content.

That said, media commentator Harry Jessell (2018) advises stations to pursue OTT streaming, but to lower their expectations that it would transform their business. He suggests that they "develop a local OTT news product that capitalizes on the medium's attributes—the ability to be live and on-demand at the same time, to reach viewers on multiple devices (TV sets, desktops and smartphones) and to keep in touch with younger viewers who are more prevalent in that universe" (4).

I agree with Jessell's overall caution. If stations can accomplish the innovations that I outlined previously, I think OTT can provide a significant boon to the future of local television. Just think—compelling storytelling combined with a promising way to engage a diverse audience.

But the innovations and making local journalism more viable will take money.

Paying for Local Journalism

It seems everyone now extolls the virtue of local journalism and the absolute necessity to bring it back. The money is impressive, as well as the commitment. The Knight Foundation has had a long and distinguished history in supporting journalism for communities. At the Knight Media Forum in February 2019, the participants focused on the importance and the urgency for community foundations and regional place-based funders to "rebuild healthy media ecosystems in the face of challenging trends in journalism" (Stehle 2019, 1). In fact, in the keynote address, Heinz Endowment President Grant Oliphant emphasized, "community, community, community is where we must and can do this work" (1).

And there have been major investments in that cause. The Knight Foundation doubled its contributions over the next five years to $300 million. Facebook said in January 2019 that it was committing $300 million to support news with an emphasis on local news. In 2018 Google distributed $16 million among various journalism nonprofit support organizations such as the Pulitzer Center, Report for America, the Local Media Association, the Local Media Consortium, and the American Journalism Project, among others (Schmidt 2019a). In late 2018 the Knight Foundation and the Lenfest Institute each contributed $10 million to support the Knight-Lenfest Newsroom Initiative, a Philadelphia-based collaboration first launched in 2015 as Table Stakes that included the newsrooms of four metropolitan newspapers to manage the transition to digital technology. The new initiative will include twelve newsrooms and create a technology resource hub (Schmidt 2018a).

Certainly, this largesse is welcome. However, there have been a number of attempts to finance local news that have not achieved their goals. Christine Schmidt (2018b) identifies them as:

For-profit newspaper and TV stations that siphoned off advertising dollars. She cites the experience of Tronc (the once and future Tribune Publishing) whose managers saw the newspapers as a financial asset rather than a civic-minded institution (Benton 2018).

Billionaire benefactors who don't always play nice. Example—in November 2018 billionaire Joe Ricketts abruptly shut down two popular local news networks that he funded because the employees voted to unionize.

Start-from-scratch scraggly independent outlets started by bought-out or laid-off reporters. These are the hyperlocal reporting outlets that came to life as reporters simply could not see themselves doing anything else but journalism.

A chain-based model scattered across towns with appealing demographics. The Patch experience is the most obvious example as it tried to literally "patch" together an army of journalists across twenty states (Doctor 2013).

Organizations drawing support solely from foundations and crossing fingers that it lasts. Further, foundations affect the "boundaries of journalism" (Scott, Bunce, and Wright 2019).

Chasing virality (although that goes for pretty much the entire news industry).

Given this litany of failures and difficulties, perhaps the most innovative approach to funding local journalism is *venture philanthropy* (Schmidt 2018b). Venture philanthropy occupies a middle ground between venture capital firms and foundations. In venture capital firms, the partners invest in promising startups for which they expect or hope for a payout in return. Foundations, on the other hand, make grants to organizations and do not expect a return on that investment aside from the public benefit that it generates. A venture philanthropy firm "draws in capital from mission-minded individuals or groups and invests in promising social enterprises while also heavily coaching them along the way—and not necessarily expecting a financial ROI [return on investment]" (Schmidt 2018b, 6). The American Journalism Project has already collected $42 million of its initial $50 million goal (Stehle 2019).

There is another idea about how to solve the local news crisis—treat it as a library. Journalist Don Day harkens back to the generosity of Andrew Carnegie who gave away 90 percent of his wealth. A major focus of that giving was 1,700 libraries in the United States. Day (2018) argues that libraries and journalism have much in common as institutions that bind the community together and serve information needs. His formula calls for the creation of an $8 billion fund that could generate 5.5 percent in dividends per year, $440 million. Using an average cost of $80,000 per reporter nationwide, the fund would provide support for journalists in each of the 210 television markets in the United States, based on their size. That would mean that in the largest market, New York, a news operation would have almost $28 million to spend each year on local news. In total, the fund would support annually almost five thousand journalists who would not be captured by the profit-making apparatus of private media firms.

Local Television in Local Journalism

All of this promise and activity, however, will benefit local television news only if it can reinvent itself. The foundation funds that are being made available, for the most part, will not go to local television stations. If local television news can accomplish the innovations that allow for collaboration with the local entities that will receive support, it can ride part of the local journalism revitalization wave. But I have my doubts. The head-long and continuing push toward consolidation in the local television space mitigates against that innovation because it costs money. In announcing the consolidation deals, the consolidators always state their commitment to advancing local journalism. That reference only occurs after they make the case for the economics of the deal—the returns on investment, the stock prices, the economies of scale. We should not be surprised by that claim or that calculus. Local television stations are private entities with a fiduciary responsibility to their stockholders. That is especially so as hedge funds increasingly become major players in the local television landscape. They are in it for the money. Therefore, their opportunities, let alone their suitability, to benefit from the infusion of money to support local journalism are constrained by their own design.

Political Ads Online?

My questions for the book revolved around the information that citizens got about political races from local television news. Even in this age of the Internet, it has remained a dominant source of local political news. Yes, television news is losing audience share, but that is happening slowly, and that loss is not evenly distributed among age groups or markets. And there is the drumbeat that political ads will move to the web. In fact, political consultant Marc Levitt (2018, 1) says that the "heyday of television ads is over and that politicians ought to act like it." He makes the charge that using television to broadcast political ads is the product of a "warped set of economic incentives" (1). Political consultants get paid a lot of money as part of the amount of television time that candidates purchase—"The more ads, the more income. Although this structure helps address the industry's usual risks—campaigns fold, paydays are sporadic—it creates a push to generate the most TV ads possible" (1). The economic incentives of the consulting industry drive up the costs of campaigns. Levitt predicts that these days are over as the political ad systems moves online.

Political ads will increasingly move to the web. And those ads will be personalized as campaigns will come to know much more about their ad targets. We already see that at work in the early stages of the 2020 campaign. As of the middle of September 2019 (fourteen months prior to the election), digital ads far outpace those on broadcast. At that point, about $61 million had been spent on Facebook and Google combined on presidential contenders. Trump lead the spending pack with almost $16 million. The closest to him was Tom Steyer at $6.6 million. Steyer is the billionaire who launched the media campaign to impeach Trump. The digital spending is compared to only $11.4 million spent on broadcast to that point (Wesleyan Media Project 2019).

But it is very early in the campaign and we should not be too hasty in writing off broadcast political ads, particularly for local races. BIA Advisory Services estimates that $6.55 billion will be spent on local political advertising in 2020 with almost half ($3.08 billion, 47 percent) going to over-the-air television. Online and digital outlets will realize about $1.37 billion or 21 percent (Miller 2019c). They also identify Los Angeles, Phoenix, and Philadelphia as the top political revenue generating markets in the country (Miller 2019c).

Former New York mayor and billionaire Michael Bloomberg has already shaken up the political ad spending calculus. Since joining the Democratic race in November 2019, he has spent an average of $25.5 million per week to influence Democratic voters. That level of spending dwarfs all of the other candidates' efforts. His activity has had a marked effect on political ad advertisement rates around the country, which have increased on average about 22 percent. In the Houston market his $1 million ad buy increased political spending in the market tenfold and caused advertising rates to soar by 45 percent, the highest of any market in the country (Campanile 2019).

Political ad expert, Steve Passwaiter, vice-president and GM of the research firm Kantar CMAG, echoes BIA's assessment that most of the political ad spending in 2020 will go to broadcast television. He puts the total political ad spend a bit lower (at $5.6 billion) with $3.2 billion going to television stations and cable and digital getting equal parts of the remaining $2.4 billion. But he cautions that broadcasting's share will fall from two-thirds of political ad spending in 2016 to about 57 percent in 2020 (Jessell 2019c).

Passwaiter also makes extremely important observations about the changes in which states are considered in the battleground group. Arizona, Florida, and North Carolina were battleground states in 2016. However, Iowa and others may draw more money than expected as the Democrats might think they can flip Georgia and Texas and the Republicans have their sights on New Mexico and Minnesota (Jessell 2019c). Presidential candidate Bernie Sanders made his first buy of television political ads to run in Iowa in the first two weeks of October 2019. The cost was $1.3 million (Eggerton 2019i).

All of this spending is for the presidential race. There is no information so far about the political ad spending for down-ballot races. Of course, it is much too early for that. As we saw in 2016, that is where the overwhelming majority of political ads were aired and where the political ad money was spent.

There is a feature of Internet ads that may mitigate their utility. They are presented through platforms that prey on what Nobel Prize winner Daniel Kahneman, in his research on human cognition, calls System One thinking—"fast instinctive thought, requiring minimal mental exertion or concentration, which makes the thinking process highly efficient, comes at the expense of errors that could be avoided by further reflection" (Ghonim 2018). System Two thought is that reflective process that demands further engagement. The personalized engagement-driven algorithms on which the Internet is based put a premium on that System One thinking. As such, attention to the ads might be fleeting, or avoided altogether. Who wants to stop for an ad, pushing whatever politician or platform, when you're in the middle of search for the latest gadget or news tidbit?

Television news is consumed differently. Each story or ad is seen in a series. In order to get to item three on the newscast, you must see items one and two. Chances are that the news consumer will see the entire ad—most probably several of them, one after the other, on the newscast. That is also the case with the stories on the broadcast. As the audience sees the ads, there is the possibility that a political story will also appear somewhere in the newscast that questions the claims of the ad or covers a public issue that the ads addressed. The audience would also see that story in the process of watching the newscast. Given what I found in this research, the chance of encountering and consuming such a story is slim. However, with the freedom of the click on the web, as users can avoid ads, so too can they avoid stories.

In the medium term—for the next two presidential election cycles—local television will still be a major player. I think that it will be a major player in down-ballot races for a longer period than that. Local television is the least ideological place to put political ads. By its very nature, it does not garner an audience that is identified with one political bent or another. Further, television reaches all of the households in the market in the political jurisdiction; the Internet reaches about 84 percent and cable, on average, reaches less than half.

Crucial Facts

First, there was a significant imbalance in how political ads were distributed across the presidential and down-ballot races—both in terms of the number of ads and the money that was spent to air them.

Second, the local television station owners accepted over $220 million in exchange for that airing. That money, realized in just sixty-four days, accounted for a significant proportion of their *yearly* revenue. For a station in Las Vegas, it was 35 percent.

Third, political ads were much more prominent, in terms of numbers and time, than political stories. That difference was vast when it came to the time devoted to political ads compared to the time devoted to political stories that addressed issues in the campaign.

Fourth, the stations made no investment in producing stories that critically examined the claims of the ads that appeared on their programs. The tension between profit and the public interest is most taut when it comes to balancing political ads and political stories. There is much money to be made in the political ad game. So much so that station groups have consolidated and assumed substantial debt to realize those profits. Even hedge funds are getting in on the action.

Fifth, even when the stations produced campaign stories, almost nine out of ten of them were directed at the presidential race. The down-ballot races were almost forgotten when it came to campaign stories. This may be indicative of the "nationalization" of journalism that may be taking place. Increasingly, as large station groups take over more stations to get even larger, there is an incentive to distribute production costs across as large an audience as possible. Virtually all of the political stories on the stations that were campaign status reports by network affiliate reporters were national stories that were repurposed for the local audience. They were simply introduced by the local anchor. But there was nothing "local" about them.

This "nationalization" of journalism is consistent with the "nationalization" of politics to which I referred previously. National candidates increasingly call for voters to support them by voting for local candidates who espouse their same political stance, regardless of the merits of local political issues. That is precisely what happened in the 2018 mid-term campaign when Trump made the election a referendum on him. He lost, but that is beside the point. He emphatically made the link between local candidates and national issues. Democrats made the same argument in 2018. Both are making the argument for 2020.

One could argue that the actions of Trump and the polarization of our electorate make this type of politics inevitable. I think that is true—to a point. But this has been a trend in our politics for over thirty years. From 1988 to 2016 the proportion of senators elected whose party was the same as the state's presidential choice increased from 60 percent to perfect symmetry (100 percent) with Trump in 2016.

What does this mean for political communication and for what citizens learn about the candidates and advocates who vie for their attention, support, and money? The short answer is that political reality is bought. Political ads spout their versions of the truth and, with all that money, the sponsors make their claims over and over again. The repetition works. There seems to be a perverse calculus in play. Stations make ever increasing profits from content that, by its very nature, does not represent a neutral reality. That is the right of the political advertisers. The station owners' public interest obligation as license holders should press them to offer critical analyses of that very content. The local television journalism that I examined in the ten markets, either by incapacity or unwillingness, did not challenge those claims. In so doing, citizens were left to their own devices to ferret out fact from fiction. Their devices are fundamentally dependent on an active and challenging press. Our democracy depends on that very arrangement. Which citizen can follow a candidate around to determine if her actions match the positions she espouses on her ads? Which citizen can file a claim for public information to verify one or another reality? Which citizen can take the place of journalism?

It is true that citizenship requires effort. It should. And there is the argument that citizens have untold ways now to pursue information. That is also true. But that does not abrogate the public interest obligation that television station owners have, and claim to protect, in the defense of their broadcast licenses. I do not begrudge the media firms' pursuit of profit. They are private firms delivering a public good called news. From my examination of these ten markets, political stories could not compete with political ads, particularly for the down-ballot races. As a result, on those newscasts, political reality was dominated by those who had the resources to buy it.

Acknowledgments

The ideas that sustained this book were the result of countless conversations about democracy, the media, political communication, public policy, urban places and citizenship that I have had over time with my colleagues, friends, and family. I will try to acknowledge all of them here, but I cannot fully convey my gratitude or my debt to them—not by a long shot.

Many of the ideas for the book came from a collaboration with Allison Becker, former graduate student at the Biden School and now a colleague and very dear friend. Ally has an abiding interest in the media's role in society, especially as it relates to citizenship and public policy. We started looking at the relationship among political ads, money, and news in Philadelphia during the 2014 mid-term elections. Ally served as the coding director for that project. We learned much from the Philly work and we fashioned this research to reflect critical questions about political communication in local places. She helped to develop the coding scheme, trained all of the coders, and ensured the intercoder reliability that is crucial to content analysis. Ally's contribution to the research was enormous. Her imprint on the book is unmistakable. I am deeply grateful to her.

If there was ever a savior of a book, it is my colleague here at the Biden School, Professor Ed Ratledge. Because of a glitch, the political ad information we had gathered did not include the US House of Representatives races (we had the US Senate data). Ed provided the funding that I needed to secure those data and his critical insights and perspective throughout the process of completing the research and writing the book were the reality check that kept everything on track. He is a true colleague and friend; words cannot express how much I owe him.

This book is about local news content and the only way to understand that is to conduct a rigorous content analysis of newscasts. That begins with the coding of those broadcasts—1,552 of them to be exact. That coding was accomplished by dedicated students in the Biden School of Public Policy and Administration and the Department of Communication at the University of Delaware. Undergraduate students Devin Bulgar, Emily Goodman, Eli Gordy-Stith, Jeremy Hidalgo, Abigail Kane, Emily Moore, Ashley Pipari, Keri Taranto, Morgan Windish, and Gina Zappone and graduate students Ben Chun and Oscar de Paz were magnificent in their work. We met at night, during the day, on weekends—all in the tremendous effort to get it right. They were committed, passionate and tireless and have my enduring gratitude.

I also benefited greatly from the advice of two wonderful colleagues: Roger Macdonald, Television Archive Fellow at the Internet Archives, and veteran journalist Kathy Kiely, then of the Sunlight Foundation and now Lee Hills Chair in Free-Press Studies in the School of Journalism at the University of Missouri. Their insight, advice and candor infused the Philly research and that guided how I approached the work of this book.

I have had many conversations over time about the media, society, citizenship, and public policy with some the most insightful thinkers (whom I gratefully count as my friends) on the subject—Phil Napoli, Shepley Professor of Public Policy at the Sanford School of Public Policy and the DeWitt Center for Media and Democracy at Duke University; Lew Friedland, Vilas Distinguished Achievement Professor at the School of Journalism and Mass Communication at the University of Wisconsin-Madison; and Mark Lloyd, Clinical Professor of Communication at the Annenberg School of Communication and Journalism at the University of Southern California Their insights and critical views have greatly influenced my thinking, my approach and my understanding of these issues. I owe them much and I look forward to our continued conversation.

Thanks also to Steve Passwaiter, vice president and general manager of Campaign Media Analysis Group at Kantar Media, was wonderfully generous in providing the political ad database that I needed for the research.

My colleagues here in the Biden School were wonderful. Steve Peuquet supported my work through the Center for Community Research and Service. He was always ready to engage the conversation and I took advantage of that dozens of times. Maria Aristigueta, the director of the Biden School, faculty colleagues John McNutt, Andrea Pierce, Dan Rich, and Tibor Toth provided advice and guidance with kindness and generosity. I extend to them my heartfelt gratitude.

I owe much gratitude to the reviewers of the book. Their suggestions for revisions were insightful and forthright.

The staff at Fordham University Press provided the crucial support to get the book started and then to see it through. My conversations with Fred Nachbaur and Will Cerbone about my ideas were critical to my pursuit of the project. They listened with patience and grace as I worked to organize my thoughts and to frame the book. I am also indebted to compositor Susan Mark for getting the book to print on an accelerated schedule. My work with editor Michael Koch has been one of the most satisfying professional relationships in my career. First, before we made any changes, we talked about what I wanted the book to say. His sharp eye, clear instructions for changes, lightning fast responses, and wicked sense of humor made our work a true collaboration. The book is immensely better because he worked on it. He has my deepest gratitude. Lucky for me, now I have a friend who just happens to be a crackerjack editor.

None of this would be possible without my family. And being a Serbian-American, that means my *kumovi* as well. It is the strongest thing that I know, and it has shaped who I am. Their love and support are manifest in a thousand ways. My cousin Beba, Dr. Beverly Yanich, and our adopted cousin and Kuma, Dr. Linda Wolf, insightfully probed my logic, my methods, and my conclusions in countless conversations on the porch in Cape May. They were as unsparing in their constructive criticism as they were generous in the spirit in which they offered it.

My Dad, Ben Yanich, was a voracious reader of history, a decorated World War II veteran and a steelworker. He did not have the opportunities that he and my Mom, through their uncompromising sacrifice, provided to me. That expression of their love made all the difference. He passed away in 2005, yet his indelible mark is in these pages. Večnaja pamjat.

My brother Tosh, Ted Yanich, is the person to whom I go to ground myself in our common experience of growing up together and using that bond to understand the present and to accept the future. He listened as I talked about the book and posed my questions about how I would accomplish it. From playing ball as kids in the Lower End of Steelton to now, Tosh has been my unwavering support. I love him for it.

The person who lived with this book as much as I is my partner in life, Rosemarie Paolinelli. She quietly, and sometimes not so quietly, endured my preoccupation with the work. It was more than not being able to do things together. Too often, even if we were in the same room, I simply was not present. My mind was elsewhere. I think that is the most difficult consequence of the writing process. But throughout the time, Ro was always my support, full of love, encouragement, wisecracks, and thousands of hugs. I love her for every one of them. This book is as much hers as it is mine.

—D.Y.
Newark, Delaware
January 2020

Reference List

Abdul-Razaak, Nour, Carlo Prato, and Stephane Wolton. 2017. "How Outside Spending Shapes American Democracy." Paper presented at the MPSA Annual Meeting.

Abramowitz, Allen, and Steven Webster. 2016. "The Rise of Negative Partisanship and the Nationalization of US Elections in the 21st Century." *Electoral Studies* 41: 12–22. doi:10.1016/j.electstud.2015.11.001.

AdAge. 1999. "John Wannamaker." AdAge. March 29. www.adage.com/article/special-report-the-advertising-century/john-wannamaker.

Adilov, Nodir, Peter Alexander, and Keith Brown. 2007. "From Many, One: Cross-Media Ownership and Story Choice in Local News." ReseearchGate. February 15. https://www.researchgate.net/publication/265521649.

Ahmed, Nabila, and Kiel Porter. 2019. "Apollo Is Nearing Deal for Group of Nexstar Stations." Bloomberg. Updated on February 14, 2019. https://www.bloomberg.com/news/articles/2019-02-13/apollo-is-said-to-be-nearing-deal-for-group-of-nexstar-stations.

Alexander, Peter J., and Kevin Brown. 2004. *Do Local Owners Deliver More Localism? Some Evidence from Local Broadcast News.* Washington, DC: Federal Communications Commission.

Allard, Nicholas W. 2016. "Money and Speech: Practical Perspectives." *Journal of Law and Policy* 25, no. 1: 255–272.

Allen, Barbara, Daniel P. Stevens, Gregory Marfleet, John Sullivan, and Dean Alger. 2007. "Local News and Perceptions of the Rhetoric of Political Advertising." *American Politics Research* 35, no. 4: 506–540.

Ansolabehere, Stephen, and Brian F. Schaffner. 2017. CCES Common Content, 2016. https://doi.org/10.7910/DVN/GDF6Zo.

Ariens, Chris. 2011. "New Year Brings Changes to Idaho Falls." Adweek. January 3. https://www.adweek.com/tvspy/new-year-brings-change-to-idaho-falls/5741/.

Bagdikian, Ben. 2004. *The New Media Monopoly*. Boston, MA: Beacon Press.

Baker, Liana B., and Greg Roumeliotas. 2019. "Exclusive: Apollo Nears $3 Billion Deal to Buy Cox TV Stations - Sources." Reuters. February 10. https://www.reuters.com/article/us-coxtv-m-a-apollo-glo-mgmt/exclusive-apollo-nears-3-billion-deal-to-buy-cox-tv-stations-sources-idUSKCN1PZ0QX.

Ballotpedia. 2016. "U.S. Senate Battlegrounds, 2016." Ballotpedia. https://ballotpedia.org/U.S._Senate_battlegrounds,_2016.

Banerjee, Mousumi, Michelle Capozzoli, Laura McSweeney, and Debajyoti Sinha. 1999. "Beyond Kappa: A Review of Interrater Agreement Measures." *Canadian Journal of Statistics* 27, no. 1: 3–23.

Barthel, Michael, Elizabeth Grieco, and Elisa Shearer. 2019. "Older Americans, Black Adults and Americans with Less Education More Interested in Local News." Pew Research Center. August 14. https://www.journalism.org/2019/08/14/older-americans-black-adults-and-americans-with-less-education-more-interested-in-local-news/.

Barthel, Michael, Jesse Holcomb, Jessica Mahone, and Amy Mitchell. 2016. "Civic Engagement Strongly Tied to Local News Habits." Pew Research Center. November 3. http://www.journalism.org/2016/11/03/civic-engagement-strongly-tied-to-local-news-habits/.

Beaudet, Mike, and John Wihbey. 2019. "Reinventing Local News." Shorenstein Center on Media, Politics and Public Policy and Northeastern University. February 12. https://shorensteincenter.org/reinventing-local-tv-news/.

Beckel, Michael. 2016. "Team Clinton Sponsored 75 Percent of TV Ads in 2016 Presidential Race." Center for Public Integrity. Updated November 16. https://www.publicintegrity.org/2016/11/08/20452/team-clinton-sponsored-75-percent-tv-ads-2016-presidential-race.

Bennett, W. Lance. 2005. "News as Reality TV: Election Coverage and the Democratization of Truth." *Critical Studies in Media Communication* 22, no. 2: 171–177. doi:10.1080/07393180500093802.

———. 2016. *News: The Politics of Illusion*. 10th ed. Chicago: University of Chicago Press.

Benton, Joshua. 2018. "Requiem for a Tronc." NiemanLab. October 5. http://www.niemanlab.org/2018/10/requiem-for-a-tronc/.

Benoit, William L. 2000. "A Functional Analysis of Political Advertising Across Media, 1998." *Communication Studies* 51, no. 3: 274–295.

Berenson, Tessa. 2016. "New Clinton Ad Highlights Donald Trump's Remarks About Women." Time. November 1. http://time.com/4553101/hillary-clinton-ad-donald-trump-women/.

BIA/Kelsey. 2018. Personal communication. August 2, 2018.

Bienstock, David. 2012. *Ex Parte Presentation of Target Enterprises: In the Matter of Standardized and Enhanced Disclosure Requirements for Television Broadcast Licensee Public Interest Obligations*. Washington, DC: Federal Communication Commission.

Blackwell, Matthew. 2013. "A Framework for Dynamic Causal Inference in Political Science." *American Journal of Political Science* 57, no. 2: 504–520. doi:10.1111/j .1540-5907.2012.00626.x.

Bode, Karl. 2017. 3 "Million Dish Customers May Miss Thanksgiving Football in Latest Example of TV Industry Dysfunction." Techdirt. November 22. https:// www.techdirt.com/articles/20171121/11384638660/3-million-dish-customers-may -miss-thanksgiving-football-latest-example-tv-industry-dysfunction.shtml.

Bond, Paul. 2016. "Leslie Moonves on Donald Trump: 'It may not be good for America, but it's damn good for CBS.'" *Hollywood Reporter*. February 29. https://www.hollywoodreporter.com/news/leslie-moonves-donald-trump -may-871464.

Bowie, Blair, and Adam Lioz. 2013. "Billion Dollar Democracy: The Unprecedented Role of Money in the 2012 Elections." Dēmos. January 17. https://www.demos.org/ sites/default/files/publications/BillionDollarDemocracy_Demos.pdf.

Brader, Ted. 2005. "Striking a Responsive Chord: How Political Ads Motivate and Persuade Voters by Appealing to Emotions." *American Journal of Political Science* 49, no. 2: 388–405.

———. 2006. *Campaigning for Hearts and Minds: How Emotional Appeals in Political Ads Work*. Chicago: University of Chicago Press.

Branswell, Helen. 2018. "When Towns Lose Their Newspapers, Disease Detectives Are Left Flying Blind." STAT. March 20. https://www.statnews.com/2018/03/20/ news-deserts-infectious-disease/.

Campanile, Carl. 2019. "Michael Bloomberg's Massive Ad Spending Greatly Affects TV Markets." *New York Post*. December 27. https://nypost.com/2019/12/27/ michael-bloombergs-massive-ad-spending-greatly-affecting-tv-markets/.

Campbell, Angela. 2009. *Complaint and Request for Emergency Relief Regarding Shared Services Agreement Between Raycom Media and MCG Capital for Joint Operation of Television Stations KHNL, KFVE, and KGMB, Honolulu, Hawaii*. Washington, DC: Institute for Public Administration, Georgetown University Law Center.

Cassino, Kip. 2017. "The Final Analysis: What Happened to Political Advertising in 2016 (and Forever)." January 3. https://www.borrellassociates.com/shop/the-final -analysis-political-advertising-in-2016-detail.

Center for Responsive Politics. 2018. "Cost of Election." OpenSecrets.org. https:// www.opensecrets.org/overview/cost.php.

———. 2019. "Blue Wave of Money Propels 2018 Election to Record-Breaking $5.2 Billion in Spending." OpenSecrets.org. October 29. https://www.opensecrets.org/ news/2018/10/2018-midterm-record-breaking-5-2-billion/.

Champlin, Dell, and Janet Knoedler. 2002. "Operating in the Public Interest or in Pursuit of Private Profits? News in the Age of Media Consolidation." *Journal of Economic Issues* 36, no. 2: 459–468.

Chermak, Steven. 1995. *Victims in the News: Crime and the American News Media*. Boulder, CO: Westview Press.

Christin, Angèle. 2014. "When It Comes to Chasing Clicks, Journalists Say One Thing but Feel Pressure to Do Another." NiemanLab. August 29. http://www .niemanlab.org/2014/08/when-it-comes-to-chasing-clicks-journalists-say-one -thing-but-feel-pressure-to-do-another/.

Citizens United v. Federal Election Commission. 2010. 558 U.S. 310. January 21.

Coleman, Price. 2010. "Hot Trend: Outsourcing Station Management." TVNewsCheck. August 25. https://tvnewscheck.com/article/44718/ hot-trend-outsourcing-station-management/.

Cook, Timothy E. 2006. "The News Media as a Political Institution: Looking Backward and Looking Forward." *Political Communication* 23, no. 2: 159–171. doi:10.1080/10584600600629711.

Coren, Michael. 2018. "Americans Can Barely Buy a Coffee with What They Spend Per Year on Public Media." Quartz. September 9. https://qz.com/1383503/ americans-could-barely-buy-a-coffee-with-what-they-spend-per-year-on-public -media/.

Coster, Helen. 2019. "Big Broadcasters Sue Non-Profit That Streams TV Channels for Free." Reuters. July 31. https://www.reuters.com/article/us-usa-broadcasters -lawsuit/big-broadcasters-sue-non-profit-that-streams-tv-channels-for-free -idUSKCN1UQ2FT.

Coulson, David C., Daniel Riffe, Stephen Lacy, and Charles R. St. Cyr. 2001. "Erosion of Television Coverage of City Hall? Perceptions of TV Reporters on the Beat." *Journalism and Mass Communication Quarterly* 78, no. 1: 81–92.

Daunt, Tina. 2012. "Political Ads: TV's $ 2.9 Billion Battle." *Hollywood Reporter.* September 25. https://www.hollywoodreporter.com/news/political-ads-tvs-29 -billion-373761.

Day, Don. 2018. "How to Solve the Local News Crisis? Look It Up in the Library." Medium. June 7. https://medium.com/jsk-class-of-2018/ how-to-solve-the-local-news-crisis-look-it-up-in-the-library-b3ad39b17edb.

de Vreese, Claes. 2004. "The Effects of Frames in Political Television News on Issue Interpretation and Frame Salience." *Journalism and Mass Communication Quarterly* 81, no. 1: 36–52.

de Vreese, Claes, and Hajo Boomgaarden. 2006. "News, Political Knowledge and Participation: The Differential Effects of News Media Exposure on Political Knowledge and Participation." *Acta Politica* 41: 317–341.

Decker, Cathleen. 2016. "A Republican Senator's Strategy to Save His Seat in One of the Country's Tightest Races: Avoid Trump." *Los Angeles Times.* October 24. http:// www.latimes.com/politics/la-na-pol-pennsyvlania-senate-20161023-snap-story.html.

Delli Carpini, Michael, and Scott Keeter. 1996. *What Americans Know About Politics and Why It Matters.* New Haven, CT: Yale University Press.

Derderian, Jeff. 2011. "Exclusive: Layoffs at Channel 6 Start." GoLocalProv. April 15. https://www.golocalprov.com/business/exclusive-layoffs-at-channel-6-start/.

Desilver, Drew. 2018. "More and More, Senate Elections Reflect States' Presidential Votes. FactTank: News in the numbers." Pew Research Center. June 26. http:// www.pewresearch.org/fact-tank/2018/06/26/more-and-more-senate-elections -reflect-states-presidential-votes/.

Doctor, Ken. 2013. "The Newsonomics of Patch's Unquilting." NiemanLab. August
    19. http://www.niemanlab.org/2013/08/the-newsonomics-of-patchs-unquilting-2/.
Domonoske, Camila. 2018. "Video Reveals Power Of Sinclair, As Local News
    Anchors Recite Script In Unison." NPR. April 2. https://www.npr.org/sections/
    thetwo-way/2018/04/02/598794433/video-reveals-power-of-sinclair-as-local-news
    -anchors-recite-script-in-unison.
Donald, Ralph, Riley Maynard, and Thomas Spann. 2008. *Fundamentals of
    Television Production.* London: Pearson/Allyn and Bacon.
Douglas, Anna. 2016. "Republican Ad Hits NC Senate Hopeful Ross for ACLU
    Argument in Rape Case." McClatchy. October 11. http://www.mcclatchydc.com/
    news/politics-government/election/article107460962.html.
Dowling, Conor M., and Amber Wichowsky. 2015. "Attacks without Consequence?
    Candidates, Parties, Groups, and the Changing Face of Negative Advertising."
    American Journal of Political Science 59, no. 1: 19–36. doi:10.1111/ajps.12094.
Dunaway, Johanna, Kathleen Searles, Erika Fowler, and Travis Ridout. 2019.
    "The Effects of Political Advertising: Assessing the Impact of Changing
    Technologies, Strategies and Tactics." In *Mediated Communication:
    Handbooks of Communication Science*, vol. 7, edited by Philip Napoli. Berlin:
    Mouton de Gruyter.
Dunaway, Johanna, and Regina G. Lawrence. 2015. "What Predicts the Game
    Frame? Media Ownership, Electoral Context, and Campaign News." *Political
    Communication* 32, no. 1: 43–60. doi:10.1080/10584609.2014.880975.
Eggerton, John. 2011. "NABET Takes Aim at Joint Station Agreements."
    Broadcasting+Cable. Updated March 16. https://www.broadcastingcable.com/
    news/nabet-takes-aim-joint-station-agreements-59470.
———. 2017. "FCC Deregulates Broadcast Ownership." Broadcasting+Cable.
    Updated March 16. https://www.broadcastingcable.com/news/fcc-deregulates
    -broadcast-ownership-170163.
———. 2018a. "ACA Seeks Early Sinclair Station Renewals." Multichannel News.
    November 27. https://www.multichannel.com/news/aca-seeks-early-sinclair
    -station-renewals.
———. 2018b. "Enforcement Bureau OK with Ending Sinclair-Tribune Hearing."
    Broadcasting+Cable. August 14. https://www.broadcastingcable.com/news/
    enforcement-bureau-ok-with-ending-sinclair-tribune-hearing.
———. 2018c. Nexstar Settles DoJ Ad Info Investigation. Broadcasting+Cable.
    December 13. https://www.broadcastingcable.com/news/nexstar-settles-doj-ad
    -info-investigation.
———. 2019a. "Court Deals Blow to Pai Dereg." Broadcasting+Cable. Updated
    September 23. https://www.broadcastingcable.com/news/court-deals-blow
    -to-pai-dereg.
———. 2019b. "DOJ to Look at Impact of Edge on Local TV Ads." Broadcasting+
    Cable. January 29. https://www.broadcastingcable.com/news/doj-to-look-at
    -impact-of-edge-on-local-tv-ads.
———. 2019c. "FCC ALJ Drops Sinclair Hearing." Broadcasting+Cable. March 5.
    https://www.broadcastingcable.com/news/fcc-alj-drops-sinclair-hearing.

———. 2019d. "FCC Approves Nexstar-Tribune Merger." Broadcasting+Cable. Updated September 16. https://www.broadcastingcable.com/news/fcc-approves -nexstar-tribune-merger.

———. 2019e. "FCC Challenges Court's Broadcast Dereg Smackdown." Multichannel News. November 7. https://www.multichannel.com/news/fcc -challenges-courts-broadcast-dereg-smackdown.

———. 2019f. "FCC's O'Rielly: Time to Jettison Myopic Vision of Broadcast Market." Broadcasting+Cable. February 26. https://www.broadcastingcable.com/ news/fccs-orielly-time-to-jettison-myopic-vision-of-broadcast-market.

———. 2019g. "Locast Expands Outlets for Free Online TV." Broadcasting+Cable. May 1. https://www.broadcastingcable.com/news/locast-expands-outlets-for-free -online-tv.

———. 2019h. "Nexstar, Tribune to FCC: Cap Should Be at Least 78%." Broadcasting+Cable. March 11. https://www.broadcastingcable.com/news/ nexstar-tribune-to-fcc-cap-should-be-at-least-78.

———. 2019i. "Sanders Buying $1.3M TV Time in Iowa." Broadcasting+Cable. October 1. https://www.broadcastingcable.com/news/sanders-buying-1-3m-tv -time-in-iowa.

Enda, Jodi, Katerina Matsa, and Jan Lauren Boyles. 2014. "America's Shifting Statehouse Press." Pew Research Center. July 10. http://www.journalism.org/ 2014/07/10/americas-shifting-statehouse-press/.

Entman, Robert M. 1996. *Democracy Without Citizens: Media and the Decay of American Politics.* New York: Oxford University Press.

———. 2006. "Blacks in the News: Television, Modern Racism, and Cultural Change." *Communication and Law: Multidisciplinary Approaches to Research* 69, no. 2: 205–227.

Epstein, Reed J. 2016. "Rob Portman May Provide Reverse Coattails for Donald Trump in Ohio." *Wall Street Journal.* Updated September 29. https://www.wsj .com/articles/ rob-portman-may-provide-reverse-coattails-for-donald-trump-in-ohio-1475181035.

Evers-Hillstrom, Karl. 2020. "More Money, Less Transparency: A Decade Under Citizens United." OpenSecrets.org. January 14. http://www.opensecrets.org/news/ reports/a-decade-under-citizens-united.

Fallows, James. 1996. *Breaking the News: How the Media Undermine American Democracy.* New York: Pantheon Books.

Farrell, Michael. 2018. "CBS Stations, CBS Interactive Launch Streaming News Service." Multichannel News. December 13. https://www.multichannel.com/ news/cbs-stations-cbs-interactive-launch-streaming-news-service.

Farrell, Michael. 2019a. "Meredith Stations Go Dark to Dish Customers." Broadcasting+Cable. July 17. https://www.broadcastingcable.com/news/meredith -stations-go-dark-to-dish-customers.

———. 2019b. "Nexstar Wage Retrans Battle on Two Fronts." Broadcasting+Cable. January 2. https://www.broadcastingcable.com/news/nexstar-wages-retrans -battles-on-two-fronts.

———. 2019c. "Small TV Stations Locked in Retrans Dispute with DirecTV." Broadcasting+Cable. June 2. https://www.broadcastingcable.com/news/small -tv-stations-locked-in-retrans-dispute-with-directv.

———. 2017. *Report and Order in the Matter of Elimination of the Main Studio Rule.* Washington, DC: Federal Communications Commission. http://transition.fcc .gov/Daily_Releases/Daily_Business/2017/db1024/FCC-17-137A1.pdf.

———. 2019. *Applications of Tribune Media Company and Sinclair Broadcasting Group.* Washington, DC: Federal Communication Commission Retrieved from https://docs.fcc.gov/public/attachments/FCC-19M-01A1.pdf.

Fenton, Jacob. 2014. "Denver TV Station Pulls Biggest Political Ad Order from Public Site." Colorado Independent. June 24. http://www.coloradoindependent .com/147908/denver-tv-station-pulls-biggest-political-ad-order-from-public-site.

Fico, Frederick, Stephen Lacy, Steven S. Wildman, Thomas Baldwin, Daniel Bergan, and Paul Zube. 2013. "Citizen Journalism Sites as Information Substitutes and Complements for United States Newspaper Coverage of Local Governments." *Digital Journalism* 1, no. 1: 152–168. doi:10.1080/21670811.2012.740270.

Filla, Jackie, and Martin Johnson. 2010. "Local News Outlets and Political Participation." *Urban Affairs Review* 45, no. 5: 679–692.

Fowler, Erika, and Travis Ridout. 2009. "Local Television and Newspaper Coverage of Political Advertising." *Political Communication* 26, no. 2: 119–136. doi:10.1080/ 10584600902850635.

Fowler, Erika, Michael Franz, and Travis Ridout. 2016. *Political Advertising in the United States.* Boulder, CO: Westview Press.

Fowler, Erika, Kenneth Goldstein, Matthew Hale, and Martin Kaplan. 2007. "Does Local News Measure Up." *Stanford Law and Policy Review* 18, no. 410: 410–431.

Fowler, Erika, Travis Ridout, and Michael Franz. 2016. "Political Advertising in 2016: The Presidential Election as Outlier?" *Forum* 14, no. 4: 445–469. doi:10.1515/ for-2016-0040.

Fratrik, Mark. 2018. "Raising the National Cap to 50%: An Economic Analysis." Chantilly, VA: BIA Advisory Services.

Freedman, Paul, Michael Franz, and Kenneth Goldstein. 2004. Campaign Advertising and Democratic Citizenship. *American Journal of Political Science* 48, no. 4: 723–741. doi:10.1111/j.0092-5853.2004.00098.x.

Freedman, Paul, and Kenneth Goldstein. 1999. "Measuring Media Exposure and the Effects of Negative Campaign Ads." *American Journal of Political Science* 43, no. 4: 1189–1208. doi:10.2307/2991823.

Fridkin, Kim, Patrick Kenney, and Amanda Wintersieck. 2015. "Liar, Liar, Pants on Fire: How Fact-Checking Influences Citizens' Reactions to Negative Advertising." *Political Communication* 32, no. 1: 127–151. doi:10.1080/10584609.2014.914613.

Friedland, Lewis, Philip Napoli, Katherine Ognyanova, Carola Weil, and Ernest J. Wilson III. 2012. "Review of the Literature Regarding Critical Information Needs of the American Public." FCC (website). July 25. https://www.fcc.gov/news -events/blog/2012/07/25/review-literature-regarding-critical-information-needs -american-public.

Friendly, Fred. 1967. "The television 'fiasco': Interview with Fred Friendly, TV Authority." *US News and World Report*, June 12, 58–62.

Fuhrman, Mike. 2019. "Political Advertising Rules in Local TV Buying: 6 Common Misconceptions." MMi. July 8. https://www.mediaaudit.com/post/political -advertising-rules-in-local-tv-buying-6-common-misconceptions.

Gao, Pnegjie, Chang Lee, and Dermot Murphy. 2018. "Financing Dies in Darkness? The Impact of Newspaper Closures on Public Finance." SSRN, May 15. https:// dx.doi.org/10.2139/ssrn.3175555.

Gardner, Eriq 2019. "Locast Accuses the Major Broadcasters of Antitrust Violations." *Hollywood Reporter*. September 26. https://www.hollywoodreporter.com/thr-esq/ locast-accuses-major-broadcasters-antitrust-violations-1243822.

Garzik, Jeff. 2004. "No. 71: The Duration in Office of the Executive." In *The Founding Papers*, vol. 2, *The Federalist Papers*, edited by J. Garzik. New York: Lulu Enterprises.

Geer, John G., and Lynn Vavreck. 2014. "Negativity, Information, and Candidate Position-Taking." *Political Communication* 31, no. 2: 218–236. doi:10.1080/10584 609.2013.828140.

Gentzkow, Matthew. 2006. "Television and Voter Turnout." *Quarterly Journal of Economics* 121, no. 3: 931–972. doi:10.1162/qjec.121.3.931.

Gerber, Alan S., James G. Gimpel, Donald P. Green, and Daron R. Shaw. 2011. "How Large and Long-lasting Are the Persuasive Effects of Televised Campaign Ads? Results from a Randomized Field Experiment." *American Political Science Review* 105, no. 1: 135–150. doi:10.1017/s000305541000047x.

Gilliam, Franklin D. Jr., and Shanto Iyengar. 1998. "The Crime Script in Local Television News." www.kidscampaign.org/cac. (Site discontinued.)

———. 2000. "Prime Suspects: The Influence of Local Television News on the Viewing Public." *American Journal of Political Science* 44, no. 3: 560–573.

Glassman, James K. 2017. "Local Broadcast News Knows America Better Than Cable." The Hill. Updated July 20, 2018. https://thehill.com/blogs/congress-blog/ politics/320143-local-broadcast-news-knows-america-better-than-cable.

Ghonim, Wael. 2018. "Transparency: What Went Wrong With Social Media and What Can We Do About It." Shorenstein Center on Media, Politics and Public Policy. March 27. https://shorensteincenter.org/transparency-social-media-wael -ghonim/.

Gottfried, Jeffrey, and Michael Barthel. 2018. "Almost Seven-in-Ten Americans Have News Fatigue, More Among Republicans." Pew Research Center. June 5. http://www.pewresearch.org/fact-tank/2018/06/05/ almost-seven-in-ten-americans-have-news-fatigue-more-among-republicans/.

Gottfried, Jeffrey, and Elisa Shearer. 2017. "American's' Online News Use Is Closing in on TV News Use." Pew Research Center. September 7. http://www.pewresearch .org/fact-tank/2017/09/07/americans-online-news-use-vs-tv-news-use/.

Graber, Doris. 2001. *Processing Politics: Learning from Television in the Internet Age*. Chicago: University of Chicago Press.

———. 2010. *Mass Media and American Politics*. 8th ed. Washington, DC: CQ Press.

Greeley, Paul. 2014. "CSD Survey, Pt. 1, Ownership, Local News Quality, Marketing Effectiveness." TVNewsCheck. July 7. https://marketshare.tvnewscheck.com/ 2014/07/07/ownership-local-nws-quality-marketing-effectiveness-what-creative -services-directors-think-part-1/.

Green, Elizabeth. 2018. "What I Wish Everyone Who Cared About Local News Knew About Local News." Medium. September 28. https://medium.com/trust -media-and-democracy/what-i-wish-everyone-who-cared-about-local-news-knew -about-local-news-acbdd544469a.

Grieco, Elizabeth. 2018. "Newsroom Employment Dropped Nearly a Quarter in Less Than 10 Years, with Greatest Decline at Newspapers." Pew Research Center. https://www.pewresearch.org/fact-tank/2019/07/09/u-s-newsroom -employment-has-dropped-by-a-quarter-since-2008/.

Hale, Matthew, Erika Fowler, and Kenneth M. Goldstein. 2007. "Capturing Multiple Markets: A New Method of Capturing and Analyzing Local Television News." *Electronic News* 1, no. 4: 227–243.

Hamilton, James T. 2004. *All the News That's Fit to Sell: How the Market Transforms Information into News.* Princeton, NJ: Princeton University Press.

Hargreaves, Ian, and James Thomas. 2002. *New News, Old News: Broadcasting Standards Commission.* London: Independent Television Commission.

Harris and Bowser v. McCrory and Howard. 2016. 1:13–CV-00949 C.F.R. June 2.

Hart, Roderick P. 1999. *Seducing America: How Television Charms the Modern Voter, Revised Edition.* Thousand Oaks, CA: Sage.

Hayes, Danny, and Jennifer Lawless. 2015. "As Local News Goes, So Goes Citizen Engagement: Media, Knowledge,and Participation in the US House." *Journal of Politics* 77, no. 2: 447–462.

———. 2018. "The Decline of Local News and Its Effects: New Evidence from Longitudinal Data." *Journal of Politics* 80, no. 1: 332–336. doi:10.1086/694105.

Healy, Patrick, and James Martin. 2016. "Ted Cruz Stirs Convention Fury in Pointed Snub of Donald Trump." *New York Times.* July 20. https://www.nytimes .com/2016/07/21/us/politics/ted-cruz-donald-trump-mike-pence-rnc.html.

Hellman, Deborah. 2010. "Money Talks but It Isn't Speech." *Minnesota Law Review* 95: 953–1002.

Herman, Edward S., and Noam Chomsky. 1988. *Manufacturing Consent: The Political Economy of the Mass Media.* New York: Pantheon Books.

Hooghe, Marc. 2002. "Watching Television and Civic Engagement Disentangling the Effects of Time, Programs, and Stations." *Harvard International Journal of Press/Politics* 7, no. 2: 84–104.

Huber, Gregory, and Kevin Arceneaux. 2007. "Identifying the Persuasive Effects of Presidential Advertising." *American Journal of Political Science* 51, no. 4: 957–977. doi:10.1111/j.1540-5907.2007.00291.x.

Iyengar, Shanto. 2011. *Media Politics: A Citizen's Guide* New York: W. W. Norton.

Jackson, Robert A., Jeffery J. Mondak, and Robert Huckfeldt. 2009. "Examining the Possible Corrosive Impact of Negative Advertising on Citizens' Attitudes toward Politics." *Political Research Quarterly* 62, no. 1: 55–69. doi:10.1177/1065912908317031.

Jacobson, Gary C. 2015. "It's Nothing Personal: The Decline of the Incumbency Advantage in US House Elections." *Journal of Politics* 77, no. 3: 861–873. doi:10.1086/681670.

James, Meg. 2011. "Cable Telvision Gaining in Advertising Revenues, but Political Dollars." *Los Angeles Times* (blog). June 17. https://latimesblogs.latimes.com/entertainmentnewsbuzz/2011/06/cable-television-gaining-in-advertising-revenue-but-not-political-dollars.html.

Janeway, Michael. 2001. *Republic of Denial: Press, Politics, and Public Life.* New Haven, CT: Yale University Press.

Jessell, Harry A. 2018. "Stations Need to Forge Ahead with OTT." TVNewsCheck. December 17. https://tvnewscheck.com/article/top-news/227013/stations-need-forge-ahead-ott/.

———. 2019a. "FCC Approves Gray's Top 4 Duop in Sioux Falls." TVNewsCheck. September 24. https://tvnewscheck.com/article/top-news/239374/fcc-approves-kdlt-purchase-by-gray/.

———. 2019b. "Musings About Apollo-Cox-Northwest-Nexstar." TVNewsCheck. February 25. https://tvnewscheck.com/article/top-news/230791/musings-apollo-cox-northwest-nexstar/.

———. 2019c. "Ohio May Be Left Out Of 2020 Presidential Spend." TVNewsCheck. September 30. https://tvnewscheck.com/article/top-news/239507/ohio-may-be-left-out-of-2020-presidential-spend/.

———. 2019d. "Retrans Accounts For 50% of Nexstar Revenue Mix." TVNewsCheck. May 8. https://tvnewscheck.com/article/top-news/234787/retrans-accounts-for-5-of-nexstar-revenue-mix/.

Johnson, Ted. 2018. "Appeals Court Dismisses Challenge to FCC's 'UHF Discount.'" *Variety.* July 25. https://variety.com/2018/politics/news/fcc-uhf-discount-appeals-co-1202883885/.

Jones, Alex. 2009. *Losing the News: The Future of the News That Feeds Democracy.* New York: Oxford University Press.

Jones, Jeffrey. 2006. "A Cultural Approach to the Study of Mediated Citizenship." *Social Semiotics* 16, no. 2: 365–383.

Jones, Michael, and Paul Jorgensen. 2012. "Mind the Gap? Political Advertisements and Congressional Election Results." *Journal of Political Marketing* 11, no. 3: 165–188.

Kahn, Kim F., and Patrick J. Kenney. 1999. "Do Negative Campaigns Mobilize or Suppress Turnout? Clarifying the Relationship Between Negativity and Participation." *American Political Science Review* 93, no. 4: 877–889. doi:10.2307/2586118.

Kaniss, Phyliss. 1995. *The Media and the Mayor's Race: The Failure of Urban Political Reporting.* Bloomington: Indiana University Press.

Kaplan, Martin, Kenneth Goldstein, and Matthew Hale. 2005. "Local News Coverage of the 2004 Campaigns: An Analysis of Nightly News Broadcasts." Local News Archive. February 15. http://www.localnewsarchive.org/pdf/LCLNA Final2004.pdf.

Kaplan, Martin, and Matthew Hale. 2010. "Local TV News in the Los Angeles Media Market: Are Stations Serving the Public Interest?" Norman Lear Center. March 11. https://learcenter.org/pdf/LANews2010.pdf.

Kaplan, Noah, David Park, and Travis Ridout. 2006. "Dialogue in American Political Campaigns? An examination of issue convergence in candidate television advertising." *American Journal of Political Science* 50, no. 3: 724–736.

Keum, Heejo, et al. 2004. "The Citizen-Consumer: Media Effects at the Intersection of Consumer and Civic Culture." *Political Communication* 21, no. 3: 369–391.

Kirkpatrick, Dan. 2018. "Political Broadcasting QandA." CommonLawBlog. February 27. https://www.commlawblog.com/2018/02/articles/deadlines/political-broadcasting-rules-qa/.

Klumpp, Tilman, Hugo M. Mialon, and Michael A. Williams. 2016. "The Business of American Democracy: Citizens United, Independent Spending and Elections." *Journal of Law and Economics* 59 (February): 1–43.

Knight Commission. 2009. *Informing Communities: Sustaining Democracy in the Digital Age.* Washington, DC: Aspen Institute.

Knight Foundation. 2018. *Indicators of News Media Trust.* https://knightfoundation.org/reports/indicators-of-news-media-trust.

Kolhatkar, Sheela. 2018. "The Growth of Sinclair's Conservative Media Empire. The New Yorker." *New Yorker.* October 15. https://www.newyorker.com/magazine/2018/10/22/the-growth-of-sinclairs-conservative-media-empire.

Kovach, Bill, and Tom Rosenstiel. 2010. *Blur: How to Know What's True in the Age of Information Overload.* New York: Bloomsbury USA.

Krupnikov, Y. 2011. "When Does Negativity Demobilize? Tracing the Conditional Effect of Negative Campaigning on Voter Turnout." *American Journal of Political Science* 55, no. 4: 796–812. doi:10.1111/j.1540-5907.2011.00522.x.

Kuchinskas, Susan. 2019. "Don't Overlook Antenna TV Viewers." Videa. July 31. website: https://videa.tv/2019/07/dont-overlook-antenna-tv-viewers/.

Kull, Steven. 2018. "Americans Evaluate Campaign Finance Reform." College Park: University of Maryland.

Lafayette, Jon. 2018a. "More TV Stations Sold in 2017, Says BIA/Kelsey." Broadcasting+Cable. Updated March 16. https://www.broadcastingcable.com/news/more-tv-stations-sold-2017-says-biakelsey-171217.

———. 2018b. "Post-Sinclair, Tribune Media Reports Third-Quarter Profit." Broadcasting+Cable. November 9. https://www.broadcastingcable.com/news/post-sinclair-tribune-media-reports-third-quarter-profit.

———. 2019a. "Sinclair Launching Stirr With National, Local Programming." Broadcasting+Cable. January 16. https://www.broadcastingcable.com/news/sinclair-launching-stirr-with-national-local-programming.

———. 2019b. "Sinclair Reports Lower Earnings for 4th Quarter." Broadcasting+Cable. February 27. https://www.broadcastingcable.com/news/sinclair-reports-lower-earnings-for-4th-quarter.

Lafayette, Jon, and John Eggerton. 2018. "Master Station Consolidator Nexstar Aims to Live Large." Broadcasting + Cable. December 10. https://www.broadcasting cable.com/news/master-station-consolidator-nexstar-aims-to-live-large.

Lau, Richard R., David J. Andersen, Tessa M. Ditonto, Mona S. Kleinberg, and David P. Redlawsk. 2017. "Effect of Media Environment Diversity and Advertising Tone on Information Search, Selective Exposure, and Affective Polarization." *Political Behavior* 39, no. 1: 231–255. doi:10.1007/s11109-016-9354-8.

Lau, Richard R., Lee Sigelman, and Ivy B. Rovner. 2007. "The Effects of Negative Political Campaigns: A Meta-Analytic Reassessment." *Journal of Politics* 69, no. 4: 1176–1209. doi:10.1111/j.1468-2508.2007.00618.x.

Lee, Chisun, Brent Ferguson, and David Earley. 2014. *After Citizens United: The Story in the States*. New York: Brennan Center for Justice.

Lee, Francis E. 2016. *Insecure Majorities: Congress and the Perpetual Campaign*. Chicago: University of Chicago Press.

Levitt, Mark. 2018. "The Heyday of Television Ads Is Over. Political Campaigns Ought to Act Like It." *Washington Post.* November 6. https://www.washington post.com/outlook/2018/11/06/heyday-television-ads-is-over-political-campaigns -ought-act-like-it/.

Lipsitz, Keena, and John G. Geer. 2017. "Rethinking the Concept of Negativity: An Empirical Approach." *Political Research Quarterly* 70, no. 3: 577–589. doi:10.1177/ 1065912917706547.

Lloyd, Mark. 2006. *Prologue to a Farce: Communication and Democracy in America.* Urbana: University of Illinois Press.

Locast. 2020. "Watch Your Local Broadcast TV for Free!" January 20. https://www .locast.org.

Lovett, Mitchell J., and Ron Shachar. 2011. "The Seeds of Negativity: Knowledge and Money." *Marketing Science* 30, no. 3: 43–446. doi:10.1287/mksc.1110.0638.

Lowry, Dennis. 1971. "Agnew and the Network News: before.after Content Analysis." *Journalism Quarterly* 48, no. 40 (Summer): 205–210.

Mahtesian, Charles. 2016. "What Are the Swing States in 2016?" Politico. June 15. https://www.politico.com/blogs/swing-states-2016-election/2016/06/what-are-the -swing-states-in-2016-list-224327.

Mak, Tim, and Libby Berry. 2018. "Russian Influence Campaign Sought to Exploit Americans' Trust in Local News." NPR. July 12. https://www.npr.org/2018/07/12/ 628085238/russian-influence-campaign-sought-to-exploit-americans-trust-in -local-news.

Malloy, Liam C., and Shanna Pearson-Merkowitz. 2016. "Going Positive: The Effects of Negative and Positive Advertising on Candidate Success and Voter Turnout." *Research and Politics* 3, no. 1: 15. doi:10.1177/2053168015625078.

Malone, Michael. 2010. "Scripps CEO: Let Us Run Your News Operation." Broadcasting+Cable. Updated March 16, 2018. https://www.broadcastingcable .com/news/scripps-ceo-let-us-run-your-news-operation-42648.

———. 2013. "The Rise of the Station Super-Groups. Broadcasting and Cable."
Broadcasting+Cable. Updated March 16, 2018. https://www.broadcastingcable
.com/news/rise-thestation-super-groups-43886.

Mann, Thomas, and Norman Ornstein. 2013. *It's Even Worse Than It Looks: How
the American Constitutional System Collided with the Politics of Extremism*. New
York: Basic Books.

Martin, Gregory J., and Joshua McCrain. 2019. "Local News and National Politics."
American Political Science Review 113, no. 4: 1–13. doi:10.1017/S0003055418000965.

Matsa, Katarina Eva. 2014. "Interest in Midterms May Be Low, but Local TV Awash
in Political Ad Spending." Pew Research Center. October 31. http://www.pew
research.org/fact-tank/2014/10/31/interest-in-midterms-may-be-low-but-local-tv
-awash-in-political-ad-spending/.

———. 2017. "Buying Spree Brings More Local TV Stations to Fewer Big Companies."
Pew Research Center. May 11. http://www.pewresearch.org/fact-tank/2017/05/11/
buying-spree-brings-more-local-tv-stations-to-fewer-big-companies/.

Matsa, Katarina Eva, and Sophia Fedeli. 2018. "State of the News Media: Local TV
News Fact Sheet." Pew Research Center. http://www.pewresearch.org/topics/
state-of-the-news-media/.

———. 2019. "Local TV News Fact Sheet." Pew Research Center. June 25. http://
www.journalism.org/fact-sheet/local-tv-news/.

McChesney, Robert W. 1999. *Rich Media, Poor Democracy*. Chicago: University of
Chicago Press.

———. 2004. *The Problem of the Media: U.S. Communications Policy in the 21st
Century*. New York: Monthly Review Press.

———. 2008. *The Political Economy of the Media: Enduring Issues, Emerging
Dilemmas*. New York: Monthly Review Press.

———. 2012. "A Real Media Utopia." Paper presented at the American Sociological
Association, New Orleans, LA.

McCutcheon v. Federal Elections Commission. 2014. 572 C.F.R. April 2.

McGann, Anthony J., Charles Anthony Smith, Michael Latner, and J. Alex Keena.
2015. "A Discernable and Manageable Standard for Partisan Gerrymandering."
Election Law Journal: Rules, Politics, and Policy 14, no. 4: 295–311. doi:10.1089/
elj.2015.0312.

McLeod, Jack M., Katie Daily, Zhongshi Guo, William P. Eveland, Jan Bayer,
Seungchan Yang, and Hsu Wang. 1996. "Community Integration, Local Media
Use, and Democratic Processes." *Communication Research* 23, no. 2: 179–209.

McManus, John H. 1994. *Market-Driven Journalism: Let the Buyer Beware*.
Thousand Oaks, CA: Sage Publications.

———. 2017. *Detecting Bull: How to Identify Biased, Fake and Junk Journalism in the
Digital Age*. 3rd ed. Sunnyvale, CA: Unvarnished Press.

Micheli, Carolyn. 2018. "Scripps to Acquire 15 Television Stations in 10 Markets
from Cordilerra Communications." Scripps. October 29. https://scripps.com/

press-releases/1198-scripps-to-acquire-15-television-stations-in-10-markets-from
-cordillera-communications/.

Miller, Mark. 2016. "Nexstar Jumps to No. 3 in Annual Ranking." TVNewsCheck.
June 1. https://tvnewscheck.com/article/95107/nexstar-jumps-to-no-3-in-annual
-ranking/.

———. 2018a. "Over $3B Spent On Midterm Local TV Ads." TVNewsCheck.
November 7. https://tvnewscheck.com/article/225083/3b-spent-midterm-local
-tv-ads/.

———. 2018b. "Tribune Kills Sinclair Merger, Files Suit." TVNewsCheck. August 9.
https://tvnewscheck.com/article/top-news/220320/tribune-kills-sinclair-merger/.

———. 2019a. "BIA: 2020 Local Political Adv. to Top $6.5B." TVNewsCheck. August
5. https://tvnewscheck.com/article/top-news/237520/bia-2020-local-political-adv
-to-top-6-5b/.

———. 2019b. "CBS Launches CBSN Boston." TVNewsCheck. September 24.
https://tvnewscheck.com/article/239354/cbs-launches-cbsn-boston/.

———. 2019c. "Gray Buys Three United Stations In Two Markets." TVNewsCheck.
February 11. https://tvnewscheck.com/article/top-news/230061/gray-buys-three
-united-stations-two-markets/.

———. 2019d. "Gray's Fourth Quarter Revenue Climbs 40%." TVNewsCheck.
February 28. https://tvnewscheck.com/article/top-news/231039/grays-fourth
-quarter-revenue-climbs-40/.

———. 2019e. "Nexstar 4Q Revenue Soars 22% To $798M." TVNewsCheck.
February 26. https://tvnewscheck.com/article/top-news/230851/nexstar-4q-revenue
-soars-22-798m/.

———. 2019f. "Record Political Ups Tegna's 4Q Rev 31%." TVNewsCheck. March 1.
https://tvnewscheck.com/article/top-news/231153/record-political-ups-tegnas
-4q-rev-31/.

———. 2019g. "Scripps 4Q Local Media Revenue Climbs 39%." TVNewsCheck.
March 1. https://tvnewscheck.com/article/top-news/231157/scripps-4q-local-media
-revenue-climbs-39/.

———. 2019h. "Sinclair 4Q Media Revejue Climbs 25.4%." TVNewsCheck. February
27. https://tvnewscheck.com/article/top-news/230977/sinclair-4q-media-revenue
-climbs-25-4/.

Mitchell, Amy, Jeffrey Gottfried, Michael Barthel, and Elisa Shearer. 2016. "The
Modern News Consumer: News Attitudes and Practices in the Digital Era."
Pew Research Center. July 7. http://www.journalism.org/2016/07/07/the-modern
-news-consumer/.

Mitchell, Amy, and Dana Page. 2014. "Acquisitions and Content Sharing Shapes
Local TV News in 2013." Pew Research Center. March 26. http://www.pewresearch
.org/wp-content/uploads/sites/8/2014/03/Local-News-Aquisitions-and-Content
-Sharing-Shapes-Local-TV-News-in-2013_Final.pdf.

Montero, Frank. 2014. "On Censoring Political Ads." CommLawBlog. October 16.
https://www.commlawblog.com/2014/10/articles/broadcast/on-censoring
-political-ads/.

Napoli, Philip M. 2001. "The Localism Principle in Communications Policymaking and Policy Analysis: Ambiguity, Inconsistency, and Empirical Neglect." *Policy Studies Journal* 29, no. 3: 372–387. doi:10.1111/j.1541-0072.2001.tb02099.x.

———. 2003. *Foundations of Communications Policy: Principles and Process in the Regulation of Electronic Media*. Cresskill, NJ: Hampton Press.

———. 2004. "The Localism Principle in Communications Policymaking: An Annotated Bibliography." New York: Fordham University, Donald McGannon Communication Research Center.

Napoli, Philip M., Matthew Weber, Katie McCollough, and Qun Wang. 2018. "Assessing Local Journalism: News Deserts, Journalism Divides and the Determinants of the Robustness of Local News."

National Popular Vote. 2016. "Two-Thirds of Presidential Campaign Is in Just 6 States." https://www.nationalpopularvote.com/campaign-events-2016.

Newman, Nic, David Levy, and Rasmus Nielsen. 2015. *Reuters Institute Digital News Report 2015: Tracking the Future of News*. Oxford: Reuters Institute.

Newsday Staff. 2016. "Donald Trump Speech, Debates and Campaign Quotes." Newsday. November 9. https://www.newsday.com/news/nation/donald-trump -speech-debates-and-campaign-quotes-1.11206532. (Page removed.)

Nichols, John, and Robert W. McChesney. 2013. *Dollarocracy: How the Money and Media Election Complex Is Destroying America*. New York: Nation Books.

Nielsen. 2016. "Local Television Market Universe Estimates." Radio Television Digital News Association. September 24. https://www.rtdna.org/uploads/files/ 2016-2017-nielsen-local-dma-ranks.pdf.

———. 2017. "The Nielsen Local Watch Report Q1 2017: Television Trends in Our Cities." Nielsen. September 14. https://www.nielsen.com/us/en/insights/report/ 2017/q1-2017-local-watch-report-tv-trends-in-our-cities/.

Norris, Pippa. 2000. *A Virtuous Circle: Political Communications in Postindustrial Societies*. Boston, MA: Cambridge University Press.

———. 2010. "Evaluating Media Performance." In *Public Sentinel: News Media and Governance Reform*, edited by P. Norris, 3–29. Washington, DC: World Bank.

O'Neill, Brenda. 2010. "The Media's Role in Shaping Canadian Civic and Political Engagement." *Policy and Society* 29, no. 1: 37–51.

O'Rielly, Michael. 2019. *Statement of Commissioner Michael O'Rielly on Third Circuit Court Decision*. FCC. September 23. https://docs.fcc.gov/public/ attachments/DOC-359806A1.pdf.

Olsen, Hanna Brooks. 2017. "Stop Watching Your Local News." Medium. November 27. https://medium.com/@mshannabrooks/stop-watching-your-local-news-e898f 397a90f.

OpenSecrets.org. 2019. "Most expensive midterm ever: Cost of 2018 election surpasses $5.7 billion." OpenSecrets.org. February 6. https://www.opensecrets .org/news/2019/02/cost-of-2018-election-5pnt7bil/.

Opportunity Nation. 2016. "Opportunity Index 2016: Summary of Findings for States and Counties." New York: Measure of America, Social Services Research Council.

Oxenford, David. 2012. "Political Broadcasting Refresher Part 5—Why Don't TV
Stations Pull More SuperPAC Ads? Is There Potential Liability for These Ads?"
Broadcast Law Blog. https://www.broadcastlawblog.com/?s=Political+broadcasting
+refresher+part+5.

———. 2019. "Reminder—FCC Political Rules Apply to Off-Year Elections for State
and Local Offices." Broadcast Law Blog. September 20. https://www.broadcast
lawblog.com/2019/09/articles/reminder-fcc-political-rules-apply-to-off-year
-elections-for-state-and-local-offices/.

Padgett, Jeremy, Johanna Dunaway, and Joshua P. Darr. 2019. "As Seen on TV? How
Gatekeeping Makes the U.S. House of Representatives Seem More Extreme."
Journal of Communication 69, no. 6 (December): 1–24. doi:10.1093/joc/jqz039.

Pai, Ajit. 2019. Chairman Pai Statement on the Third Circuit's Media Ownership
Decision. FCC. September 23. https://docs.fcc.gov/public/attachments/DOC
-359794A1.pdf.

Papper, Bob. 2017. RTNDA Research: The Business of News. Radio Television Digital
News Association. May 8.https://www.rtdna.org/article/rtdna_research_the
_business_of_tv_news_2017.

———. 2018. 2018 RTNDA/Hofstra University Newsroom Survey: Local News by the
Numbers. Radio Television Digital News Association. https://rtdna.org/uploads/
files/2018%20Local%20News%20Research.pdf.

Patterson, Thomas. 1993. Out of Order. New York: Alfred A. Knopf.

Perez, Sarah. 2018. "U.S. Cord Cutters to Reach 33 Million This Year, Faster Than
Expected." TechCrunch. July 25. https://techcrunch.com/2018/07/25/u-s-cord
-cutters-to-reach-33-million-this-year-faster-than-expected/.

Peterson, Erik. 2017. "Paper Cuts: How Reporting Resources Affect Political News
Coverage. Program in Quantitative Social Science." Paper. Dartmouth College.

Pew Research Center. 2003. "Does Ownership Matter in Local Television News:
A Five-Year Study of Ownership and Quality." Pew Research Center. Updated
April 29. http://www.pewresearch.org/wp-content/uploads/sites/8/legacy/
ownership.pdf.

Pickard, Victor. 2015. America's Battle for Media Democracy: The Triumph of
Corporate Libertarianism and the Future of Media Reform. New York: Cambridge
University Press.

Plouffe, David. 2009. The Audacity to Win: The Inside Story and Lessons of Barack
Obama's Historic Victory. London: Penguin.

Poindexter, Paula M., and Maxwell E. McCombs. 2001. "Revisiting the Civic Duty
to Keep Informed in the New Media Environment." Journalism and Mass
Communication Quarterly 78, no. 1: 113–126.

Poor, Jack. 2014. "Politics 2014: Local Market TV and the Next Political Cycle."
TVB. January 15. http://www.tvb.org/media/file/Political_Cycle_2014_pc.pdf.
(File removed.)

Postman, Neil. 1986. Amusing Ourselves to Death: Public Discourse in the Age of
Show Business. New York: Penguin Books.

Price, Hank. 2019. "Retrans Boom Bodes Well For Stations' Future." TVNewsCheck. May 19. https://tvnewscheck.com/article/top-news/235142/retrans-boom-bodes -well-for-stations-future/.

Putnam, Robert D. 2000. *Bowling Alone: The Collapse and Revival of American Community*. New York: Simon and Schuster.

Redlawsk, David, and Kyle Mattes. 2017. "How Voters Process Facts." Paper presented at the Annual meeting of the Midwest Political Science Association, Chicago, IL.

Richey, Sean. 2013. "Random and Systematic Error in Voting in Presidential Elections." *Political Research Quarterly* 66, no. 3: 645–657. doi:10.1177/106591 2912459565.

Ridout, Travis, and Erika Fowler. 2012. "Explaining Perceptions of Advertising Tone." *Political Research Quarterly* 65, no. 1: 62–75. http://journals.sagepub.com/ doi/abs/10.1177/1065912910388189.

Ridout, Travis, and Michael Franz. 2011. *The Persuasive Power of Campaign Advertising*. Philadelphia: Temple University Press.

Ridout, Travis, and Rob Mellen Jr. 2007. "Does the Media Agenda Reflect the Candidates'Agenda?" *Harvard International Journal of Press/Politics* 12, no. 2: 44–62. doi:10.1177/1081180x07299799.

Ridout, Travis, and Glen R. Smith. 2008. "Free Advertising: How the Media Amplify Campaign Messages." *Political Research Quarterly* 61, no. 4: 598–608. doi:10.1177/1065912908314202.

Ridout, Travis, Michael Franz, and Erika Fowler. 2013. "Are Interest Group Ads More Effective?" Paper presented at the American Political Science Association.

———. 2014. "Advances in the Study of Political Advertising." *Journal of Political Marketing* 13, no. 3: 175–194. doi:10.1080/15377857.2014.929889.

Riffe, Daniel, Stephen Lacy, and Frederick Fico. 2014. *Analyzing Media Messages: Using Quantitative Content Analysis in Research*. 3rd ed. New York: Routledge/ Taylor and Francis Group.

Robinson, Michael J. 1976. "Public Affairs Thelevision and the Growth of Political Malaise: The Case of Selling the Pentagon." *American Political Science Review* 70, no. 2: 409–432. doi:10.2307/1959647.

Rosenblum, Mort. 1993. *Who Stole the News?* New York: John Wiley and Sons.

Sass, Erik. 2014. "Americans Sick of Gossip, Sports in News Coverage, Want More Susbstance." MediaPost. October 21. http://www.mediapost.com/publications/ article/236675/americans-sick-of-gossip-sports-in-news-coverage.html.

Schaffner, Brian, and Pat Sellers. 2003. "The Structural Determinants of Local News Coverage." *Political Communication* 20, no. 1: 41–57. doi:10.1080/10584600 3901365.

Schmidt, Christine. 2018a. "$20 Million Is Heading Toward Local News From the Lenfest Institute and Knight Foundation." NiemanLab. September 16. http:// www.niemanlab.org/2018/09/20-million-is-heading-toward-local-news-from-the -lenfest-institute-and-knight-foundation/.

———. 2018b. "Venture Philanthropy for Local News Might Not Be as Scary as It Sounds." NiemanLab. October 10. http://www.niemanlab.org/2018/10/venture -philanthropy-for-local-news-might-not-be-as-scary-as-it-sounds/.

———. 2018c. "What Kind of Information—Not Just Content—Do You Need as a News Consumer?" NiemanLab. July 12. http://www.niemanlab.org/2018/07/ what-kind-of-information-not-just-content-do-you-need-as-a-news-consumer/.

———. 2019a. "Facebook Is Committing to Spending $300 Million to Support News, With an Emphasis on Local." NiemanLab. January 15. http://www.niemanlab. org/2019/01/facebook-is-committing-300-million-to-support-news-with-an -emphasis-on-local/.

———. 2019b. "Local TV Is Still the Most Trusted Source of News. So How Do You Collaborate With a Station?" NiemanLab. February 20. http://www.niemanlab .org/2019/02/local-tv-is-still-the-most-trusted-source-of-news-so-how-do-you -collaborate-with-a-station/.

Schuck, Andreas R. T., Rens Vliegenthart, and Claes H. de Vreese. 2016. "Who's Afraid of Conflict? The Mobilizing Effect of Conflict Framing in Campaign News." *British Journal of Political Science* 46, no. 1: 177–194. doi:10.1017/s0007 123413000525.

Scott, Ben. 2004. "The Politics and Policy of Media Ownership." *American University Law Review* 53, no. 645: 645–677.

Scott, David, Robert Gobetz, and Mike Chanslor. 2008. "Chain Versus Independent Television Ownership." *Communication Studies* 59, no. 1: 84–98.

Scott, Martin, Mel Bunce, and Kate Wright. 2019. "Foundation Funding and the Boundaries of Journalism." *Journalism Studies* 20, no. 1: 1–19. doi:10.1080/14616 70X.2018.1556321.

Semetko, Holli A., and Patti M. Valkenburg. 2000. "Framing European Politics: A Content Analysis of Press and Television News." *International Journal of Communication* 50, no. 2: 93–109.

Severns, Maggie, and Derek Willis. 2018. "The Hidden Money Funding the Midterms." Politico. Updated December 21. https://www.politico.com/inter actives/2018/hidden-money-funding-midterms-superpacs/.

Seyler, Dave. 2019. "Investors Put Their Chips On Television." TV CheckNews. April 8. https://tvnewscheck.com/article/top-news/233489/investors-put-their -chips-on-television/.

Shearer, Elisa, and Elizabeth Grieco. 2019. "Americans Are Wary of the Role Social Media Sites Play in Delivering the News." Pew Research Center. October 2. https://www.journalism.org/2019/10/02/ americans-are-wary-of-the-role-social-media-sites-play-in-delivering-the-news/.

Sherman, Alex. 2018. "Private Equity Mulling Local TV Companies Tribune, Nexstar, Sinclair." CNBC. August 21. https://www.cnbc.com/2018/08/21/private -equity-mulling-local-tv-companies-tribune-nexstar-sinclair.html.

Shover, David, Lisa Danetz, Martin Redish, and Scott Thomas. 2006. "Corporations and Political Speech: Should Speech Equal Money Symposium: Corporations and the First Amendment; Examining the Health of Democracy." *Seattle University Law Review* 30: 930–958.

Siders, David. 2018. "Devin Nunes Creates His Own Alternative News Site." *Politico*. February 11. https://www.politico.com/story/2018/02/11/devin-nunes-alternative-news-site-402097.

Sides, John, Keena Lipsitz, and Matthew Grossmann. 2010. "Do Voters Perceive Negative Campaigns as Informative Campaigns?" *American Politics Research* 38, no. 3: 502–530. doi:10.1177/1532673x09336832.

Sigelman, Lee, and Emmett Buell Jr. 2004. "Avoidance or Engagement? Issue Convergence in the U.S. Presidential Campaigns, 196–2000." *American Journal of Political Science* 48, no. 4: 65–661. doi:10.1111/j.0092-5853.2004.00093.x.

Smith, Bradley A. 1997. "Money Talks: Speech, Corruption, Equality, and Campaign Finance." *Georgetown Law Journal* 86, no. 1: 45–100.

Snyder, James, and David Stromberg. 2010. "Press Coverage and Political Accountability." *Journal of Political Economy* 118, no. 2: 355–408.

Sohn, Gigi, and Andrew Schwartzman. 1994. "Broadcast Licenses and Localism: At Home in the 'Communications Revolution.'" *Federal Communications Law Journal* 47, no. 2: 383–389.

Statista. 2019a. "Most Likely Sources of Fake News Stories in the United States as of January 2017." Statista. https://www-statista-com.udel.idm.oclc.org/statistics/697774/fake-news-sources/.

———. 2019b. "Outside Group Spending in United States Political Cycles From 1990 to 2016 (in U.S. dollars)." Statista. January 15. https://www-statista-com.udel.idm.oclc.org/statistics/611303/outside-spending-in-us-political-cycles/.

Stehle, Vincent. 2019. "Knight Media Forum Underscores Urgency of Rebuilding Local News Infrastructure." Media Impact Funders. February 28. https://mediaimpactfunders.org/knight-media-forum-underscores-urgency-of-rebuilding-local-news-infrastructure/.

Stevens, Daniel, Dean Alger, Barbara Allen, and John L. Sullivan. 2006. "Local News Coverage in a Social Capital Capital: Election 2000 on Minnesota's Local News Stations." *Political Communication* 23, no. 1: 61–83. doi:10.1080/10584600500477062.

Stewart, Emily. 2016. "Donald Trump rode $5 billion in free media to the White House." The Street. November 20. https://www.thestreet.com/politics/donald-trump-rode-5-billion-in-free-media-to-the-white-house-13896916.

Stratmann, Thomas, and J. W. Verret. 2015. "How Does Corporate Political Activity Allowed by Citizens United v. Federal Election Commission Affect Shareholder Wealth?" *Journal of Law and Economics* 58, no. 3: 545–559. doi:10.1086/684226.

Strömbäck, Jesper, and Adam Shehata. 2018. "The Reciprocal Effects Between Political Interest and TV News Revisited: Evidence from Four Panel Surveys." *Journalism and Mass Communication Quarterly* 92, no. 2: 473–496.

Stucke, Maurice E., and Allan P. Grunes. 2009. "Toward a Better Competition for the Media: The Challenge of Developing Antitrust Policies That Support the

Media Sector's Unique Role in Our Democracy." *Connecticut Law Review* 42, no. 1: 101–129.

Sullivan, Kathleen M. 1996. "Political Money and Freedom of Speech Edward L. Barrett, Jr. Lecture on Constitutional Law." *UC Davis Law Review* 30: 663–690.

Svitek, Patrick. 2018. "With More Competitive Races Than Usual, Texas Saw Deluge of Outside Spending." Texas Tribune. November 6. https://www.texas tribune.org/2018/11/06/texas-elections-outside-spending/.

The Commission on Freedom of the Press. 1947. *A Free and Responsible Press: A General Report on Mass Communication: Newspapers, Radio, Motion Pictures, Magazines, and Books*. Chicago, IL: University of Chicago Press.

Tompkins, Al. 2018. "Gray Broadcasting to buy Raycom to create 3rd largest local TV owner." Poynter. June 25. https://www.poynter.org/news/gray-broadcasting -buy-raycom-create-3rd-largest-local-tv-owner.

Turner, S. Derek. 2014. "Cease to Resist: How the FCC's Failure to Enforce Its Rules Created a New Wave of Media Consolidation." Washington, DC: Free Press.

TVB, and Keller Fay Group. 2015. "The American Conversation Study." TVB. Updated September 24, 2018. https://www.tvb.org/Default.aspx?TabID=2203.

United States Election Project. 2019. "Voter Turnout Demographics." US Election Project. http://www.electproject.org/home/voter-turnout/demographics.

University of Wisconsin Population Health Institute. 2016. "County Health Rankings and Roadmaps." https://www.countyhealthrankings.org/explore-health -rankings/rankings-data-documentation/national-data-documentation-2010-2017.

Valentino, Nicholas, Vincent Hutchings, and Dmitri Williams. 2004. "The Impact of Political Advertising on Knowledge, Internet Information Seeking and Candidate Preference." *Journal of Communication* 54, no. 2: 337–354.

van der Wurff, Richard, and Klaus Schoenbach. 2014. "Civic and Citizen Demands of News Media and Journalists: What Does the Audience Expect From Good Journalism?" *Journalism and Mass Communication Quarterly* 91, no. 3: 433–451.

Van Zuylen-Wood, Simon. 2017. "Oy, the Traffic. And It's Poring. Do I Hear Sirens?" *Columbia Journalism Review*. https://www.cjr.org/local_news/tv-news-broadcast -jacksonville.php.

Varona, Anthony E. 2004. "Changing Channels and Bridging Divides: The Failure and Redemption of American Broadcast Television Regulation." *Minnesota Journal of Law, Science and Technology* 6, no. 1: 3–116.

Video Advertising Bureau. 2018. "It's a Matter of Trust: Media's Influence on Voters." VAB. August. https://s3.amazonaws.com/media.mediapost.com/uploads/Matter OfTrust.pdf.

Vogel, Pam. 2018. "Sinclair's 'Terrorism Alert Desk' Segments Are Designed to Gin Up Xenophobia via Local News." Media Matters. March 1. https://www.media matters.org/research/2018/03/01/sinclair-s-terrorism-alert-desk-segments-are -designed-gin-xenophobia-local-news/219517.

Waldman, Steven. 2011. *The Information Needs of Communities*. FCC. July. https:// transition.fcc.gov/osp/inc-report/The_Information_Needs_of_Communities.pdf.

———. 2015. "Report for America." Medium. June 9. https://medium.com/@steven waldman/report-for-america-bc65a707c395.

Wenger, Debora, and Bob Papper. 2018. *Local TV News and the New Media Landscape*. Knight Foundation. https://knightfoundation.org/reports/local-tv -news-and-the-new-media-landscape.

Wesleyan Media Project. 2019. "Digital Spending Dominates in Early 2020 Presidential Race." September 19. http://mediaproject.wesleyan.edu/releases -091919/.

West, Darrell. 2010. *Air Wars: Television Advertising in Election Campaigns, 1952–2008*. 5th ed. Washington, DC: Congressional Quarterly Press.

———. 2017. *Air Wars: Television Advertising and Social Media in Election Campaign, 1952–2016*. 7th ed. Thousand Oaks, CA: Sage.

Wheel, Robert. 2017. "Did Bernie Sanders Cost Hillary Clinton the Presidency?" October 12. Sabato's Crystal Ball. http://www.centerforpolitics.org/crystalball/ articles/did-bernie-sanders-cost-hillary-clinton-the-presidency/.

White, Joseph. 2018. "Why I flamed out of TV news." Medium. August 1. https:// medium.com/@JoeWhiteNTS/why-i-flamed-out-of-tv-news-a59aa26de240.

Wright, J. Skelly. 1975. "Politics and the Constitution: Is Money Speech." *Yale Law Journal* 85: 1001–1021.

Yan, Michael Zhaoxu. 2006. "Newspaper/Television Cross-Ownership and Local News and Public Affairs Programming on Television Stations." McGannon Center Working Paper Series. October. https://fordham.bepress.com/mcgannon_working _papers/18/.

Yan, Michael Zhaoxu, and Yong Jin Park. 2005. "Duopoly Ownership and Local Informational Programming on Television: An Empirical Analysis." Paper presented at the Telecommunication Policy Research Conference, Washington, DC.

Yanich, Danilo. 2001. "Location, Location, Location: Urban and Suburban Crime on Local TV News." *Journal of Urban Affairs* 23, nos. 3–4: 221–241.

———. 2004. "Crime Creep: Urban and Suburban Crime on Local TV News." *Journal of Urban Affairs* 26, no. 5: 535–563.

———. 2011. *Local TV News and Service Agreements: A Critical Look*. Newark, DE: Center for Community Research and Service, University of Delaware.

———. 2013a. *Local TV, Localism and Service Agreements*. Newark, DE: Center for Community Research and Service, University of Delaware.

———. 2013b. "Local TV News Content and Shared Services Agreements: The Honolulu Case." *Journal of Broadcasting and Electronic Media* 57, no. 2: 242–259.

———. 2016. "Same Ol', Same Ol': Consolidation and Local Television News." In *The Communication Crisis in America and How to Fix It*, edited by M. Lloyd and Lewis Friedland. New York: Palgrave Macmillan.

Yin, Leon, Franziska Roscher, Richard Bonneau, Jonathan Nagler, and Joshua A. Tucker. 2018. *Your Friendly Neighborhood Troll: The Internet Research Agency's Use of Local and Fake News in the 2016 Presidential Campaign*. Social Media and Political Participation. https://s18798.pcdn.co/smapp/wp-content/uploads/ sites/1693/2018/11/SMaPP_Data_Report_2018_01_IRA_Links.pdf.

Index

administrative law judge, 183–184
advertisements. *See* political ads
affective intelligence, 57
affiliation, 72, 72–73
age, 20–21
aggregation theory, 55–56
Amazon, 219
American Cable Association, 184
anchors, on television, 104–105, *105*
Apollo Global Management, LLC, 200, 203
The Apprentice, 4
Assessing Local Journalism (Napoli), 29–30
AT&T, 194
Atwater, Lee, 40
audiences: citizens as, 81–83, *82–84*; for media, 28–29; news for, 102–103; for political ads, 19–21; viewing time of, 21, 22
Axelrod, David, 39
Ayotte, Kelly, 6

Balchunis, Mary Ellen, 138
battleground states, 63, *64*
Bennet, Michael, 150
Bilirakis, Gus, 147
Bipartisan Campaign Reform Act (BCRA), 44–45
Bloomberg, Michael, 223
Blum, Rod, 154
Boehne, Rich, 187–188
Boehner, John, 210–211
Boyle, Brendon, 138
Brady, Robert, 138
Broadcasters State Leadership Conference, 196

broadcast samples: political ads in, 64–65, 100–102, *101*, 105–107, *106*; political stories in, 98–100, *99–100*, 107
broadcast television, 223–224
Buchanan, Vern, 147–148
Buckley v. Valeo, 43–45
Budd, Tedd, 143
Burr, Richard, 142–143
Bush, George H. W., 5, 40
Bush, George W., 5, 40–41
business, of news, 174–182, 209
Butterfield, G. K., 143

cable television, 19–20; for Clinton, H., 44–45; Internet and, 196; news on, 21, 22; retransmission fees for, 192–193
campaign finance, 42–44, 46, 51–52, 223–224
campaigns: BCRA for, 44; campaign finance, 42–44, 46, 51–52, 223–224; *Citizens United* for, 44–51; for communities, 23; data on, 36; events in, 118–121, *121*, 176; FECA for, 42–44, 62; finance reform for, 89, *89*–90, 213–214; on local television, 78–79, *79*; in market profiles, 174; as news, 129–130; pacing of, 76–77, *77*; PACs for, 16; period of, 62; political ads and, 1–2, 8–10, 35–36, 56–57, 114, *115*–117, *116*, 172; political stories and, 16, 114, *115*–117, *116*, *136*, 140, 145, 149, 153, 156, 160, 163, 167, 170, 172–173; for president, 10, 63, *64*; public funding for, 43; by Republicans, 40; for Senate, 132, 137, 142, 147, 150, 154, 157, 161, 164, 168; for Supreme Court, 43; television and, 17; in Texas, 6, 214–215. *See also* down-ballot campaigns

Danilo Yanich is a professor of Urban Affairs and Public Policy at the Joseph R. Biden, Jr. School of Public Policy of the University of Delaware. He is the associate director of the school and directs the master's program in Urban Affairs and Public Policy. He is a two-time Presidential Fellow of the Salzburg Seminar; his research focuses on the relationship among the media, citizenship, and public policy.